AGAINST CALVINISM

AGAINST CALVINISM

ROGER E. OLSON

ZONDERVAN®

ZONDERVAN.com/
AUTHORTRACKER
follow your favorite authors

ZONDERVAN

Against Calvinism

This title is also available as a Zondervan ebook. Visit www.zondervan.com/ebooks.

This title is also available in a Zondervan audio edition. Visit www.zondervan.fm.

Requests for information should be addressed to:

Zondervan, *Grand Rapids, Michigan 49530*

Library of Congress Cataloging-in-Publication Data

Olson, Roger E.
Against Calvinism / Roger E. Olson.
p. cm.
Includes bibliographical references.
ISBN 978-0-310-32467-6 (softcover)
1. Calvinism. I. Title.
BX9424.3.O47 2011
230'.42 – dc22 2011007932

Cover design: Tobias Outerwear for Books
Interior design: Cindy LeBreacht

Printed in the United States of America

HB 08.15.2024

This book is dedicated to three of my theological
heroes who went to be with the Lord in 2010:
Donald Bloesch, Vernon Grounds, and Clark Pinnock

CONTENTS

Foreword (by Michael Horton) 9

Preface 12

ONE Introduction: Why This Book Now? 15

TWO Whose Calvinism? Which Reformed Theology? 26

THREE Mere Calvinism: The TULIP System 38

FOUR Yes to God's Sovereignty; No to Divine Determinism 70

FIVE Yes to Election; No to Double Predestination 102

SIX Yes to Atonement; No to Limited Atonement/ Particular Redemption 136

SEVEN Yes to Grace; No to Irresistible Grace/Monergism 155

EIGHT Conclusion: Calvinism's Conundrums 175

Appendix 1: Calvinist Attempts to Rescue God's Reputation 181

Appendix 2: Responses to Calvinist Claims 188

Notes 193

FOREWORD

Roger Olson's book *Against Calvinism* represents a contemporary presentation and defense of evangelical Arminianism that not only merits but requires careful and sympathetic reading by non-Arminians as well.

Roger is correct when he says that it is increasingly difficult to know what the label "Reformed" actually means today. Especially in America, where everyone likes to pick and choose the elements of one's personal creed, it sounds arrogant to tell other people they're not actually Reformed if they hold views that differ significantly from our confessions and catechisms. However, like other confessional traditions, Reformed teaching is determined by a common confession of believers in actual churches, not by the emphases of certain teachers or popular movements. The creeds and confessions don't speak *for* us; we speak as churches *through and with* them. Non-Calvinists should therefore evaluate these summaries and the doctrinal systems that are consistent with them rather than depend on idiosyncratic presentations.

When it comes to the doctrines of grace, our confessions reject hyper-Calvinism as well as Arminianism. Furthermore, covenant theology—including the baptism of covenant children and connectional church government led by ministers and elders—belong to our common confession along with the famous TULIP. God's glorious grace is as evident in our view of baptism and the Lord's Supper as means of grace rather than as merely human acts of commitment and remembering. For confessional Reformed and Presbyterian churches, regulating worship, ministry, outreach, and discipline on the basis of Scripture is as crucial to glorifying and enjoying God as is the doctrine of election or justification.

But this challenge cuts both ways. Although most Arminians do not subscribe to a common confession or collection of doctrinal standards, there are fairly standard representations at least of evangelical Arminian convictions. Roger Olson cuts through the caricatures, challenging misconceptions. If popular criticisms of Calvinism often trade on misunderstanding or exaggerated representations, then Calvinists should also feel sympathy for Arminians when they are falsely accused, for example, of being "Pelagians" who deny grace in favor of works-righteousness.

Neither of us is immune to the temptation of false accusations, but Roger and I agree that there has often been more heat than light in contemporary Calvinist-Arminian debates. Neither of us succumbs to the illusion that both represent partial truths that can be balanced in a noncontradictory and harmonious blend. There is no such thing as "Calminianism." Where these classic positions clash, Roger is a full-blooded Arminian and I am just as convinced that Scripture teaches what is rather infelicitously nicknamed "Calvinism." Yet we also agree that nothing is gained—in fact, much is lost—by misrepresenting each other's views. It's one thing to say that someone holds a certain view that the person explicitly rejects and another thing to argue that the view leads logically to that conclusion. This is where we often go astray on both sides: confusing our interpretations of the consequences of each other's positions with a charitable statement of each other's stated views.

On the one hand, Roger thinks that *if* I followed Calvinism to its logical conclusions, I *should* concede that the Holocaust and natural disasters are caused directly by God and that those condemned on the last day could justly blame God rather than themselves. In his view, the serious error of hyper-Calvinism is actually the position that follows most logically from Calvinism itself. In my view, it is not at all surprising that some Arminians have abandoned the classical Christian consensus concerning some divine attributes and original sin and have adopted moralistic theories of Christ's person and work as well as justification.

On the other hand, I think that *if* Roger followed Arminianism to its logical conclusion, he *should* go on to deny that salvation is entirely of God's grace; that Arminianism leads inevitably to human-centered rather than God-centered convictions if followed consistently. In other words, we each believe that the other person is inconsistent. At the end of the day, Roger suspects that monergism (e.g., God alone working) undermines God's goodness and love (as well as human agency), and I cannot see how synergism can be reconciled with *sola gratia* (grace alone). Yet Roger knows that Calvinism does not teach that God is the author of evil or that human beings have no responsibility. And it would be reckless for me to describe Arminianism as "Pelagian."

Although I'd still take exception to some of Roger's descriptions of

Calvinism, I respect his commitment to engaging real differences rather than caricatures. For my part, I have learned much from Roger about the stated positions of leading Arminian theologians and appreciate his cautions and rebukes along the way.

I also share Roger's appraisal of the state of much in contemporary evangelicalism. Far beyond Arminianism, he argues, Pelagian assumptions seem astonishingly prevalent. He agrees that "Christless Christianity" is "simply pervasive in American church life." When Arminian friends like Tom Oden, William Willimon, and Roger Olson challenge this state of affairs while some professing Reformed preachers sell their birthright for a deadly soup of folk religion, our differences—though important—are put in proper perspective. I have no doubt that James Arminius or John Wesley would be as offended as Roger Olson at what often passes erroneously for "Arminianism" today in many circles.

I am grateful to Roger for the candor, passion, and informed argumentation that this book represents. At the end of the day, Roger and I share the most important agreement: namely, that the crucial questions involved in this or any other debate must be brought to the bar of Scripture. We both believe that Scripture is clear and sufficient, even if we are confused and weak. We are all pilgrims on the way, not yet those who have arrived at our glorious destination. Only by endeavoring more and more to talk to each other as coheirs with Christ instead of about each other and past each other as adversaries can we engage with serious disagreements—and with the hope that we may also be surprised by felicitous agreements along the way.

Michael Horton

PREFACE

I write this book reluctantly; polemics is not my preferred style of scholarship. That is to say, I would rather proclaim what I am *for* than denounce what I am *against.* I value the irenic approach to theology, and I hope to be against Calvinism as irenically as possible. I want to make clear "right up front" that I am not against Calvinists. Many of my relatives are Calvinists, and I love them dearly. Although my immediate family was not theologically of that persuasion, we knew our relatives were every bit as Christian as we were. I still believe that to be the case; a person can be as marvelously saved and as dedicated a Christian as possible and be a Calvinist. Let me repeat: I am not against Calvinists.

I am well aware, however, how difficult it can be to separate one's sense of self-worth from one's passionately held beliefs. I hope my Aunt Margaret is not rolling over in her grave as this book is published! And I pray my Calvinist cousins and friends are not offended. I try as far as possible to separate myself from my theology in order to accept criticism of the latter graciously without becoming personally defensive. I can only hope and pray that my Calvinist friends and family will do the same.

This hope for a fair hearing requires that I be scrupulously fair in my handling of Calvinism. That is my intention in this little book. I promise to do my best to represent Calvinism as Calvinists themselves would represent it—without distortion or caricature. I promise not to set it up as a straw man easily cut down and burned. My motto is "Before saying 'I disagree' be sure you can say 'I understand.'" Another principle I try to follow is "Always represent the other viewpoint as its best adherents represent it." That's what I want done with my Arminianism, and I promise to do my best to do that with Calvinism.

I consider Calvinists my brothers and sisters in Christ, and it grieves me to have to write against their theology, which has a rich history and tradition. I confess that Calvinism, which I have studied from its primary sources (from Calvin through Jonathan Edwards to John Piper and numerous Reformed theologians between them), has many positive aspects. As many Calvinists love to point out, Calvinism (or Reformed theology) is not reducible to the doctrines popularly associated with it—total depravity, unconditional election, limited atonement, irresistible grace, and perseverance of the saints (TULIP). Some of those (especially the middle three) are the beliefs I will criticize in this book. Reformed thought in general, however, transcends them and is a larger whole of which they are only a part. How crucial they are to Reformed thought is much debated both by Calvinists themselves and by others.

My point here is simply to acknowledge that when I say I am "against Calvinism," I am talking only about some points of Reformed theology and not all that it stands for. Because the Reformed tradition (perhaps as distinct from some of its objectionable doctrines) is Christ-centered, I consider it a part of the rich tapestry of classical Christianity. I can and do worship with Calvinists without cringing.

In case anyone needs more persuasion about this matter, I wish to point out that I have worked and worshiped alongside Calvinists in three Christian universities and several churches (Baptist and Presbyterian) over the past thirty years without difficulty. I have voted to hire Calvinist professors and to give them tenure. I have no qualms about Calvinists being genuine Christian believers and faithful Christian scholars and teachers. I know firsthand that they often are. I admit that I am offended by some Calvinists. They are those that consider their theology the only authentically Christian (or evangelical) one and who misrepresent theologies other than their own—especially Arminianism. Unfortunately, especially in recent years, I have found those traits all too common among the "new Calvinists."

Some readers may question my credentials for writing about Calvinism. Let me reassure them. For a number of reasons I consider myself able to write fairly and accurately about a theology with which I disagree. I have taught historical theology in three Christian universities on both the undergraduate and graduate levels for almost thirty years. I studied Calvin and Jonathan Edwards and other Reformed theologians in seminary and graduate school and have always required my students to read them as part of their historical theology courses. I have also gone out of my way to invite "high Calvinists" (those committed to the entire TULIP schema) to speak to and interact with my classes. I have read John Calvin's *Institutes of the Christian Religion* as well as many of

Jonathan Edwards' treatises carefully and with extreme attentiveness to being unprejudiced.

I am well acquainted with the new Calvinism's greatest contemporary proponent—John Piper—and have read several of his books. I have studied the writings of numerous other Calvinists, including Charles Hodge, Loraine Boettner, Louis Berkhof, Anthony Hoekema, R. C. Sproul, and Paul Helm. I have attended Calvinist theological conferences, contributed to Calvinist publications, engaged in extended dialogues with Reformed thinkers, and published a major historical theology textbook that extensively engages Reformed theology.

My acquaintance with Calvinism and Reformed theology is more than a passing one. It has become a passion—and not only with the intent to refute it. My study of Reformed sources has greatly enriched my own theological and spiritual life. I lay no claim to being an expert on Calvinism, but I will defend my ability to describe and evaluate it based on thorough study of its primary sources both ancient (sixteenth century) and contemporary. I hope and expect that even well-informed Calvinists will consider my descriptions here fair if not profound.

I wish to thank several people for their invaluable help in bringing this book to completion. Calvinists all, they aided it unwittingly simply by answering my questions and engaging with me in theological dialogue. There was no subterfuge on my part; the idea for this book arose later than most of those events. First of all I want to thank Michael Horton, editor of *Modern Reformation* and astute Calvinist scholar, who has graciously conversed (sometimes debated) with me about these matters over several years. I have learned much from him. I also want to thank my Calvinist friends of Redeemer Presbyterian Church of Waco, Texas, and of the local Reformed University Fellowship. They have graciously endured my (hopefully) light-hearted heckling when they spoke to my classes and always gently corrected my errors. Finally, I thank my many Calvinist students who took my classes in spite of my well-known qualms about Reformed theology and who often contributed to my understanding of their own faith tradition.

ONE

INTRODUCTION: WHY THIS BOOK NOW?

Soon after I began teaching theology, an eager young student followed me to my office and asked to speak privately with me. Without hesitation I invited him to sit down next to my desk and tell me what was on his mind. He leaned toward me and with earnest countenance said, "Professor Olson, I don't think you're a Christian." Needless to say, I was somewhat taken aback.

"Why is that?" I asked.

"Because you're not a Calvinist," came his reply.

I asked him where he got the idea that only a Calvinist can be a Christian and he named a leading pastor and author whose church he attended. That pastor and author has since became world famous for his promotion of high Calvinism. I encouraged my student to go back and talk with his pastor about this matter, and I confirmed my confidence in being a Christian because of my faith in Jesus Christ. The student never did recant his charge that I was not a Christian. Years later, however, the pastor did deny that he ever taught that only Calvinists could be Christians.

That was the first salvo, as it were, of my long struggle with the "new Calvinism" celebrated by *Time* magazine (May 12, 2009) as one of the ten great ideas changing the world "right now." My student accuser was one of the first of a movement later labeled the "young, restless, Reformed" generation of Christians. At the time, all I knew was that many of my best and brightest theological students were gravitating toward Calvinism under the influence of the pastor the student mentioned. Many on our faculty called them "Piper cubs." But their tribe was destined to increase over the next few years.

THE YOUNG, RESTLESS, REFORMED PHENOMENON

In 2008 Christian journalist Collin Hansen published the first book-length exploration of a phenomenon most evangelical Christian leaders were talking about: *Young, Restless, Reformed: A Journalist's Journey with the New Calvinists.*[1] The roots of this movement go deep into Protestant history. Calvinism, obviously, derives its name from Protestant Reformer John Calvin (1509–1564), whose 500th birthday was recently celebrated across North America with conferences and worship events dedicated to his memory. A more recent catalyst was New England Puritan preacher, theologian, and educator Jonathan Edwards (1703–1758), who famously defended a version of Calvin's theology against what he saw as the creeping rationalism of deism in his day. One apparent aspect of the new Calvinist youth movement (not confined to youth) is the popularity of graphic T-shirts sporting the face of Jonathan Edwards and the motto "Jonathan Edwards is my homeboy."

A major contemporary catalyst of the movement is Minneapolis Baptist pastor, author, and popular speaker John Piper (b. 1946), whose numerous theological books are unusually reader-friendly and scholarly—a rare combination. His *Desiring God: Confessions of a Christian Hedonist*[2] is second only to the Bible in terms of inspiration and authority for many of the young, restless, Reformed Christians who eagerly devour Piper's books and sermons (readily available online). Piper speaks to enormous youth audiences at "Passion Conferences" and "One Day" events—sometimes attended by as many as forty thousand people under age twenty-six. What many of his followers do not know is something Piper makes no secret about—that he is simply repackaging the Calvinist theology of Jonathan Edwards for contemporary youth. (Edwards' writings can be daunting to read!)

For readers not sure what this "new Calvinism" (or perhaps even Calvinism itself) is all about, I will here present journalist Hansen's apt nutshell description. (A fuller account of Calvinism and Reformed theology will unfold throughout this book.) According to Hansen:

> Calvinists—like their namesake, Reformation theologian John Calvin—stress that the initiative, sovereignty and power of God is the only sure hope for sinful, fickle, and morally weak human beings. Furthermore, they teach that the glory of God is the ultimate theme of preaching and the focus of worship.[3]

Furthermore, Hansen explains, "Calvinism puts much stock in transcendence which draws out biblical themes such as God's holiness, glory and majesty."[4] But if these were the only emphases of the new Calvinism (or old Calvinism, for that matter), few genuinely evangelical Protestant Christians would quibble with it. What evangelical Christian denies them? For Hansen and those he studies, however, it may be a matter of emphasis. According to him, the new Calvinists are reacting to what they regard as a general decline of theology and especially emphasis on God's glory in contemporary American church life. His subjects, he says, are reacting against the "feel good theology" of many contemporary evangelical churches.[5]

Hansen refers to sociological studies of evangelical Christian young people that label their default view of God as "Moralistic Therapeutic Deism"[6]—a fancy term for a vision of God as a grandfatherly figure in heaven who demands perfection but always forgives anyway. This "God" is both a judge and a self-esteem coach. He cannot be pleased but he always forgives. This is a weak and thin vision of God by historical Christian standards, and many young Christians have figured that out and turned to the only alternative available to them—the strong and thick doctrines of Calvinism.

As a veteran teacher of Christian college and university students, I accept this critique of much contemporary evangelical church life and preaching. Far too many Christian youth grow up with almost no biblical or theological knowledge, thinking that God exists for their comfort and success in life even if he lays down a law nobody can really live up to. Like a kindly grandfather who dotes on his preteen progeny while decrying their bad grades, God may be disappointed in us but his whole goal is to make us fulfilled anyway.

That may be something of a caricature; few evangelical pastors or teachers would say that. But my experience resonates with what Hansen argues—that somehow or other most evangelical Christian young people manage to latch onto such a picture of God and fail entirely to plumb the riches of either the Bible or Christian theology to deepen their understanding of themselves and God. So many of the brightest and best become vaguely aware that something is missing in their spiritual upbringing, and when they hear the message of Calvinism, they latch onto it as their lifeboat from watery, culturally accommodated spirituality. Who can blame them? However, Calvinism isn't the only alternative;

most of them know little to nothing about either its weaknesses or historically rich, biblically faithful, and more reasonable alternative theologies.

ROOTS OF THE NEW CALVINISM

By now readers may be wondering if this new Calvinism phenomenon is a youth fad that popped up out of nowhere. I've already strongly hinted that's not the case. But something new is afoot in it—the appeal of a very old theology to a very young audience. Calvinism and Reformed theology (the distinction and relationship of those terms will be unpacked in chapter 2) used to be considered largely a Christian tradition of mostly old people. Years ago even many evangelical Christians thought of Calvinism as almost confined to the Dutch enclaves of Grand Rapids, Michigan, and Pella, Iowa (and similar communities populated mainly by Dutch immigrants). Holland was, after all, a country where Calvinism especially caught on. Grand Rapids sports a number of influential Calvinist institutions such as Calvin College and Seminary, several Reformed-leaning publishers, and numerous large Calvinist churches. In Pella, Iowa, the scene of a well-attended, annual tulip festival, one can find First, Second, and Third Reformed churches within blocks of each other. And the town boasts the fine Central College—a Reformed liberal arts school.

All that is by no means meant to demean Reformed churches or Calvinist theology; they have a rich historical tradition and a major presence within American evangelical Christianity. Many leading evangelical leaders and thinkers have been Reformed since the days of the Puritans (who were English Calvinists). However, for several generations during the twentieth century Calvinism's vitality seemed to be waning. One can sense that in the defensive tones of lofty Calvinist theologian Loraine Boettner's (1901–1990) massive tome, *The Reformed Doctrine of Predestination.*[7] (Boettner's book was long treated as a magisterial source on high Calvinism by numerous Reformed Christians even though more popularly written books that espouse the same theology have largely eclipsed it.)

Boettner, who declared that "a full and complete exposition of the Christian system can be given only on the basis of the truth as set forth in the Calvinistic system"[8] and that "our doctrine is the clearly revealed doctrine of the Scriptures,"[9] decried the decline of strong Calvinist belief among evangelical Americans. He would be delighted to see its current renaissance. But he was right. In the 1940s through the 1980s Calvinism struggled to hold onto young people; the 1970s Jesus movement was anything but Calvinistic, and the charismatic and Third Wave movements were also, for the most part, non-Calvinist. These were the popular Christian movements of my youth; many of today's Christian teenagers and university students (and older people as well) are just as excited about their newfound faith in God's absolute sovereignty as Christian young people of my generation were about "getting high on Jesus."

However, Calvinism never disappeared or even went underground. It has always been a strong force in certain segments of American church life. And the contemporary young, restless, Reformed believers are largely unaware of Calvinists before John Piper (and his popularizing young preachers and writers), who paved the way for their rediscovery of that message and lifestyle. One was Boettner—little known but influential. Another was one of my own seminary professors, James Montgomery Boice (1938–2000), who pastored the strongly Calvinistic and evangelical Tenth Presbyterian Church in Philadelphia. He was also a radio preacher, Bible commentator, Christian magazine publisher (*Eternity*), and author of numerous books mostly about Reformed theology. (Boice took a sabbatical from his church in the mid-1970s during which he taught a course at North American Baptist Seminary in Sioux Falls, South Dakota; I was one of his students during that minisemester course on preaching.) Most of the young, new Calvinists have never heard of Boice, but he was an amazingly prolific pastor-theologian-author-speaker who was, like Piper later, almost a force of nature in American evangelical life.

Another precursor and pioneer of the new Calvinism is Reformed theologian and apologist R. C. Sproul (b. 1939), founder of the influential Ligonier Ministries, which specializes in Christian apologetics. (Not all Calvinists are as fond of rational apologetics as Sproul, but there can be no doubt about his Calvinist credentials.) Sproul has taught at several leading conservative Calvinist seminaries and has appeared in person and via media at numerous Christian conferences and church events. Among his widely read expositions and defenses of Calvinist theology are *What Is Reformed Theology?* and *Chosen by God.*[10] Hansen gives Sproul great credit for paving the way for the new Calvinism even though he is not nearly as well-known among the young, restless, Reformed as John Piper.

Another popular Calvinist writer and speaker who helped set the stage for the revival of Reformed theology among the youth is radio evangelist, pastor, and Bible commentator John F. MacArthur (b. 1939), pastor of one of the original megachurches—Grace Community Church of Sun Valley, California. His radio program *Grace to You* has been in constant broadcast since 1977. In 1985 he founded his own Christian college and in 1986 his own seminary. He is the author of numerous books, all of which promote a Calvinist perspective on the Bible and theology. There can be no doubt that, like Boice and Sproul, MacArthur's influence "trickled down" to the new Calvinists who, by and large, have never heard of him.

One other precursor and pioneer must be given credit for the resurgence of Calvinism even though few of its youthful adherents know about him. That is prolific theological author and editor Michael Horton (b. 1964), who teaches theology at Westminster Theological Seminary's California campus in Escondido. He is the consummate organizer and has brought together many Calvinists (and others with similar views of God and salvation) in organizations such as the Alliance of Confessing Evangelicals, of which he was executive director. He is editor of the enormously successful *Modern Reformation* magazine and host of the *White Horse Inn* radio program—both serious but popular organs of Calvinist Bible interpretation, cultural critique, and theology. Many young Calvinists are discovering Horton and his works, such as *Christless Christianity: The Alternative Gospel of the American Church*[11]—a prophetic critique of the thin "man-centered" theology and spirituality of much contemporary evangelical Christianity.

These notable Calvinists are surrounded by a host of others who could be named as influential promoters of evangelical Calvinism and preparers for the rise of the new Calvinism in the 1990s and first decade of the twenty-first century. But one more phenomenon must be mentioned to give even a cursory accounting of its background—the "Edwards renaissance" in both philosophy and theology during the last decades of the twentieth century. For decades and perhaps a century Jonathan Edwards was known to most people, including Christians, only as the cranky Puritan preacher of the sermon "Sinners in the Hands of an Angry God." However, he was rediscovered as a profound philosopher and theologian as well as an astute observer of nature and amateur naturalist in the 1980s and beyond. Numerous books continue to fall from publishers' presses touting Edwards as "America's Theologian"—the title of one theological recommendation of Edwards and his thought.[12] During his student days at Fuller Theological Seminary, John Piper chose Edwards as his theological mentor and found in him the richest and fullest account of biblical Christianity in the modern world.[13]

None of this history includes those associated with the bastion of American Reformed thought and life—Calvin College and Seminary of Grand Rapids, Michigan. The extent to which those institutions paved the way for the new Calvinism is uncertain. Their influence is probably more remote. Moreover, some American Reformed thinkers associated with those institutions have expressed certain reservations about the new Calvinism that, interpreted in a certain way, could be taken as casting doubt on its already named precursors.

The December 1, 2009 issue of *Christian Century* magazine contained an article by Reformed theologian Todd Billings of Western Theological Seminary of Holland, Michigan (like Calvin College and Seminary, a center of the older Dutch-rooted Reformed tradition). In his article "Calvin's Comeback? The Irresistible Reformer," Billings decried the new Calvinism's one-sided focus on some of Reformed theology's more exotic doctrines and especially the TULIP scheme of total depravity, unconditional election, limited atonement, irresistible grace and perseverance of the saints. He averred that the new Calvinists use TULIP as a litmus test by which one's authenticity as Reformed is tested. In response he claims that "TULIP does not provide an adequate or even accurate distillation of Reformed theology"[14] and criticizes the new Calvinists for placing at the center what is peripheral to the tradition.

For Billings and for many other "churchly Calvinists" (a term for those associated with the older Dutch and Scottish Reformed and Presbyterian liturgical and sacramental denominations) the new Calvinists are missing the boat almost entirely. "Reformed" designates not an emphasis on predestination and certainly not on reprobation (predestination of some persons to hell)—what Calvin famously called the "horrible decree [of God]"—but on a certain catholic (with a small "c," meaning universal) and sacramental vision of Christianity that does emphasize God's sovereignty but does not play it out in celebration of God's absolute control of the minutest events including evil.

Billings' objection will no doubt be debated by other self-proclaimed Reformed Christians. I only mention it here because it well expresses a murmur against the new Calvinism one can hear emanating from the older Reformed institutions of American and European Christianity that have to some extent downplayed the TULIP system of Reformed theology. I will explore this and other aspects of Reformed and Calvinist diversity in the next two chapters.

THE NEED FOR A RESPONSE NOW

This introduction is entitled "Why This Book Now?" Indeed, why a book now *Against Calvinism*? Isn't the rise of serious theological reflection and commitment among young Christians a good thing? Why pour cold water on the revival fires of spirituality among the young? I take that objection seriously to heart.

However, I believe the time has come for someone to point out the flaws and weaknesses in this particular type of Calvinism—the type widely embraced and promoted by leaders and followers of the young, restless, Reformed movement. But the promotion of what I consider a flawed system comes not only from them. The same theology of God's absolute sovereignty can be found in Calvin (perhaps without the aspect of limited atonement), Edwards (in an extreme way as I will explain), Boettner, Boice, Sproul, and numerous other popularizers of Calvinism. So what's wrong with believing in and celebrating God's sovereignty? Absolutely nothing! But, it can be and often is taken too far—making God the author of sin and evil—which is something few Calvinists admit to but which follows from what they teach as a "good and necessary consequence" (a somewhat confusing technical phrase often used by Calvinists themselves to point out the dreaded effects they see in non-Calvinist theologies).

One can go to the Internet phenomenon called YouTube and watch numerous video clips by adherents of the new Calvinism declaring shocking beliefs about God's sovereignty, including that God causes all calamities and horrors "for his glory." John Piper famously published a sermon a few days after the Twin Towers terrorist events of September 11, 2001, declaring that God did not merely permit them but caused them.[15] He has since published other statements similarly attributing natural disasters and horrific calamities to God. Piper is not alone; many of the new Calvinists and their mentors are aggressively asserting that this view of God is the only biblical and reasonable one.

Contemporary popular Calvinism may be by-and-large consistent with Calvin and many of his followers (although I think it is even more shaped by his successor as chief pastor of Geneva, Theodore Beza [1519–1605] and his followers), but it is not the only version of Reformed theology and Calvinism. I will explain that further in the next chapter. For now, suffice it to say that even many Reformed Christians are shocked and appalled at the implications of the new Calvinism's extreme emphasis on God's sovereignty.

Of course, the definition of "Reformed" depends largely on the church or thinker claiming the label. In fact, the worldwide organization called the World Communion of Reformed Churches (WCRC) includes many denominations and churches that in no way embrace the whole TULIP system. (In fact, shockingly to some Calvinists, the WCRC includes some Arminian churches that believe in free will and deny God's meticulous, providential control of all events!) I consider myself Reformed in its broadest sense—non-Lutheran in the broad Protestant stream extending from the Swiss Reformation led originally by Ulrich Zwingli (1484–1531).

I believe someone needs finally to stand up and in love firmly say "No!" to egregious statements about God's sovereignty often made by Calvinists. Taken to their logical conclusion, that even hell and all who will suffer there eternally are foreordained by God, God is thereby rendered morally ambiguous at best and a moral monster at worst. I have gone so far as to say that this kind of Calvinism, which attributes everything to God's will and control, makes it difficult (at least for me) to see the difference between God and the devil. Some of my Calvinist friends have expressed offense at that, but I continue to believe it is a valid question worth pursuing. What I mean is that *if* I *were* a Calvinist and believed what these people teach, I would have difficulty telling the difference between God and Satan. I will unpack that in more detail throughout this book.

Some Calvinists accuse non-Calvinists of rejecting their theology of God's sovereignty because of a latent humanistic love for free will. A Calvinist colleague, who has since become a well-known author of Reformed books, once asked me seriously if I had considered whether my belief in free will was evidence of unrecognized humanism in my thinking. Needless to say, I rejected that suggestion. The fact is that I, like most non-Calvinist evangelical Christians, embrace free will for two reasons (beyond that we believe it is everywhere assumed in the Bible): it is necessary to preserve human responsibility for sin and evil, and it is necessary to preserve God from being responsible for sin and evil. I can honestly say (as most non-Calvinist evangelicals do) that I don't give a flip about free will except for those reasons.

I have no interest in man-centered theology; I am intensely interested in worshiping a God who is truly good and above reproach for the Holocaust and all other evils too numerous to mention. Too many Calvinist authors misrepresent non-Calvinist theologies as if they are all man-centered, humanistic, less-than-God-honoring, and even unbiblical without ever acknowledging the problems in their own theology. Too many young, impressionable followers have not yet figured out what those problems are.[16] I write this to help them.

So, the time has come for an irenic and loving but firm "No!" to the extreme version of Calvinism being promoted by leaders of the young, restless, Reformed generation and too often uncritically being embraced by their followers. I will demonstrate that the "No!" can be said from within Reformed theology itself and has been said by some leading Reformed theologians and biblical scholars. I will show that this extreme Calvinism, which with adherent Hansen I label "radical,"[17] is inherently flawed biblically, logically, and in terms of the wider Christian tradition.

I will put all my cards on the table here and confess that I operate with four criteria of theological truth: Scripture, tradition, reason, and experience (the so-called Wesleyan Quadrilateral). *Scripture* is the primary source and norm of theology. *Tradition* is theology's "normed norm"—a respected guidance mechanism. *Reason* is a critical tool for interpreting Scripture and weeding out absolutely incredible theological claims that contradict each other or lead to consequences that are untenable in the light of what else is believed. *Experience* is the inevitable crucible in which theology is done, but though it is a criterion for evaluation, it is not an authority, so I will hardly appeal to it at all. What I do believe about experience is that no theology is created or embraced in a vacuum; experience always colors what we believe and how we believe it.

I will argue throughout this book that high Calvinism is not the only or the best way of interpreting Scripture. It is one possible interpretation of isolated texts, but in light of the whole witness of Scripture it is not viable. Furthermore, I will argue that high Calvinism stands in tension with the ancient faith of the Christian church and much of the heritage of evangelical faith. Some of its crucial tenets cannot be found before the church father Augustine in the fifth century, and others cannot be found before a heretic named Gottschalk (d. circa 867) or from him until Calvin's successor, Theodore Beza.

Finally, I will argue that high Calvinism falls into contradictions; it cannot be made intelligible—and Christianity should be intelligible. By "intelligible" I do not mean philosophically rational; I mean capable of being understood. A sheer contradiction is a sure sign of error; even most Calvinists agree about that. The greatest contradiction is that God is confessed as perfectly good while at the same time described as the author of sin and evil. I do not say that all Calvinists admit that their theology makes God the author of sin and evil; many deny that. But I will show that it is a "good and necessary consequence" of what else they say about God.

Someone has said that no theology is worth believing that cannot be preached standing in front of the gates of Auschwitz. I, for one, could not stand at those gates and preach a version of God's sovereignty that makes the extermination of six million Jews, including many children, a part of the will and plan of God such that God foreordained and rendered it certain.[18] I want young Calvinists (and others) to know and at least come to terms with the inevitable and unavoidable consequences of what this radical form of Reformed theology teaches. And I want to give their friends and relatives and spiritual mentors ammunition to use in undermining their sometimes overconfidence in the solidity of their belief system.

TWO

WHOSE CALVINISM? WHICH REFORMED THEOLOGY?

I attended a professional society meeting of Christian theologians at which a leading Calvin scholar and Reformed theologian read a paper on Calvin's theology. Nowhere did he mention the doctrines of meticulous providence (that God controls all events including sin and evil) or predestination. In fact, the entire TULIP scheme was completely missing from his account of Calvin's theology. The emphasis was rather on gratitude toward God as a major theme of Calvin. During the discussion time that followed I asked the scholar why he said nothing about Calvin's doctrine of God's absolute and all-encompassing sovereignty. He replied almost condescendingly that this is not an essential part of Calvin's theology or Reformed theology.

This would come as quite a surprise to many young, restless, Reformed Calvinists! My experience is that most of them specialize in that doctrine; it is for them the doctrine of great comfort and the reason why they embraced Calvinism in the first place. One told me that he had a second conversion—the second one to Calvinism because of a sudden and overwhelming experience of comfort from believing that salvation is all God's doing and has nothing at all to do with his decisions, except as God gave him the gift of faith to believe in Jesus Christ. For other young Calvinists (and others) the strong doctrine of God's sovereignty allows the chaotic world to make some sense—it is all the outworking of a divine master plan.

In short, most participants in the new Calvinism movement believe firmly that God's absolute sovereignty, which rules out contingency and free will, is central to their newly discovered Reformed faith. It will come as quite a shock to them to discover that "Reformed" is an essentially contested concept. What they are calling *Reformed* is not the only version of the Reformed tradition, and it is even debatable whether what they are calling *Calvinism* was believed in its entirety by Calvin.

WHAT ARE CALVINISM AND REFORMED THEOLOGY?

Before plunging into my critique of Calvinism, it is incumbent on me to explain as carefully and precisely as possible *what Calvinism* I am criticizing and *what Reformed theology* I am against. But the categories themselves are used in such different ways by different theologians and historians that it is difficult to treat them as boxes—closed categories in which every belief either wholly fits or does not. There is much fluidity and ambiguity in these terms and the phenomena they describe.

I compare the situation to trying to sort out concepts such as "liberal" and "conservative" in American political life. Republicans are said to be conservative. Yet, historically, many of the earliest ones were radicals. Abraham Lincoln was one of America's first Republicans and was an infamous iconoclast and destroyer of the status quo. Thus, he was anything *but* conservative in any usual sense of the word. During the 1960s several leading Republican politicians were notable liberals politically and socially. Nelson Rockefeller (1908–1997) was vice president under Gerald R. Ford and was famous for being rather liberal. Yet he was a leader of the Republican Party. Also during the 1960s and 1970s many Democrats especially of the South were archconservatives politically and socially. They were called "Dixie Democrats" and sometimes "Boll Weevil Democrats" because of their defenses of Southern traditions and refusal to vote for progressive social reforms.

Political categories are not nearly as tidy as many people think. Neither are *Calvinist* and *Reformed.* When people say to me that someone is theologically Reformed, I have little idea what they mean. Among the new, youthful Calvinists it usually means the person is Calvinist in the strong sense of belief in the whole TULIP system of soteriology (doctrine of salvation). However, I know people who are solidly Reformed in their own minds and who reject crucial aspects of TULIP. Similarly, I know people who proudly identify themselves as Calvinist who would not be considered Reformed by leading authorities on what Reformed means. In some Baptist circles, *Calvinist* indicates only that a person believes in the doctrine of the eternal security of true believers—that a genuinely saved person cannot become apostate and end up in hell no matter what they do or don't do. In some Reformed circles (especially what I have called "churchly Reformed" circles) Baptists cannot be truly Reformed. The WCRC—the World Communion of Reformed Churches, an ecumenical body of 214 denominations in 107 countries—does not include any Baptist groups even though some Baptists call themselves and their churches "Reformed Baptist." Finally, many Lutherans use the label *Reformed* to designate all non-Lutheran Protestants![1]

If you're confused, don't worry about it. These terms and the categories they attempt to name are slippery. In spite of the existence of the WCRC there is no worldwide magisterium (formal authority) that has the power to decide who is and who is not Reformed or Calvinist. Practically speaking, anyone can apply these labels to themselves in any way they want to and no one can do anything about it (except reject their claims). Of course, some denominations, churches, and other Christian organizations have their own litmus tests for determining who within them is genuinely Calvinist or Reformed (or both). One traditional approach is to identify as Reformed only persons and groups that confess the "three symbols of unity" (statements of faith)—the Heidelberg Catechism, the Belgic Confession, and the Canons of Dort. But that excludes Presbyterians, most of whom identify their tradition as Reformed, and the WCRC (World Communion of Reformed Churches) includes many Presbyterian groups. (Presbyterians adhere to the Westminster Confession of Faith written by British Calvinists in 1648 largely on the basis of the previously mentioned three "symbols of unity.")

Because of this confusion of labels it will be helpful here to unpack the terms more carefully and examine the claims of new Calvinists, many of whom belong to Baptist or independent churches, to being truly representative of historical and contemporary Calvinism and Reformed theology. Many of them claim that *they* or *their leaders* are the true torchbearers of real Calvinism and Reformed theology, and they tend to place the TULIP scheme at the center of what it means to be Calvinist and Reformed. I want to make clear that I am not opposed to all Reformed theology or the whole spectrum of the Reformed Christian form of life equally. I am against the TULIP scheme of Calvinism and radical Reformed theology that embraces it and pushes it to its limits. I call that "radical Reformed theology" as opposed to moderate Reformed theology, which is more inclusive and less emphatic about TULIP.

REFORMED THEOLOGY IN HISTORICAL PERSPECTIVE

One way to approach deciding who is truly Reformed is to look at the WCRC. All lay some claim to spiritual and theological ancestry in the Swiss branch of the sixteenth-century Reformation led by Zwingli and Calvin. (However, historically speaking, the reformer of Strasburg, Martin Bucer [1491–1551], is usually considered by historical theologians an equally important early leader of the Reformed movement.) Without doubt the WCRC does celebrate the life and thought of John Calvin; that was evident during 2009—the 500th anniversary of Calvin's birth. However, its membership includes denominations that do not particularly exalt Calvin or his theology but whose historical pedigree, so to speak, reaches back to the Swiss Reformation of which Calvin was a part. The WARC (World Alliance of Reformed Churches) merged with another Reformed organization to form the WCRC in 2010; its website carried the following description, which one may assume is roughly correct of the WCRC:

> WARC is a fellowship of more than 200 churches with roots in the 16th-century Reformation led by John Calvin, John Knox, Ulrich Zwingli and many others, and the earlier reforming movements of Jan Hus and Peter Valdes. Our churches are Congregational, Presbyterian, Reformed and United. Most live and witness in the southern hemisphere; many are religious minorities in their countries. The Alliance is an interdependent network of people and churches working and worshipping together with faith in God's promise always to be with his creation.[2]

The WCRC, like the WARC before it, includes everything from the Protestant Church of Algeria (first member church listed in alphabetical order by country) to the Presbyterian Church of South Africa.[3] Among the member denominations are the Waldensian Evangelical Church of the River Plate of Uruguay, a branch of the larger Waldensian movement that harks back to the ministry of Italian reformer Peter Waldo (1140–1218), who lived long before Calvin, and the Remonstrant Brotherhood of the Netherlands—the oldest Arminian church in the world. (Jacob Arminius [1560–1609] and his followers, the Remonstrants, were fervent opponents of at least the middle three tenets of TULIP.)

Notably missing from the list are any Baptist churches, and yet, as earlier noted, many of the young, restless, Reformed leaders are

Baptists. The exclusion of Baptists from the WCRC more than hints that Reformed Christians worldwide do not consider "Reformed Baptist" a historically accurate label. Of course, Reformed Baptists (and others) can always say that the WCRC has no authority to decide who is and who is not Reformed—and that's true. It is interesting, however, that the WCRC excludes Baptists but includes many such as the Waldensians and Remonstrants, who do *not* consider themselves Calvinists! What churches are or may be included in the WCRC? According to its constitution any body (denomination) may join:

- Which accepts Jesus Christ as Lord and Saviour;
- Which holds the Word of God given in the Scriptures of the Old and New Testaments to be the supreme authority in matters of faith and life;
- Which acknowledges the need for the continuing reformation of the Church catholic;
- Whose position in faith and evangelism is in general agreement with that of the historic Reformed confessions;
- And which recognizes that the Reformed tradition is a biblical, evangelical, and doctrinal ethos, rather than any narrow and exclusive definition of faith and order.[4]

Nothing is said about which "Reformed confessions" a member denomination must be in "general agreement" with or what "agreement with" means. One can only assume they are the Heidelberg Catechism, the Belgic Confession, and the Westminster Confession or the Savoy Declaration (the Congregational version of the Westminster Confession). However, given the rather liberal theological flavor of some member denominations it is unlikely that "general agreement" means anything close to strict adherence.

The WARC seemed to regard Reformed theology as flexible; the organization highlighted the old motto "reformed and always reforming" (paraphrased in its constitution as "the continuing reformation of the Church catholic"). One evidence of this is the writings of one of its leaders—one-time WARC theological secretary Alan P. F. Sell (b. 1935). As theological secretary, Sell's own approach to Reformed theology can be trusted to lie somewhere in the mainstream of contemporary worldwide Reformed thought. Sell was professor of Christian doctrine and philosophy of religion at Wales' United Theological College before his retirement.

During his career as a Reformed theologian Sell wrote many books, including a volume about the Calvinist versus Arminian debate over salvation: *The Great Debate: Calvinism, Arminianism, and Salvation.* There he criticized some aspects of traditional Calvinism without taking sides with Arminianism. According to him, "The Arminian ethical protest [against the doctrine of double predestination] cannot easily be set aside,"[5] and "on balance we feel that an amelioration of Calvinism is to be preferred to a capitulation to Arminian extremes."[6] The context makes clear that he does not so much object to ordinary Arminianism (e.g., as taught by Arminius himself) as to some rational extremes to which some have taken it. He distinguishes between "Arminianism of the heart," which he finds much more acceptable, and "Arminianism of the head"—a kind of rationalistic and even deistic religion, which he finds objectionable.

But the most intriguing comment by Sell in *The Great Debate* is the one quoted above about a desired "amelioration of Calvinism." In other words, like many others in the modern Reformed movement, Sell believes some aspects of classical "high Calvinism" must be modified. He leaves no doubt what he is driving at when he quotes Scottish Presbyterian theologian James Orr (1844–1913), who criticized Calvin's idea of God's sovereignty because in it "love is subordinated to sovereignty, instead of sovereignty to love."[7] Like Orr and many other Reformed thinkers, Sell believes Calvin got his Reformed theology partly right and partly wrong. In one telling statement Sell suggests that Calvin's doctrine of election be reinterpreted so that "God calls not simply individuals, but *a people* for his praise" (i.e., corporate election).[8] This is what Arminius believed about election; most Arminians throughout history have interpreted it this way.

In a three-volume set of semi-systematic theology with the overarching title *Doctrine and Devotion*,[9] Sell expressed a revisionist perspective of Reformed theology that Calvin would probably not recognize as continuous with his own thought, especially in the areas of God's sovereignty in history (providence) and salvation (predestination). Throughout the three volumes Sell repeatedly rejects any form of divine determinism (the idea that God foreordains and renders certain everything that happens in history without exception) and affirms the limited free will of human persons. To be fair, it should be said that Sell also attributes all the "work" of salvation to God and none to human beings. He would no doubt point to that as evidence of his Reformed leanings. However, Arminius affirmed the same thing, as have all classical Arminians since.[10]

Here I have used Sell as a case study in what I call "revisionist Reformed theology" to point out that "Reformed theology" is by no means a monolithic structure or a closed system, as some among the new Calvinist movement (and their forerunners and mentors) would have it. It is by no means identical with the TULIP system of soteriology or with a deterministic view of God's sovereignty in either providence or predestination. In fact, many leading Reformed spokespersons have come to reject those while insisting that they are still Reformed.

Others besides Sell could be mentioned: G. C. Berkouwer (1903–1996), one of the most influential Reformed theologians of the twentieth century, fought against what he regarded as a rigid Calvinism that insisted on God's sovereignty even to the extent of affirming God's decree of reprobation against certain individual persons (that is, that God foreordained some specific human beings to hell). Hendrikus Berkhof (1914–1995) (not to be confused with Calvinist theologian Louis Berkhof [1873–1957], to whom he was not related), a prolific Dutch Reformed theologian, radically rejected the traditional Calvinist view of God's sovereignty, emphasizing instead God's self-limitation and human covenant partnership with God in the kingdom and in salvation.[11]

Another well-recognized Reformed theologian who revised Reformed theology away from classical Calvinism was James Daane, who served as professor of theology and ministry at Fuller Theological Seminary for many years. His *The Freedom of God: A Study of Election and Pulpit*[12] is a vigorous attack on divine determinism and especially the doctrine of God's decree of double predestination. For Daane, God's unconditional election is of only one individual, Jesus Christ, and otherwise of the corporate people of God—Israel and the church. And Daane radically rejects any decree of reprobation.

Finally, another influential revisionist Reformed theologian critical of high Calvinism is South African Adrio König, retired professor of theology at UNISA (University of South Africa), whose *Here Am I! A Believer's Reflection on God*[13] attacked any deterministic version of God's sovereignty and affirmed instead a self-limiting God, who suffers human rejection and evil and invites people into covenant partnership with himself without foreordaining or determining their choices. Again, as with Berkhof and the other revisionist Reformed theologians mentioned here, most if not all Arminians could gladly sign on to these Reformed visions of God's sovereignty.

I am well aware, of course, that more traditionalist Reformed and Calvinist theologians and their followers will dismiss these revisionists out of hand as defectors from the tradition. The revisionists would likely respond that the traditionalists are forgetting the Reformed motto "reformed and always reforming." Even the Reformed tradition itself needs reforming and, according to the revisionists, it has never been so brittle as to be incapable of change. Nevertheless, one has to admit that especially in America in recent years, with the rise of the new Calvinism, "Reformed" is most often used in evangelical Protestant circles for the TULIP system of soteriology (without, of course, excluding other aspects of Reformed belief). But is that necessarily an accurate use of the Reformed label? Even among evangelicals in America "Reformed" is described in quite different ways.

As my first witness I call well-known and widely recognized Reformed historian and theologian Donald McKim, a reference book editor for the Presbyterian publisher Westminster John Knox Press and former professor of theology at several Presbyterian and Reformed seminaries, including Memphis Theological Seminary (where he also served as dean) and the University of Dubuque Theological Seminary. McKim is a graduate of Westminster Theological Seminary (a bastion of conservative Reformed theology) and has a PhD from the University of Pittsburgh. During his career he edited and authored numerous books on Reformed theology, including *The Encyclopedia of the Reformed Faith*, *The Westminster Handbook to Reformed Theology*, and *Introducing the Reformed Faith*.[14] By virtually all accounts McKim is a reliable authority on Reformed theology.

According to McKim, "Each church or group of churches ... has its own definition of what it means to be 'Reformed.'"[15] In other words, according to this expert, "Reformed" is not a monolithic or closed category; it is, in fact, an essentially contested concept. And he affirms that it is a living tradition still in the making.[16] However, that does not mean it is an empty or meaningless category. Rather, according to McKim, we have to treat it as a diverse family—the "Reformed family" that traces its ancestry back to John Calvin of Geneva and further back. "The Reformed faith ... has its family tree," McKim declares, and like all family trees it is full of diversity.[17]

One aspect of that diversity, according to McKim, is the differences between Calvin's own approach to theology and that of his followers.

"Though Calvin had a brilliant systematic mind, his successors in the seventeenth century systematized his theology even further. It became more detailed and cast in the mold called scholasticism."[18] The rest of McKim's book reveals that he does not regard this development as a good thing.

Like many other scholars of the Reformed tradition McKim describes it in terms of "family resemblances" rather than as a closed system. One family resemblance is "confessionalism"—Reformed Christians frequently confess their faith using the historic creeds of Christendom (especially the Nicene Creed) and the historic Reformed confessions such as the Helvetic Consensus Formula of 1675.[19] According to McKim, however, these confessions of faith are always "relative," "temporary," and "provisional."[20] He realizes that not all Reformed people will agree and says, "Though some Reformed bodies have tended to become more narrow and almost assume that their formulations are the only means of expressing God's truth, this impulse runs counter to the genuine heartbeat of Reformed faith."[21] An example of the "more narrow" approach to Reformed confessions might be the work of Sproul whose books such as *What Is Reformed Theology?* almost treat the Westminster Confession of Faith as an authority equal with Scripture itself. (Of course Sproul would deny that, but he appeals to it often as if it were an incorrigible authority for Christian and especially Reformed thought.)

McKim's treatment of Reformed faith underscores its common ground with other branches of Christianity; he includes chapters on Scripture as the Word of God, the Trinity, and the person of Christ, where nothing distinctively Calvinist is found. In the chapters on providence and salvation, where one would expect to find heavy emphasis on Calvinist distinctives, McKim provides modest accounts of Reformed doctrine. For example, when discussing God's sovereignty over history (providence), he acknowledges that Reformed people traditionally emphasize that "God's plan and purposes guide the creation, human history, and human lives. The God who *knows* all things also *wills* all things."[22] However, when he turns to the problem of God and evil, he explicitly denies what many consider the central controversial point of high Calvinism—that God even foreordains and renders certain ("sends") evil: "We do not speak of God 'sending' evil upon us or causing those things in our lives that are against the purposes of God's gracious love and justice as we know these in Jesus Christ."[23]

Of course, most Reformed theologians deny that God actually "causes" evil in any straightforward sense, but as I will show below many Calvinists *do* affirm that even sin and evil are parts of the foreordained divine plan and are rendered certain by God to fit into God's purposes for history. McKim seems to want to avoid any implication that evil is part of God's plan or that God renders it certain. His is a softened version of God's sovereignty that would probably not satisfy many of the new Calvinists and their mentor theologians.

Most surprisingly, perhaps, McKim does not even mention limited atonement (the "L" in TULIP), also called "particular redemption" by many Calvinists. His book includes an entire chapter on the "Work of Christ" in which he discusses the Reformed doctrine of atonement. But one searches in vain for limited atonement—something that would shock many Calvinists.

In his chapter on "Salvation: Receiving God's Gift," McKim claims to describe "Reformed emphases," but says little about unconditional election or irresistible grace. He places the stress on corporate election to service rather than individual election to salvation, only briefly mentioning the latter: "Some believe; others do not. The explanation for this is in the eternal election of God."[24] Finally, near the end of his book, McKim makes my point clearly: "Not all Reformed Christians today subscribe to [the] 'Five Points of Calvinism.'"[25]

The contrast between this account of Reformed faith and Sproul's in *What Is Reformed Theology?* (and other, similar books) is bewildering. There Sproul virtually equates Reformed theology with the high Calvinism of TULIP and as strong and absolute a doctrine of God's sovereignty as possible: "If God is not sovereign, then he is not God. It belongs to God as God to be sovereign."[26] The context makes clear that by "sovereign" Sproul means God is the absolute determiner and controller of everything down to the minutest details. The rest of his book reads very differently from McKim's; it expounds the Reformed faith in terms of TULIP, including double predestination—God's decree of reprobation of some to eternal torment in hell.[27]

Here, then, we have two renowned scholars of the Reformed tradition, Donald McKim and R. C. Sproul, defining and describing it in very different ways. The only things they seem to have in common are historical lineage of the Reformed heritage, including but not exclusively determined by Calvin and an emphasis on divine sovereignty regarded as somehow missing in non-Reformed theologies. Of course, even Sproul would admit that "Reformed" includes more than just TULIP (as McKim tirelessly argues), but that soteriological system serves him as the distinctive feature of Reformed theology whereas it does not for McKim.

An American Reformed theologian who seems to walk a line somewhere between McKim and Sproul is Fuller Theological Seminary president Richard Mouw, whose little book *Calvinism in the Las Vegas Airport*[28] is a delightful tour of Reformed theology as understood by the author. Mouw affirms TULIP without placing it front and center as the be-all and end-all of Reformed theology; for him the Reformed vision of a transformed society seems more important than a particular doctrine of God's sovereignty. Nevertheless, he says he subscribes to the TULIP doctrines while admitting they "have a harsh feel about them."[29] It is easy to discern that Mouw is uncomfortable with the classical Calvinist emphasis on TULIP and especially with the ways in which it is often expressed. "I must ... say up front that ... I find many Calvinists lacking in gentleness and respect. I even find these qualities missing in Calvinists' interactions with other *Christians*. Indeed, Calvinists are often not very gentle and respectful when debating fine points of doctrine with fellow *Calvinists*."[30]

Mouw's discomfort with some points of TULIP is apparent in his chapter on the "L" in TULIP—limited atonement or particular redemption, that is, the idea that Christ's atoning death on the cross was intended by God only for some sinners (the elect). He calls it his "shelf doctrine," by which he means a part of his belief system that doesn't function in his life on a day-to-day basis.[31] While continuing to affirm it (in a somewhat revised fashion), Mouw wishes to leave it mostly alone and only bring it down "off the shelf" once in a while, and then to put it back again. One can only wonder why anyone would want to hold onto a "shelf doctrine."

But my point is that Mouw represents a third type of evangelical Reformed theologian in America (and perhaps throughout the world). The first is represented by McKim, whose Reformed theology is flexible and open to revision and does not regard TULIP as central. The second is represented by Sproul, whose Reformed theology seems quite closed and revolves around a strong view of God's sovereignty (that I call divine determinism) and TULIP. The third is represented by Mouw, who affirms all the historic elements of Calvinism but is somewhat embarrassed by at least some of them and does not regard TULIP or absolute divine sovereignty as the signature themes of Reformed faith.

Thus, the problem of defining "Reformed" continues and will probably always continue. As I said earlier (and hope to have now proven) it is an essentially contested concept. Still, it is not empty or meaningless. Drawing on the resources I have mentioned so far here are my theses about the meaning of "Reformed." First, it is an ideal type of Protestant theology tied to a historical branch of the Protestant Reformation stemming from the reforming efforts of primarily the Swiss theologians Ulrich Zwingli and John Calvin (and their associates) but also of Strasburg theologian Martin Bucer. Strains of it may be found in denominations as diverse as Congregationalism and Anglicanism.

Second, common to all Reformed theologies is an emphasis on God's supremacy and sovereignty, although this is interpreted in different ways. "Reformed" is not synonymous with TULIP, although TULIP is present within the Reformed tradition and all Reformed people tend to deal with it in some way (even if only by rejecting it as the central feature of their faith).

Third, the Reformed faith is confessional (per McKim) and tends to look back in some way to certain Reformed confessions of faith such as the Heidelberg Catechism and the Westminster Confession of Faith. (Whether Baptists can be Reformed I leave as an open question while pointing out that many Baptists adhere to the Second London Baptist Confession of Faith of 1689, which was heavily influenced by the Westminster Confession and in turn influenced later Baptist confessions such as the New Hampshire Confession of Faith.)

I wish to make clear that *I am not against Reformed faith in general.* But closely related to the new Calvinism of the young, restless, Reformed movement is what I call a "radical Reformed theology" that is not representative of all Reformed people or their theological traditions. I will expound more on that in chapter 3.

THREE

MERE CALVINISM: THE TULIP SYSTEM

Too many people (especially in the young, restless, Reformed movement of the new Calvinism) simply equate Calvinism with Reformed theology as if they were synonymous. As I explained above, that is simply not the case. However, sometimes common usage outruns correct use of words, and the habit of equating the two is so pervasive as to be almost beyond correction. Nevertheless, it is important to distinguish the two as many people who legitimately consider themselves Reformed do not adhere to what is usually considered Calvinism in all its features. Calvinism is a part of the history of the Reformed tradition, but it is not all of it and, for many Reformed people anyway, it can be dispensed with.

Here I want to explicate the essential features of historical Calvinism as a belief system. While "Reformed" designates a branch of the Reformation and a broad and diverse family of Protestants, "Calvinism" designates a set of beliefs about God's sovereignty especially in relation to the doctrines of providence and predestination. It is far from monolithic, but it is more unified than Reformed. There are essential features of Calvinism without which it would not be recognizable as such, but within that commonality exists a diversity that often gives rise to debates even among Calvinists.

Before getting into those areas of diversity, however, I want to allow leading Calvinists to explain what I call "garden variety Calvinism" or "mere Calvinism." Surprisingly it is *not* tied precisely or exactly to whatever Calvin happened to teach, although it is historically and theologically indebted to Calvin. What we usually call "Calvinism" today includes some elements Calvin himself did not emphasize if he believed them at all. One example is "limited atonement." Some historical theologians believe Calvin would be displeased with the overly systematic and scholastic nature of the Calvinism developed by his followers. I will explain these matters more fully in this chapter.

A leading Calvinist theologian and reliable guide to this general Calvinist outlook on God's sovereignty is Loraine Boettner. Although he is not well-known, a half century after the peak of his productivity as an author, his influence on contemporary Calvinists is profound. He is widely considered by Calvinist theologians in America a great "father figure" who packaged and handed down the Calvinist faith to them. He is certainly not regarded as infallible, and some Calvinists will disagree with some of his teachings, but few Calvinist theologians of the twentieth century can stand shoulder-to-shoulder with him in terms of influence and respect.

According to Boettner, Calvinism begins with a vision of God derived from Scripture that is also consistent with philosophical theism: "The very essence of consistent theism is that God would have an exact plan for the world, would foreknow the actions of all the creatures He proposed to create and through His all-inclusive providence would control the whole system."[1] Boettner nails it down further by asserting that God "very obviously predetermined every event which would happen" so that "even the sinful acts of men are included in this plan."[2] For Boettner (and many other Calvinists) this belief in meticulous divine providence (which I will call "divine determinism" and explain why in chapter 4) is grounded in God's infinity (philosophical theism) and Scriptures such as Amos 3:6, "When disaster comes to a city, has not the Lord caused it?"

Virtually all Calvinists (as distinct from some in the Reformed tradition and especially what I have called "revisionist Reformed" theologians) affirm a strong or high view of God's sovereignty such as Boettner's. Did Calvin himself affirm such? In Calvin's *Institutes of the Christian Religion*, Geneva's chief pastor wrote about God's providence: "We ought undoubtedly to hold that whatever changes are discerned in the world are produced from the secret stirring of God's hand ... what God has determined must necessarily so take place."[3] The surrounding context, including a vivid illustration about a merchant robbed and killed by thieves, makes absolutely clear that Calvin believed nothing at all can happen that is not foreordained and rendered certain by God. He says that a Christian will realize that nothing is truly an accident, as everything is planned by God.

This, then, is the first point of mere Calvinism: the total, absolute, meticulous sovereignty of God in providence by which God governs the entire course of human history down to the minutest details and renders everything certain so that no event is fortuitous or accidental but fits into God's overall plan and purpose. Boettner expresses it well: "There is nothing casual nor contingent in the world"[4] because "the world as a whole and in all its parts and movements and changes was brought into a unity by the governing, all-pervading, all-harmonizing activity of the divine will, and its purpose was to manifest the divine glory."[5] Few, if any, real Calvinists would quibble with any of this. (I say "real Calvinists" because it is not difficult to find people who claim to be Calvinists who are not. For example, many Southern Baptists think they are Calvinists just because they believe in the eternal security of the believer—the fifth point of the TULIP system. But that by itself hardly makes one a Calvinist!)

I will expound and critique this Calvinist view of God's sovereignty in the next chapter. It is not what all Christians believe. All Christians have always believed that nothing at all can happen without God's permission, and almost all Christians have always believed God foreknows whatever will happen. But Calvinists typically go further and claim that whatever happens is planned and rendered certain by God. Calvin explicitly denied mere foreknowledge or permission by God—even of evil.[6]

Some readers might wonder if I have simply chosen an extreme Calvinist—Boettner—to represent garden variety or mere Calvinism. Not at all. All of these ideas about God's sovereignty in history and salvation can be found in contemporary Calvinists such as Sproul and Piper. I will quote them when I turn to my critique in the next chapter. Here I am simply using Boettner as a model to expound mainstream, "garden variety," mere Calvinism.

According to Boettner (and most Calvinists) God is not only supreme and absolutely in control (and controlling) in history; he is also absolutely controlling regarding who will and who will not be saved. This is where we turn to the famous (or infamous) acrostic TULIP to describe the Calvinist system of soteriology. Readers should know the origin of TULIP. It is an acrostic developed in the nineteenth century to help students remember the so-called "five points of Calvinism" as they were stated in the Canons of the Synod of Dort in 1618/1619.

Dort was a gathering of Calvinist "divines" (theologians, scholars, pastors) in the Dutch city of Dordrecht to respond to the beliefs of the Remonstrants—followers of Jacob Arminius. The Remonstrants presented the leaders of the Reformed Church of the Netherlands a "Remonstrance" or protest against certain common Calvinist ideas. Some historians (especially Calvinists) have misrepresented this document as if it rejected all five of the beliefs represented by TULIP (total depravity, unconditional election, limited atonement, irresistible grace, perseverance of the saints). In fact, it only rejected the middle three, leaving total depravity and perseverance of the saints open to further discussion. (There were various versions of the "Remonstrance" written and published throughout the decade after Arminius's death and the Synod of Dort, and some left perseverance open while others seemed to close it off as wrong. But all affirmed total depravity.)

The Synod of Dort rejected the Remonstrants' "Remonstrance" and affirmed the so-called five points of Calvinism that later came to be summed up using the heuristic device TULIP. The Canons (decrees) of Dort included much more than TULIP, but those five beliefs were the ones thought to be denied by the Remonstrants so they are usually treated as the essence of the pronouncements of the Synod of Dort.

Ever since Dort Calvinism has been summarized by Calvinists themselves using the five points, and Boettner follows them rather closely in his exposition of the Calvinist faith. So do numerous other Calvinist authors whose book titles reveal the centrality of TULIP: *The Five Points of Calvinism* by Christian Reformed pastor-theologian Edwin H. Palmer[7] and *The Five Points of Calvinism: Defined, Defended and Documented* by David N. Steele and Curtis C. Thomas.[8] Other books do not have the five points in their titles but nevertheless organize their expositions of Calvinism according to TULIP. One example is Sproul's *What Is Reformed Theology?* (One notable exception is H. Henry Meeter, *The Basic Ideas of Calvinism*,[9] which barely mentions TULIP. This book seems to be more of an exposition of Reformed theology and social thought in general than Calvinist soteriology in particular.)

Many, if not all, Calvinists agree with Boettner about the five points as a system. They are, he wrote, a "simple, harmonious, self-consistent system," and "prove any one of them false and the whole system must be abandoned."[10] One question that will arise later is whether this system can be found in Calvin. I will argue it cannot be and that at least the "L" is created and inserted into the system after him. But that doesn't bother most Calvinists as they do not think their Calvinism must adhere slavishly to whatever Calvin believed or wrote.

"T" FOR TOTAL DEPRAVITY

The first point of the Calvinist system is "T" for total depravity. This is a widely misunderstood concept; it does not mean that human beings are as evil as they can possibly be. The "total" is what misleads people to think that. Rather, typically, it means that every part of every human person (except Jesus Christ, of course) is infected and so affected by sin that he or she is utterly helpless to please God before being regenerated (born again) by the Spirit of God. According to Boettner, the natural person, before and apart from the regenerating grace of God, always freely sins and delights in it[11] because "he is an alien by birth, and a sinner by choice."[12] The "natural virtues" of people do not count as good because they are done with wrong motives; depravity lies in the condition of the heart inherited from Adam.[13] Human beings are born with a corrupt nature but are nevertheless fully responsible for the sins they cannot avoid because of this condition.[14] Boettner claims that "only Calvinists seem to take this doctrine of the fall [original sin] very seriously."[15]

Again, is this strongly pessimistic view of humanity consistent with Calvin's own teachings? Without any doubt it is. Calvin wrote that because of the fall of Adam "the whole [of every] man is overwhelmed—as by a deluge—from head to foot, so that no part is immune from sin and all that proceeds from him is to be imputed to sin. As Paul says, all turnings of the thoughts ... are enmities against God ... and therefore death."[16]

Is this also consistent with contemporary Calvinist teaching after Boettner? Indeed it is. Sproul expresses it succinctly: "In our corrupt humanity we never do a single good thing."[17] Like Boettner and Calvin before him Sproul attributes this hopeless and helpless condition of the natural person apart from God's regenerating grace to the fall of Adam. For all of them—at least for most, if not all Calvinists—all humans except Jesus Christ inherit Adam's corrupted nature and are accounted guilty for Adam's sin. Boettner writes: "Adam's sin is imputed to his descendents."[18] Sproul sums up the dour Calvinist view of humanity because of the fall this way: "Man is incapable of elevating himself to the good without the work of God's grace within. We can no more return ourselves to God than an empty vessel can refill itself with water."[19]

Many Calvinists explain the human condition after the fall and before regeneration by the Holy Spirit as literally spiritually dead, basing that on Ephesians 2. In other words, for typical Calvinism, the natural, fallen human person is utterly incapable of even desiring God or the things of God. There is no moral ability (as opposed to a hypothetical natural ability that does not exist in spiritual matters) to reach out to God or to accept God's offer of salvation. Everything that flows from the dead person is putrid and filthy even if it seems to be virtuous. The reason is that true virtue is defined by the motive, and the sinner's heart, blackened by sin, has a constant disposition toward self rather than toward God or neighbor. This account of the human condition is important to keep in mind because it is *why* Calvinists argue that no one can be saved without unconditional election and irresistible grace.

Like Calvin, Calvinists typically acknowledge the existence of "civic virtues" in fallen, natural people who are spiritually dead. Calvin waxed eloquent about the "natural gifts" of fallen people, who are able by the help of God's Spirit through common grace to achieve great things in the arts and sciences.[20] Of course, none of these abilities or achievements has anything to do with salvation. Sproul comments on the reality of "civil virtue" by which people outwardly conform to the law of God and perform acts of charity, but he denies that these are any signs of spiritual life because they are all done out of self-interest.[21] The natural, fallen person may achieve great things, but he or she cannot please God because the heart is still corrupt and self-centered. Sin lies in the motives, and they are entirely wrong until the Holy Spirit regenerates the person.

"U" FOR UNCONDITIONAL ELECTION

The second point of TULIP is unconditional election. "Election" is another biblical word for predestination to salvation (or service); they are synonymous. All Christians believe in election; Calvinists believe in it in a particular way. Boettner expresses it clearly: "The Reformed Faith has held to the existence of an eternal, divine decree which, antecedently to any difference or desert in men themselves, separates the human race into two portions and ordains one to everlasting life and the other to everlasting death [hell]."[22] This is, of course, what is commonly known as "double predestination."

Some Calvinists will deny this teaching in favor of a "single predestination," often called "mild" or "moderate Calvinism." (These terms are also sometimes used for other permutations of Calvinism.) Single predestination is belief that God chooses some fallen persons to save while simply "passing over" others and "leaving them" to their deserved damnation. In other words, according to this idea there is no decree of God by which he foreordains anyone to hell. That is, there is no "decree of reprobation" but only one of election to salvation.

Boettner and other Calvinists scoff at the idea of single predestination. He pointed out, rightly I judge, that for God to predestine some to salvation *is* to predestine some to damnation. He wrote of reprobation that "this, too, is of God."[23] He explained it this way: "We [Calvinists] believe that from all eternity God has intended to leave some of Adam's posterity in their sins, and that the decisive factor in the life of each is to be found only in God's will."[24] This may be putting the matter a little more strongly than many Calvinists wish to put it, but it courageously clings consistently to belief in the absolute sovereignty of God in all things. Note what Boettner is saying here: the "decisive factor" in some people's going to hell is God's will. Boettner was impatient, to say the least, with Calvinists who argue for single predestination: "'Mild Calvinism' is synonymous with sickly Calvinism, and sickness, if not cured, is the beginning of the end."[25]

What did Calvin say? Did he believe in this double predestination, including God's sovereign reprobation of certain human persons to hell? He wrote: "God once established by his eternal and unchangeable plan those whom he long before determined once for all to receive into salvation, and those whom, on the other hand, he would devote to destruction."[26] Lest anyone misunderstand him, Calvin drove his point home by ridiculing those who accept election but reject reprobation, calling that an "absurd" notion: "Therefore, those whom God passes over, he condemns; and this he does for no other reason than that he wills to exclude them from the inheritance which he predestines for his own children."[27] Calvin notoriously recognized and affirmed the highly objectionable character of this double predestination and especially the reprobation side of it, calling it "the horrible decree."[28]

What about other Calvinists? Sproul unequivocally affirms unconditional election of some to salvation and predestination of others to damnation:

> It [the Calvinist view of predestination] teaches that from all eternity God has chosen to intervene in the lives of some people and bring

> them to saving faith and has chosen not to do that for other people. From all eternity, without any prior view of our human behavior, God has chosen some unto election and others unto reprobation.... The basis for God's choice does not rest in man but solely in the good pleasure of the divine will.[29]

To those who say that God elects some to salvation but does not predestine anyone to damnation Sproul responds: "If there is such a thing as predestination at all, and if that predestination does not include all people, then we must not shrink from the necessary inference that there are two sides to predestination. It is not enough to talk about Jacob; we must also consider Esau [referring to Romans 9]."[30]

Sproul carefully explains that these two decrees of God—election and reprobation—are not equal. He rejects what he calls "hyper-Calvinism," which believes in "equal ultimacy" of the decrees of election and reprobation. (Here is one area of diversity among Calvinists, although Sproul declares what he calls "hyper-Calvinism" as being "anti-Calvinist!"[31]) As he explains it, the decree of election is positive while the decree of reprobation is negative. In other words, God positively puts faith in the hearts of the elect while purposefully neglecting to do so with the reprobate. The only difference is that God does not create unbelief in the hearts of the reprobate; he simply leaves them alone in their condemnation while he creates belief in the hearts of the elect.[32]

One can only wonder how big a difference this really is. How does this make the two decrees not equally ultimate? Both are unconditional in the sense that God's choice is not based on anything God sees in the persons chosen or passed over. As I will explain in chapter 5, calling one decree "positive" and the other "negative" does not seem to lessen the awfulness of reprobation. Sproul accuses hyper-Calvinism of doing "radical violence to the integrity of God's character."[33] A critic of Sproul's high Calvinist view would say the same about his view.

Some readers who have come to embrace Calvinism (or are considering that) by hearing or reading John Piper may be asking whether *he* embraces this "dreadful decree" of reprobation. That is, does Piper believe predestination is unconditional and double? Without doubt he does. In *The Pleasures of God* he discusses "The Pleasure of God in Election" and leaves no doubt that he agrees with Calvin, Boettner, and Sproul. Election, he says, is unconditional because "it is not based on what someone does after birth. It is free and unconditional."[34] He does not dwell long on the nonelect but affirms that God chooses some not to save even though he has compassion on them.[35] I will deal with this claim in the next chapter; it seems contradictory to me and to most, if not all, non-Calvinists.[36]

The main point of the "U" of TULIP, for Calvinists, is the *unconditional* nature of election to salvation (which would also be true of reprobation). God's predestination of the eternal destinies of individual human beings *has nothing whatever to do with their foreseen character or choices.* Every Calvinist author emphatically drives this point home. Boettner declares that God's choice is not based on anything God sees in a person, including his foreknowledge of their faith or repentance. Even faith and repentance are gifts of God to the elect and cannot be the basis of their election.[37] For Calvinists this is a doctrine of mercy and grace—that God sovereignly chooses to save some undeserving sinners and does all the saving himself without any cooperation from them. Critics believe they choose to overlook the dark side of this doctrine, which is that God *could* save everyone—since election to salvation is unconditional—but does not. Boettner attempts to explain why:

> The condemnation of the non-elect is designed primarily to furnish an eternal exhibition, before men and angels, of God's hatred for sin, or, in other words, it is to be an eternal manifestation of the justice of God.... This decree displays one of the divine attributes which apart from it could never have been adequately appreciated.[38]

Many Calvinists prefer to appeal to mystery at this point and not offer any suggestion as to why God doesn't save everyone. Perhaps this is one isolated element in some Calvinists' theology that could rightly be called extreme or radical. Boettner's belief (and other Calvinists' similar answers) raises this question: Was not the cross of Jesus Christ a sufficient manifestation of God's justice and hatred toward sin? (Not that Jesus was a sinner but the sin of the world was laid on him partly to display how seriously God takes sin.) Boettner's and other Calvinists' speculative reason for reprobation would seem to lessen the glory of the cross.

"L" FOR LIMITED ATONEMENT

The third element of TULIP is "limited atonement"—also and preferably called by many Calvinists "particular redemption." This is the one point of TULIP contested by many self-identified Calvinists and *per-*

haps totally missing from Calvin's own thought. (This will be discussed in detail in chapter 6.) Many Calvinists say they are "four pointers" or "four-point Calvinists." They mean they believe in T and U and I and P but not in L. However, the L—limited atonement, particular redemption—is part of the historical Calvinist system of soteriology, and many high Calvinists argue it cannot be dropped without doing violence to the whole Calvinist scheme of salvation.

Before expounding this point of TULIP, I should note that all Calvinists accept the "penal substitution theory" of the atonement. That is, they believe with Calvin and the Puritans and most evangelical Christians that God punished Jesus for the sins of the people God wanted to save—either the whole world including all people (the typical Arminian view) or the elect (the typical Calvinist view). In other words, Jesus Christ satisfied the justice of God by bearing the deserved punishment of every person God wanted to save. That's what makes them "savable." Many non-Calvinists affirm this doctrine of the atonement as well, but Calvinists typically argue that the belief that Christ bore the punishment for every person's sins leads inevitably to universalism—belief in the salvation of all.

Boettner strongly endorses limited atonement, arguing that it is logically connected with unconditional election. With most Calvinists he emphatically asserts that the *value* of Christ's death was *sufficient* for the salvation of all people, but that it was *efficient* to save only the elect.[39] Another way of putting that is that the benefits of Christ's death on the cross, though sufficient for the salvation of all people, were *intended by God* only for the elect. The limited nature of the atonement, then, was in its *scope* and not in its *value*. This is why many Calvinists prefer the term "particular redemption" or "definite atonement." It was particularly intended by God for particular people (as opposed to everyone indiscriminately), and it definitely secured or accomplished the salvation of those for whom it was intended—the elect.[40]

In true Calvinist fashion, Boettner starkly states the doctrine of particular redemption as it applies to the nonelect: "It [the cross] was not, then, a general and indiscriminate love of which all men are equally objects, but a peculiar, mysterious, infinite love for the elect, which caused God to send His Son into the world to suffer and die."[41]

What about other Calvinists? Do they affirm this limited atonement doctrine as Boettner did (and perhaps Calvin did not)? John Piper definitely affirms it: "He [Christ] did not die for all men in the same sense. The intention of the death of Christ for the children of God [the elect] was that it purchased far more than the rising of the sun and the opportunity to be saved. The death of Christ actually saves from ALL evil those for whom Christ died 'especially.'"[42] Sproul definitely affirms it. He prefers to call this doctrine "purposeful atonement": "The atonement's ultimate purpose is found in the ultimate purpose or will of God. This purpose or design does not include the entire human race. If it did, the entire human race would surely be redeemed."[43]

Answers to these Calvinists' charges against belief in universal atonement (e.g., that it logically requires belief in universal salvation) will be answered in chapter 6. In my opinion, they are simply wrong. There is no logical connection between universal atonement and universal salvation anymore than there is a logical connection between the president of the United States declaring an unconditional amnesty for Vietnam War protesters who fled to Canada to escape the draft and every one of them automatically availing himself of that amnesty and coming back to the U.S. (This actually happened under President Jimmy Carter, and many who could have come home because all was forgiven did not return.) This is only a brief overview of TULIP. I'll address complex issues in more depth in subsequent chapters. Here it is simply important to note, for readers' understanding of Calvinism, that most Calvinists deny that God intended the cross for all people, which means, of course, that he does not love everyone in the same way.

Boettner and Piper do affirm that the cross benefits everyone in some way. Thus, it is true to say (at least for them) that Christ died for all. Boettner wrote that "certain benefits" of the cross extended to all humanity in general. These are "temporal blessings" only and have nothing to do with salvation.[44] Piper teaches that Christ did die "for all" but not in the same way. Attempting to take seriously the "all" passages of Scripture (which will be dealt with in more detail later) he says:

> We do not deny that all men are the intended beneficiaries of the cross in some sense. 1 Timothy 4:10 says that Christ is "the Savior of all men, especially of those who believe." What we deny is that all men are intended as the beneficiaries of the death of Christ in the same way. All of God's mercy toward unbelievers—from the rising sun (Matthew 5:45) to the worldwide preaching of the gospel (John 3:16)—is made possible because of the cross.[45]

Of course, as I will point out and discuss in more detail in chapter 6, one might legitimately wonder how beneficial the cross really is for those to whom God denies its saving power. How does the cross accomplish anything for the nonelect? How is the rising of the sun accomplished by the cross of Christ, and of what benefit is the preaching of the gospel to the nonelect? How does it accomplish the former and of what benefit is the latter to the nonelect? One can only suspect that both Piper and Boettner (and other Calvinists who claim that Christ died for the nonelect "in some sense") simply want to turn aside accusations that their view of limited atonement clashes with Scriptures that say Christ died for all.

Furthermore, especially Piper (and no doubt other Calvinists) wishes to say that God has genuine compassion on the nonelect for whom Christ did not die as an atoning sacrifice. "There is a general love of God that he bestows on all his creatures,"[46] but this is *not* the love God has for his elect. And, according to Piper, God has sincere compassion even for the nonelect so that he desires their salvation, even though he declines to provide for it on the cross.[47] To paraphrase John Wesley, this seems to be such a love and compassion as makes the blood run cold. What love refuses to save those who could be saved because election to salvation is unconditional? What compassion refuses to provide for their salvation when it could be provided for?

The point is that garden-variety, mere Calvinism typically, but not always, restricts the saving intention of God in the cross of Christ to the elect; it is not intended by God for the salvation of the reprobate, the nonelect. They are excluded from the atonement *except* in some attenuated sense of receiving some kind of temporal blessings from it that are left mostly unexplained. Thus, some Calvinists will refuse to say to a crowd of people or to strangers, "Christ died so that you can be saved" or "Christ died for your sins." That would be presumptuous; there is no way to know that. However, cleverly, Piper and some other Calvinists who believe in limited atonement can say to anyone and everyone, "Christ died for you," without meaning "Christ died for your sins" or "Because Christ died for you, you can be saved." Some might consider this a subterfuge, disingenuous.

On the basis of what Scriptures do Calvinists affirm limited atonement? Many critics, including some Calvinists who call themselves "four pointers," argue that this doctrine has no scriptural basis. However,

Boettner, Sproul, Piper, and others point to passages such as John 10:15; 11:51–52; and 17:6, 9, 19, in which Jesus says things such as "I lay down my life for the sheep." A main point of chapter 6, devoted to limited atonement, will be that the verse here that talks about Christ's dying for his people, his sheep, or the ones given to him by his Father does not necessarily exclude him from dying for others. In fact, 1 John 2:2 clearly states that he, Jesus, is the atonement for the sins of the whole world. Piper and others claim this refers to the children of God scattered throughout the world and not everyone.

"I" FOR IRRESISTIBLE GRACE

The fourth point of TULIP is variously called irresistible grace, effectual grace (Sproul's favored term for it), or efficacious grace (Boettner's favored term for it). A closely related term is monergism—belief that God is the sole active agent in salvation. Monergism is the opposite of synergism—the belief that salvation includes cooperation by the person being saved. Irresistible grace does not mean that all grace is always irresistible or efficacious. Rather, only saving grace given to the elect to regenerate them and to give them new birth is irresistible and effectual. A person chosen by God for salvation will not, because he or she cannot, resist the "inward call" of God because God "bends their will." It is not a matter of coercion; the Holy Spirit does not overwhelm and force the person to repent and believe; rather, the Holy Spirit transforms the person's heart so that he or she wants to repent and believe.

Boettner and other Calvinists link this aspect of their soteriology closely to total depravity:

> As Calvinists we hold that the condition of men since the fall is such that if left to themselves they would continue in their state of rebellion and refuse all offers of salvation. Christ would then have died in vain. But since it was promised ... the work of God in redemption has been rendered effective through the mission of the Holy Spirit who so operates on the chosen people that they are brought to repentance and faith, and thus made heirs of eternal life.[48]

They base this on their doctrine of total depravity as absolute spiritual deadness such that not even an elect person has the ability to respond to God, let alone reach out to God, until and unless God breathes new life into them in regeneration and Scripture. The main Scripture passage they typically point to is John 6:44, where Jesus says, "No one can come to me unless the Father who sent me draws him." Calvinists argue that the Greek word translated "draw" *always* means "compels" (but not "coerces"). To counter any idea that it means "coerce" (either in John 6 or in Calvinist theology) Sproul writes: "The whole point of irresistible grace is that rebirth quickens someone to spiritual life in such a way that Jesus is now seen in his irresistible sweetness."[49]

Boettner agrees: "This change [regeneration by means of irresistible grace through inward calling] is not accomplished through any external compulsion but through a new principle of life which has been created within the soul and which seeks after the food which alone can satisfy it."[50] This reliable Calvinist guide also states unequivocally that the work of the Holy Spirit in regenerating grace, although irresistible, never violates the person's free agency: "The elect are so influenced by divine power that their coming is an act of voluntary choice."[51] This seems peculiarly paradoxical, but that doesn't bother Boettner or other Calvinists.

With regard to Calvinists' appeal to John 6:44, in chapter 7 I will discuss whether the Greek word translated "draw" really means "compel" or "drag" or "draw irresistibly" as Sproul and other Calvinists argue. As with so many other proof texts used by Calvinists for their distinctive doctrines, this one is open to other and even better interpretations. For example, if the Greek word for "draw" in John 6:44 can only mean "drag" or "compel" rather than "woo" or "call," then John 12:32 must be interpreted as teaching universal salvation. There Jesus says "And I, when I am lifted up from the earth, will draw all people to myself." The Greek word translated "draw" there is the same one used in John 6:44. Thus, if the word has to be interpreted "compel" or "drag," then Jesus would be saying in John 12:32 that he will compel or drag all men to himself. That's not how the verse is understood even by Calvinists!

Did Calvin believe and teach irresistible grace? Although he doesn't use the term, Calvin clearly did teach the concept at the end of a lengthy discussion of how God works in the elect to bring them to himself: "To sum up: by free adoption God makes those whom he wills to be his sons; the intrinsic cause of this is in himself, for he is content with his own good pleasure."[52]

Sproul expresses this doctrine strongly: "God unilaterally and monergistically does for us what we cannot do for ourselves."[53] In true Calvinist fashion he places regeneration by the Holy Spirit (being born again) *before* conversion (in logical order of the events of salvation). That is, before a person is even able to receive the gifts of faith and repentance, he or she must be made a new creature in Christ Jesus through the "effectual inward call" of God, which is comparable with a creation out of nothing.[54] In other words, God does not take some existing potential and build on it or draw it out to work salvation in a person's life. Rather, God takes a person dead in trespasses and sins and brings him or her to life spiritually.

Sproul, like all Calvinists, distinguishes between the "outward call," which is the gospel preached to everyone, and the "inward call," by which the Holy Spirit regenerates a person. Only the elect receive the latter, and it always results in their salvation and cannot do otherwise.[55] Regeneration, then, must precede conversion (repentance and faith) because no one would ever respond to God with repentance and faith unless he or she is first born again. The saved person usually is not aware of the priority of regeneration; he or she may sense that being born again *follows* upon faith and repentance, but theologically the Calvinist knows that cannot be the case.

This is a distinctive of the Calvinist scheme and, so far as I know, all Calvinists subscribe to it. Others might subscribe to it as well, but only if they believe that infant baptism regenerates a child (baptismal regeneration), as in Episcopal and Lutheran theology. However, many Protestants such as Baptists and Pentecostals believe that faith precedes regeneration in the logical order of salvation. The ordinary message of the gospel for most evangelical Christians is "believe and be saved," based on Scripture passages such as John 3:1–21, in which Jesus tells Nicodemus that he must be born again and that belief in him will accomplish that (v. 14). There is really no way to reconcile this passage with belief that regeneration precedes faith.

"P" FOR PERSEVERANCE

The fifth aspect of TULIP Calvinism is perseverance of the saints. This is perhaps the least controversial aspect of Calvinism because many non-Calvinists believe in it as well, based on Scripture passages such as Romans 8:35–39. Even Jacob Arminius (1560–1609), the great opponent of Calvinism, declared that he was unable to decide about this doctrine and left it for further study.[56] He died before finally making up his mind. The first Remonstrant statement of faith of 1610 did not include a denial or affirmation of it. Later, especially Wesley and his followers

(Methodists, Wesleyans) rejected it on the basis of Scriptures such as Hebrews 6. Still, this does not seem to be a particularly objectionable doctrine for many non-Calvinists because it does not touch on the central issue of disagreement: the character of God.

Nevertheless, it is worth briefly expounding this fifth point of TULIP as Calvinists believe it. Sproul rightly notes that the term "perseverance of the saints" is better expressed as "preservation of the saints" because the eternal security of the true believer is God's work entirely and not theirs.[57] All Calvinists believe that a truly elect person cannot ever be finally or fully lost because God will keep him or her from falling. Another term for this doctrine is "inamissable grace." It follows logically from the other points of TULIP. (Lutherans, however, who generally agree with monergism, reject this doctrine.)

Some non-Calvinists will argue vehemently against this belief; for the most part they are strong Arminians who are in reaction against Calvinism. For example, many Baptist churches are called "Free Will Baptists" precisely because they reject this doctrine held strongly by some even non-Calvinist Baptist churches. In fact, it would probably be safe to say that most Baptists, especially in the South, are not Calvinists but adhere fervently to inamissable grace under the phrase "eternal security." Free Will Baptists oppose not only Calvinism but also this doctrine as it is widely held by other Baptists.

We have just been on a "tour," as it were, of garden-variety or mere Calvinism. But it is not the whole story of Calvinism. In the next section I want to explore diversity among Calvinists more fully by examining some varieties of "mere Calvinism."

VARIETIES OF TULIP

It should be clear by now that I consider "Reformed" a more flexible category with much greater diversity than "Calvinism." Clearly, by contemporary worldwide standards such as the WCRC, the two categories are not inextricably linked *except* in the sense that all Reformed people claim a religious family tree that reaches back to the Swiss Reformation of the sixteenth century, including the work of John Calvin. But they do not all agree with TULIP or even much that Calvin said about God's sovereignty. Calvinism is not so much a family or heritage as it is a system of theological beliefs. It is firmly embedded in the Reformed tradition, but it is not identical with it.

Many in the Reformed tradition are uncomfortable with Calvinism (as were some Swiss reformers during Calvin's lifetime!), and Calvinism extends outside the worldwide Reformed community of churches into, for example, Baptist life. It can even be found here and there among the so-called Free Churches (e.g., Evangelical Free Church of America, which has in recent years been leaning more and more toward Calvinism) and occasionally even among Pentecostals. I recently met a Calvinist pastor of a large Assembly of God church; this was unheard of in the past and still would probably shake up the hierarchy of the AG denomination! This pastor's associate pastor is clearly a member of the young, restless, Reformed movement even though for an AG person, that is something of a misnomer and definitely an anomaly. To call someone both "Reformed" *and* Pentecostal seems more than odd.

I will here write about diversity among Calvinists *about* Calvinism rather than diversity *of* Calvinism. Why? Diversity is always of people; Calvinism is not a group of people but a theological construct that gets interpreted and lived out in various ways by various people—some within the Reformed family and some outside of it. The sketch of garden-variety or mere Calvinism given above focused on an ideal type of Calvinism shared by many Calvinists, but not all. All real Calvinists look to TULIP as a relatively accurate description of their soteriology, but some reject one point (always "L"), and some who accept all five points apply them to practices such as evangelism in different ways. And then there is the old argument between "supralapsarian" and "infralapsarian" Calvinists, which I will discuss shortly.

I have already mentioned the fact that many Calvinists reject the "L" in TULIP in favor of a combination of universal atonement and particular election and effectual grace. These "four point" Calvinists step out from the rest and argue that in spite of electing only some persons to salvation and only drawing some persons irresistibly to faith, God sent Christ to die for the sins of the whole world and not only for the sins of the elect. Criticism of limited atonement will come later here; for now I will restrict myself simply to pointing out that many Calvinists agree with Arminians and Lutherans (and perhaps others) that Christ's substitutionary death on the cross was actually intended by God for all people. In other words, he bore the punishment for the sins of the whole world without exception.

One notable Calvinist theologian of the Baptist tradition who accepted all points of TULIP except "L" was August Hopkins Strong (1836–1921), longtime professor of theology at Rochester Theological Seminary and author of numerous books, including the widely used and influential textbook *Systematic Theology*. On the basis of Scripture passages such as 1 John 2:2 Strong argued that "the atonement of Christ has made objective provision for the salvation of all, by removing from the divine mind every obstacle to the pardon and restoration of sinners, except their willful opposition to God and refusal to turn to him."[58]

Following Strong in true Baptist style, later Calvinist Baptist theologian Millard Erickson (b. 1932) argued similarly: "We conclude that the hypothesis of universal atonement is able to account for a larger segment of the biblical witness with less distortion than is the hypothesis of limited atonement."[59] Numerous others, especially Baptist and Free Church Calvinists, agree with Strong and Erickson. It was probably the majority Calvinism among non-Reformed evangelicals throughout much of the twentieth century—until the rise of the young, restless, Reformed movement under the influence of John Piper and others who argue strongly for limited atonement.

But what about theologians *within* the traditionally Reformed communities, such as conservative Presbyterian and Christian Reformed? Do they all affirm the "L" in TULIP? Hardly. One notable example is theologian James Daane, mentioned above, a member of the Christian Reformed Church. In *The Freedom of God* this Fuller Seminary professor blasted the Synod of Dort for citing "no Scripture passages to prove 'limited atonement'" and for virtually eliminating mystery from Reformed theology through scholastic modes of thought that focus on *number* rather than *community*. Of much traditional Calvinism he wrote:

> All ... attempts to employ number—the idea of limitation—to understand the nature of election, the election of the church, the nature of divine grace, and of Christ's atonement are really attempts to reduce the mystery of Christian truths to boundaries that we can rationally manage. Down this road all mystery disappears—the mystery of unbelief and no less the mystery of Christ and of the church.[60]

Critics may dismiss Daane as influenced by Swiss revisionist Reformed theologian Karl Barth (1886–1968), but his main influence was Dutch Reformed theologian Berkouwer, who is generally considered much more traditional than Barth. In any case, Daane represents someone *not Baptist* and fully within the Reformed family and an evangelical (not liberal or neoorthodox) who rejected limited atonement.

Perhaps the oldest and deepest division among Calvinists is over the order of the divine decrees. The debate goes back at least to Calvin's successor in Geneva, Theodore Beza. This is a somewhat subtle area of theology that puts off many novices, so I will take time and space here carefully to explain what it is all about and why Calvinists divide over this.

Soon after Calvin's death some of his followers adopted a style of theological work foreign to Calvin himself. It has generally been labeled "scholastic," referring back to the medieval theologians' tendency to use philosophy and logic to speculate about matters left unmentioned by Scripture. (The common example, though somewhat extreme, is, "How many angels can dance on the head of a pin?") One manifestation of this scholastic approach to Calvinism was an attempt to discern the logical (not temporal or chronological) order of God's decrees expressing his sovereignty over creation and redemption. The background question was: "Did God decree the election and reprobation of persons *before* or *after* the decree to permit the fall?" Here is another, and perhaps better, way of putting it: "Did God decree the election and reprobation of persons *in light of the fall* or *prior to and not in light of it*?

If this seems like a wholly speculative endeavor, even many Calvinists would agree. However, once some Calvinists later called "supralapsarians"—who argued that God's first and foremost decree was to save some persons yet to be created and damn others—appeared with their version of Calvinism, everyone had to weigh in. The "infralapsarians" were and are those who argue that God decreed to create and allow the fall (which all agree he actually foreordained!) first and only then decreed to elect some fallen persons to salvation and predestine others to damnation.

When the Synod of Dort met in 1618/1619, this was debated and the assembly of Reformed divines ultimately decided to allow both views without marginalizing either one as heresy. There were some present, however, who considered the supralapsarian view heresy because it seemed to make God the author of sin and evil. Boettner sides with supralapsarianism, calling it "high Calvinism."[61] (It should be noted, however, that this in no way makes his overall account of Calvinist theology in general, that is TULIP, different from infralapsarianism.) Sproul, by contrast, condemns supralapsarianism calling it "hyper-Calvinism" and "anti-Calvinism." This view, he says, makes God the author of sin by "involving God in coercing sin" and thus does "radical violence to the ... character of God."[62]

A supralapsarian could easily argue that Sproul is guilty of living in a glass house while throwing rocks. How does supralapsarianism any more make God the author of sin than infralapsarianism? The difference would seem to lie elsewhere. The supralapsarian simply wishes to exalt God's supremacy by not making anything about him, including his decrees, dependent on something that happens in the world. The supralapsarian thinks the infralapsarian has done just that by subordinating the decree of election and reprobation to the decree to permit the fall. If only in light of the fall does God work out his plan of redemption, then, the supralapsarian says, redemption is a kind of "Plan B" in God's mind. This comes too close for comfort to Arminianism, so says the supralapsarian, because it makes God indirectly dependent on the world.

However, as I will show, making God dependent on the world might just be part and parcel of Calvinism—especially what I will call radical or extreme Calvinism, whether supra- or infralapsarian. That is because *some* in *both* camps emphasize that the entire program of creation and redemption (including reprobation and hell) is said to be "for God's glory." Does God need the world to glorify himself? Or is creation rather the result of the overflowing trinitarian love of God?

One more area of diversity among Calvinists has to do with whether God only "permits" sin and evil or actually in some sense brings it about. All Calvinists agree that God foreordains sin and evil because everything is foreordained by God. (Admittedly some untutored people who think they are Calvinists may not believe this, but every Calvinist theologian going back to Calvin himself affirms it.) Sproul represents those Calvinists who adamantly deny that God is in any sense the author of sin or evil. Calamities, yes; moral evil, never.

The problematic situation is set up by Sproul's (and other Calvinists') assertion of absolute divine sovereignty (meticulous providence and what I will call divine determinism even though he does not like that terminology): "If there is one single molecule in this universe running around loose, totally free of God's sovereignty, then we have no guarantee that a single promise of God will ever be fulfilled.... Maybe that one molecule will be the thing that prevents Christ from returning."[63] So the question inevitably arises: "Is God, then, the author of evil and of sin?" Sproul says no: "One thing is absolutely unthinkable, that God could be the author or doer of sin."[64] He affirms that God *allowed* the entrance of sin and evil into his good creation but *did not coerce it.*[65]

Another well-known Calvinist who says that God allows or permits sin and evil without causing it or being its author is Paul Helm, a British evangelical philosopher and theologian who teaches at Canada's Regent College. In his book *The Providence of God*, this Calvinist, like Sproul, expresses a high view of God's sovereignty: "Not only is every atom and molecule, every thought and desire, kept in being by God, but every twist and turn of each of these is under the direct control of God."[66]

But, of course, this raises to an intense pitch the question of God's relationship to sin and evil. Is God the author of them? Helm says no. Because of God's "impeccable nature" he cannot be the author of sin, but because he is sovereign he must *allow* sin and evil if they are to exist. But Helm argues this permission of sin and evil is "specific permission" (similar or identical to what Boettner calls "willing permission"). That is, God never takes the spectator posture when he allows things, including sin and evil. Without causing them he specifically wills them in such a way as to assure they will happen without actually causing them:

> God ordains all those circumstances which are necessary for the performance by a person of a particular morally evil action (say, an action of cruelty at a particular time and place). God does not himself perform that action, nor could he, for the reasons already given [viz., his impeccable nature]. Nevertheless, he *permits* that action to take place. He does not prevent it to stop it. So in circumstances ordained by God someone does an evil action; the circumstances are ordained, but the evil is permitted.[67]

Many Calvinists would say "amen" to this account of God's relationship with sin and evil. No more than anyone else do they want to say that God is the cause or author of sin and evil.

Boettner includes a lengthy chapter on this issue in *The Reformed Doctrine of Providence* and, like Helm, argues (but even more vehemently) that although God ordains everything, he is not the cause or author of sin or evil. I will probe this further in chapter 4, so I will put aside for now any lengthy discussion of the inherent problems in this view. Let it be known for now that I agree with the second view held by some Calvinists that their doctrine of God's sovereignty necessarily implies or teaches that God *is* the author of sin and evil *or at least* actively assures it in some causal sense so that language of "permission" is not sufficient.

It is not at all difficult to find Calvinists on the Internet (e.g., bloggers) who boldly state that Calvinism requires confession that God *is* the author of sin and evil. One such person is Vincent Cheung, who writes about Calvinism *as a Calvinist* at his website www.vincentcheung.com. (I know little about this person except that he is a prolific commentator on subjects related to theology from a Calvinist perspective.) Like many others one can easily find on the web, Cheung ridicules fellow Calvinists who say God is not the author of sin.[68] He then says that "when someone alleges that my view of divine sovereignty makes God the author of sin, my first reaction tends to be 'So what?' ... there is no biblical or rational problem with him being the author of sin."[69] Cheung goes on to argue that the typical Calvinist account of God's absolute sovereignty necessarily leads to God as being the author of sin in any ordinary sense of "author."

Another Calvinist who affirms that God more than merely permits sin and evil, but without actually calling God the "author of sin," is John Frame (b. 1939). Frame taught for many years at Westminster Theological Seminary and now holds a chair in theology at Reformed Theological Seminary. He is the author of numerous books, many of them on Reformed theology (from a strongly Calvinist perspective). In an interview with Andy Naselli published on the internet in 2009 Frame answered a question about God's not causing but only permitting evil. Although he demurs from saying God causes or authors evil, Frame says the language of permission is not strong enough and prefers to say that God "actually brings evil about."[70]

Another Calvinist who does not think the language of God's merely permitting sin and evil is strong enough to do justice to God's sovereignty is John Piper. While he does not reject the language of permission, he often goes beyond it in explaining God's role in disasters, evil, and even sin. In a sermon published at his website soon after the terrorist attacks on New York and Washington, D.C., on September 11, 2001, Piper rejected mere permission explanations of God's role and affirmed that, in some sense, God "designed," "ordained," and "governed" those events.[71] During a sermon preached to a youth conference in 2005 he emphasized God's absolute sovereignty over all things and said, "Even a 'dirty bomb' that levels Minneapolis would be from God."[72]

Many Calvinists wince at such statements as Cheung's, Frame's, and Piper's, but others regard them as the hard truth that necessarily follows from Scripture's own teaching. For example, Joseph told his brothers that they intended their act of selling him into slavery in Egypt for evil, but God intended it for good (Gen. 50:20). Then there is the event of the cross of Christ, which was foreordained by God "from before the foundation of the world." Both events involved sins. Was God not the author of these sins? No matter how you try to get around it, some Calvinists will say, there is no escaping the fact that God foreordained and rendered these events certain, so he is their author if not their direct cause. While disagreeing that these stories require belief that God rendered sin or evil certain, I agree with the Calvinists who say the typical Calvinist view of sovereignty requires confession of God as author of sin and evil.

There is one final realm of diversity in Calvinism to be mentioned. That is the debate over true "hyper-Calvinism"—correctly used (according to most Reformed theologians) of Herman Hoeksema's (1886–1965) version of Calvinism that rejected the practice of indiscriminately offering the gospel invitation to salvation to all people. Hoeksema was born in the Netherlands but emigrated to the United States as a child and settled in Grand Rapids, where he eventually pastored a large Christian Reformed church. Among other works he wrote *Reformed Dogmatics.*[73] Hoeksema sparked a controversy within the Reformed churches by arguing that indiscriminate evangelism, such as open invitations to salvation, violates the doctrine of God's sovereignty in salvation.

The controversy has been described as one over the "well-meant gospel offer" by leading Calvinist theologian and Calvin Theological Seminary professor Anthony Hoekema (1913–1988) (notice the different spelling from Hoeksema; they were not related). According to Hoekema, Hoeksema taught that "the gospel call is never an offer" of salvation.[74] It is rather a proclamation of what God has done; God alone will decide what to do with it, and he always decides to use it to draw the elect to himself. But it is *not* a well-meant offer of salvation to everyone because "God does not desire the salvation of all to whom the gospel comes; he desires the salvation only of the elect."[75]

The Christian Reformed Church expelled Hoeksema over this, maintaining that "the preaching of the gospel is a well-meant offer of salvation, not just on the part of the preacher, but on God's part as well, to all who hear it, and that God seriously and earnestly desires the salvation of all to whom the gospel call comes."[76]

Reformed theologian Daane attributes Hoeksema's extreme Calvinism not to an aberrant interpretation of high Calvinism but to that theology itself—a theology he calls "decretal theology," which includes reprobation as a decree of God.[77] One does have to wonder what logic prevents a person who believes in TULIP from moving to Hoeksema's position. Why would God earnestly desire the salvation of everyone and how can the gospel call be a well-meant offer of salvation to all indiscriminately, including the nonelect, if God has decreed that only some will be saved?

RADICAL REFORMED THEOLOGY

Given the manifest diversity of the Reformed community and among Calvinists, when I say I am "against Calvinism" and want to rescue God's reputation from "radical Reformed theology," whose Calvinism and which Reformed theology am I talking about? There are so many kinds! Indeed. Well, here I want to explain what kind I am against; the rest of the book will explain why in detail.

By "Calvinism" as that which I am against I am referring to the "high Calvinism" of TULIP, whether infralapsarian or supralapsarian. It really does not matter much which type one examines closely: both will be found to make God morally ambiguous at best and a moral monster at worst (in spite of Calvinists' claims to the contrary). Once again I wish to emphasize *it is not free will about which I am concerned*, except as free will is necessary to protect God's character from being impugned. What concerns me, as I will make abundantly clear, is the biblical teaching that "God is love" (1 John 4:16).

Please don't dismiss this as too facile; I am going to unpack my claim that high Calvinism, the Calvinism that affirms most or all of TULIP, directly contradicts that God *is* love. I am well aware of Calvinist objections that God's love is different from our kind of love. I've heard that many times. While there is some truth to that, it is overstated by most Calvinists. If God's love is absolutely different from the highest and best notions of love as we derive them from Scripture itself (especially from Jesus Christ), then the term is simply meaningless when attached to God. One might as well say "God is creech-creech"—a meaningless assertion.

As I hope to demonstrate, some Calvinists agree with me about the analogy between God's goodness and love and our highest and best ideas of goodness and love. Paul Helm, for example, rejects any idea that God's goodness and love is totally qualitatively different from ours (as ours is derived from Scripture, of course). Yet, I will argue, even those who agree with me cannot adequately explain how their account of God's sovereignty, especially in relation to sin, evil, and reprobation, is consistent with goodness or love.

Again, what am I against? By "against Calvinism" I mean that I am opposed to *any and every belief system that includes the "U," the "L," and/or the "I" in TULIP.* The "U" and the "I" *always* appear together even when the "L" is rejected. I object most strenuously to the "L," but I think it is necessarily implied by the "U" and the "I," so I agree with those Calvinists who argue that it is inconsistent to leave it out. The "flower," so to speak, is damaged beyond recognition or recovery by pulling off that petal!

Also, I believe, affirmation of unconditional election necessarily implies affirmation of reprobation in spite of some Calvinists' denials. Reprobation is the "good and necessary consequence" of unconditional election *unless one affirms universal salvation.* (An example of this is the great Swiss Reformed theologian Karl Barth, who, I believe, did affirm universalism.) As I cannot affirm universal salvation, I judge unconditional election with its necessary correlate reprobation unacceptable because it impugns the character of God as unconditionally good.

Irresistible grace does the same thing. It impugns the goodness of God. If God calls and draws sinners irresistibly to himself so that they escape hell simply because he overwhelms them and regenerates them without any act of free will on their part, then a good God would do that for everyone! I am not content to leave the "why" question in the realm of mystery here. I acknowledge mystery in revelation, but not one that requires belief in a hidden or secret will of God that makes him a moral monster. Only a moral monster would refuse to save persons when salvation is absolutely unconditional and solely an act of God that does not depend on free will.

When I say I am against Calvinism, then, I mean the core beliefs of garden variety, mere Calvinism *insofar* as they are taken to their logical conclusion. I realize that not all Calvinists take them to their logical conclusion; at various stages in the reasoning out process individual Calvinists stop and appeal to mystery and refuse to be logically consistent by affirming the good and necessary consequences of their beliefs. *I am not against them or their highly modified and attenuated Calvinism!* (And this is probably the case with the majority of people I meet who consider themselves Calvinists.)

However, within the young, restless, Reformed movement of the new Calvinism and among their mentors (the people they read and listen to and look up to as their heroes), *most* in my experience are taking Calvinism to its logical conclusions—or at least far in that direction. There is a boldness and even aggressiveness among them that I do not find among most Calvinists of the older generation. I am against any Calvinism (and any theology) that impugns the goodness of God in favor of absolute sovereignty, leading to the conclusion that evil, sin, and every horror of human history are planned and rendered certain by God.

What about "radical Reformed theology?" What do I mean by that and why does God's reputation need to be rescued from it? By radical Reformed theology I mean the same as consistent Calvinism described above. I mean that extreme Calvinism so evident in some Calvinist speakers and writers and their eager followers that ineluctably ends up making God the author of sin and evil, whether that language (i.e., "author") is used or not. That John Piper prefers to say that God "designs" and "governs" evil makes no difference when the context necessarily implies that God wants it to happen and renders it certain—especially when it is said that this is necessary for his full glorification.

To be perfectly blunt and to "cut right to the chase," as the saying goes, my problem is primarily and especially with divine determinism that leads to God's unconditional reprobation of certain people to eternal suffering in hell for his glory. I am opposed to any idea that, as the old Calvinist saying goes, "those who find themselves suffering in hell can at least take comfort in the fact that they are there for the greater glory of God." I recognize and freely acknowledge that few Calvinists would say this. But my argument is they should find the courage to say this because it is necessarily implied by what they do say. I will explain and defend that claim throughout this book.

Radical Reformed theology, then, is any theology that makes assertions about God that necessarily, logically imply that God is less than perfectly good in the highest sense of goodness found in the New Testament and especially in Jesus Christ, the fullest revelation of God for us.

It is consistent infralapsarianism or supralapsarianism, whether hyper-Calvinist or ordinary, mere Calvinist.

So what Reformed theology am I *not* against? I guess I would have to say the only Reformed theology I am *not* against is revisionist Reformed theology—the kind I find in Sell and Berkhof and Daane and König (although I may not agree with everything any of them taught). It is Reformed theology that explicitly rejects a divine decree of reprobation and backs up from there to reject boldly other Calvinist claims that necessarily require divine reprobation. It is Reformed theology that explicitly rejects divine determinism of every single event without exception, leaving no room for free will, and backs up from there to affirm a loving, divine self-limitation such that God is in no way responsible for the suffering of innocents in the Holocaust or similar horrors of history.

I believe it is possible to find nonradical Reformed theology commonly among Reformed people and even among some who consider themselves Calvinists. They appeal to mystery rather than divine decrees that govern every event, including the fall. They affirm God's sovereignty without extending that to sin and evil except insofar as God permits them (without that positive, willing permission spoken of by consistent Calvinists and the radical Reformed theologian who talks about God rendering them certain). They affirm election as God's gracious and unconditional choice of a people for service without unconditional determination of individuals' eternal destinies, including some to hell. They are Reformed people who agree with Adrio König, himself of Reformed pedigree, who wrote:

> Anyone who levels things out in vague generalizations by attempting to explain everything and all possible circumstances as the will of God always ends up in the impossible situation that there are more exceptions than rules, more things that are inexplicable and that clash with the picture of God that is given to us in his word, than there are comforting confirmations that he is directing everything.... Anyone who tries to use the omnipotence and providence of God to propose a meticulously prepared divine plan which is unfolding in world history (L. Boettner) will always be left with the problem that other believers might not be able to discern the God of *love* in the actual course of world events.... It must be emphatically stated that ... the Scriptures do not present the future as something which materializes

> [sic] according to a "plan" but according to the covenant.... There are distressingly many things that happen on earth that are not the will of God (Luke 7:30 and every other sin mentioned in the Bible), that are against his will, and that stem from the incomprehensible and senseless sin in which we are born, in which the greater part of mankind lives, and in which Israel persisted, and against which even the "holiest men" ... struggled all their days.... To try to interpret all these things by means of the concept of a plan of God, creates intolerable difficulties and gives rise to more exceptions than regularities. But the most important objection is that the idea of a plan is against the message of the Bible since God himself becomes incredible if that against which he has fought with power, and for which he sacrificed his only Son, was nevertheless somehow part and parcel of his eternal counsel.[78]

ALTERNATIVES TO RADICAL REFORMED THEOLOGY

One reason many young people (and perhaps others) embrace the new Calvinism (which is by-and-large radical Reformed theology as just described) is because they are convinced it is the only biblically and intellectually serious theology available. It is all too true, as some Calvinists have argued, that many American evangelical churches are almost totally devoid of theology. I have been a theology professor of thousands of students in three Christian universities over almost thirty years. During that time I have noticed a downward trend in terms of Christian students' biblical and theological awareness.

I have also noticed that trend in the churches I have attended. Whereas thirty years ago and more most evangelical churches taught Bible stories and performed some kind of catechesis with young people, most have moved to the most vapid "study" of ethical and moral issues—often substituting discussion of the possible spiritual interpretation of movies for biblical teaching and the study of doctrines.[79]

Many churches and Christian youth organizations have simply abdicated their responsibility to teach basic Christian beliefs so that Christianity seems to many Christian young people a shallow religion of self-fulfillment with God's help. This is what Calvinist intellectual Michael Horton calls "Christless Christianity,"[80] and I agree with him. It is simply pervasive in American church life. So, when intellectually curious young people who are convinced there must be something more to their faith than the folk religion they have been given encounter Calvinism for the first time (usually under the name Reformed theology), they are often impressed and sometimes swept away with it. In my experience this is partly under the influence of extremely passionate sermons delivered by scholarly popularizers of Calvinism who preach at enormous youth conferences (the sermons being podcast for relistening), as if their theology is the only one that truly honors God.

I have found that many of the new Calvinists simply are not aware there are any viable alternatives to their newfound doctrinal faith. Through reading books by their favorite pastors and teachers, many of them are convinced that all alternatives—and especially the dreaded "Arminianism"—are man-centered, biblically unsupported, and intellectually weak. Almost all alternatives to Calvinism are lumped together as Arminianism or semi-Pelagianism or both (many Calvinists such as Sproul equate the two). In his sermon on "For Whom Did Christ Die?" Piper attacks Arminianism as a theology of self-salvation. He says: "In order to say that Christ died for all men in the same way, the Arminian must limit the atonement to a powerless opportunity for men to save themselves from their terrible plight of depravity."[81]

This is, of course, a caricature of Arminianism, as I have demonstrated in *Arminian Theology: Myths and Realities*. One has to wonder what Piper was thinking when he misrepresented Arminianism in this way. Arminian theology *does not* say that people can save themselves or that the atonement is powerless. Traditional Arminian theology says that in and through the cross of Christ the sin of Adam inherited by all was forgiven (Romans 5) so that people are only condemnable for their own sins. The cross completely removes every obstacle to every human being's salvation except their own resistance to God's freely offered grace, which is given to all in some measure but especially through the preaching of the Word. I believe Piper knows this because we have communicated about it and he told me he used to be an Arminian![82]

What Piper and almost all Calvinist critics of Arminianism (and other alternative theologies of God's sovereignty and salvation) often leave out that are crucial to mention are two things: (1) any limitation of God's sovereignty is said to be a voluntary self-limitation because God is sovereign over his sovereignty, and (2) if anyone comes to Christ with repentance and faith, it is only because they are enabled by God's "prevenient grace" to do so. I rarely encounter Calvinists who fairly describe the Arminian doctrine of prevenient grace even though it is central and crucial to Arminian theology.

So what is Arminianism or Arminian theology? It is the much vilified but innocent main evangelical alternative to Calvinism. For support for the portrait of it I will paint here I point readers to *Arminian Theology*, which contains hundreds of supporting quotations from leading Arminian theologians, going back to Jacob Arminius himself, who ascribed all of salvation to the grace of God and fervently denied that he attributed any part of the work of salvation to "man" (the human person who repents and believes unto salvation). Contrary to the misrepresentations of many Calvinist critics, Arminianism does not "limit God's sovereignty" or attribute merit to "man" in salvation.

Classical Arminian theology, such as that of John Wesley (1703–1791), affirms the total depravity of human beings and their utter helplessness even to exercise a good will toward God apart from God's supernatural, assisting grace. It attributes the sinner's ability to respond to the gospel with repentance and faith to prevenient grace—the illuminating, convicting, calling, and enabling power of the Holy Spirit working on the sinner's soul and making them free to choose saving grace (or reject it). This is the Arminian interpretation of the "drawings" of God mentioned by Jesus in the gospel of John. God does not draw irresistibly but persuasively, leaving human persons able to say no.

Arminian theology does affirm divine election, but it interprets it as corporate rather than individual. Romans 9, the bedrock Scripture passage of high Calvinism, is interpreted as the early church fathers did—as referring to the service of Israel and Gentile believers in God's plan, not to the eternal destinies of individuals. Arminians affirm predestination, interpreting it with Romans 8 as God's foreknowledge of faith. They reject reprobation except insofar as it is freely chosen by people who live against the will of God revealed in nature and the law written on their hearts (Romans 1–2).

Above all Arminians insist that God is a good and loving God, who truly desires the salvation of all people. Note 1 Timothy 2:3–4: "This is good, and pleases God our Savior, who wants all people to be saved and to come to a knowledge of the truth"; and 2 Peter 3:9: "The Lord is not slow in keeping his promise, as some understand slowness. Instead he is patient with you, not wanting anyone to perish, but everyone to come to repentance." Arminians regard these and similar passages of Scripture as clearly and unequivocally pointing to God's universal desire for salvation of every person. The Greek of 1 Timothy 2:4 *cannot* be interpreted any other way than as referring to every person without limit. Some Calvinists interpret 2 Peter 2:4 as referring only to the elect, but in light of 1 Timothy 2:4, that hardly works.

Arminians believe that any limitation of God's intention for everyone's salvation, including "limited atonement," necessarily and inexorably impugns the character of God even where Calvinists insist otherwise. Arminians do not claim that Calvinists *say* God is not good or loving; they say Calvinism *implies* that necessarily, so that Calvinists *should say it* in order to be logically consistent with themselves.

The main alternative to Calvinism is classical Arminianism (which is different from what sometimes goes under that label!) as described briefly above. Again, I urge readers who are interested in exploring it further to read *Arminian Theology* and other books by Arminians about Arminianism—just as I and many Arminians have read Calvin's *Institutes* and many books about Calvinism by Calvinists. You should not believe what Calvinists say about Arminianism without checking it out for yourself in the primary sources.[83]

Is Arminian theology biblically and intellectually respectable? Is it a serious competitor with Calvinism? Of course only someone who looks into it fairly deeply in the primary sources can know for sure. But my argument is that the only reason this is seriously called into question is the vicious calumnies raised against it by Calvinists over the years; most of what Calvinists say about it is simply untrue or at least only partially true. One of the worst offenders is Sproul, who equates Arminianism with the heresy of semi-Pelagianism,[84] condemned at the Second Council or Synod of Orange in AD 529 (which also condemned any belief that God predestined sin). Virtually every book by a Calvinist expounding Calvinist theology that I have read (and I have read dozens) eventually gets around to slamming Arminianism as a shallow message of self-salvation if not actual heresy.

I urge young, restless, Reformed new Calvinists to think for themselves about Calvinism's alternatives, including especially Arminianism. But I also recommend investigation into non-Calvinist Reformed theologians such as H. Berkhof, König, and Daane, but perhaps above all the great Dutch Reformed theologian G. C. Berkouwer, who published many volumes of systematic theology in the 1950s and 1960s. Some may consider him a Calvinist, but he definitely was not one in the full TULIP, "high Calvinism" sense, especially in that he rejected any notion of divine reprobation as included in God's sovereignty.[85] Other Protestant alternatives are Lutheranism, which rejects limited atonement and unconditional perseverance, and Anabaptist theology, which focuses mainly on discipleship rather than on systematic theology but clearly includes belief in God-granted freedom of the will and rejects TULIP almost in its entirety. (Some Anabaptists accept total depravity.)

Ultimately, I hope that alternatives to Calvinism warrant serious consideration because of the serious conundrums presented by the logical extension of classical Calvinism, to which this book now turns.

FOUR

YES TO GOD'S SOVEREIGNTY; NO TO DIVINE DETERMINISM

I went to hear a famous government official, who was also a well-known evangelical Christian, speak in our college's chapel. I expected to hear him talk about the dangers of smoking because that was what he was especially known for; he was a crusader against tobacco. But that's not what he addressed in his chapel talk. Instead, for about an hour, he held forth on the subject "God killed my son." I was not totally surprised because I knew him to be a member of a large, influential Reformed church. Yet, I had never heard any Calvinist put a similar matter so bluntly. The doctor spoke eloquently and movingly about his young adult son's tragic death in a mountain climbing accident and several times stopped, looked intently at the young audience, and stated, "God killed my son."

The speaker made crystal clear what he meant. He did *not* mean God permitted his son's death or merely allowed it to happen. Rather, he meant that God planned it and rendered it certain. He stopped short of saying God caused it, but his often-repeated title certainly implied that: "God killed my son." He also made crystal clear that he did not mean this was an unusual occurrence of God's intervention; what he meant was that every such death, like every event, is planned and governed by God in such a way as to make it inevitable. (I'm certain he would say, if asked, that God uses secondary causes such as weather and moisture and faulty equipment, but to him this was not pertinent. All that he cared about was that God killed his son.) In other words, this Christian statesman was publicly declaiming that God is absolutely sovereign down to the details and that God plans every event, including tragedies, and renders them certain.

What was especially significant about this presentation of the Calvinist view of divine sovereignty in providence (God's governing of history and lives) was the speaker's *reason* for believing it so passionately. Of course, he believed it because he thought it was biblical. But he also made clear that he believed it because it was the only thing that brought him comfort and hope in the face of such a shattering tragedy. If his son's death was merely an accident and not part of God's plan, he said, he could not live with the utter randomness and meaninglessness of it. He could only find comfort in his son's death *if* it was God's doing and not at all an accident.

As I listened, I wondered what this great evangelical statesman would say if his son's death was not, as he reported, immediate and painless but rather a long, lingering, agonizing, painful death from, say, cancer. Such deaths commonly occur and sometimes to children and young people! I remember visiting my daughter's teenage friend in the hospital one day and hearing a child screaming in agony without pause for the entire thirty minutes I was there. It was bone-shattering shrieks of absolute torment echoing through the halls of the hospital. I had never heard anything like it, and it left me shaken. What if those parents asked the speaker if he believed *their* child was being killed *in that particular way* by God? What would he say? If he was consistent with himself *and his theology*, he would have to say yes.

I was working in my office one day when the phone rang. It was a pastor who had read in the student newspaper about my rejection of Calvinism. He demanded to know: "How can you not believe in God's sovereignty?"

I asked him what he meant by God's sovereignty, and he replied: "I mean the fact that God controls everything that happens."

I responded by asking him: "Does that include sin and evil?"

He paused: "No."

Then, I asked, "Do *you* really believe in God's sovereignty?" He apologized and hung up.

What I wanted to tell the pastor was that I *do* believe in God's sovereignty—with all my heart, soul, and mind. I believe, as the Bible teaches and all Christians should believe, that nothing at all can happen without God's permission. That is what some would call a "weak view" of God's sovereignty (although it has nothing to do with any "weakness" of God), whereas Calvinism typically affirms a "strong view" of God's sovereignty. Let's look into Calvinism's doctrine of divine providence—the doctrine of God's sovereignty over nature and history.

CALVINISM'S DOCTRINE OF GOD'S PROVIDENCE

Ulrich Zwingli and John Calvin

Many scholars consider the real founder of the Reformed tradition to be Ulrich Zwingli, who wrote a lengthy essay entitled *On Providence*. This essay came to be influential on Calvin and, through him, on the whole Reformed tradition (although many Reformed people, especially the ones I have labeled "revisionists," have come to reject much of it). Zwingli defined providence as God's "rule over and direction of all things in the universe. For if anything were guided by its own power or insight, just so far would the wisdom and power of our Deity be deficient."[1] Zwingli continued his exposition by denying that anything in the world is "contingent, fortuitous or accidental" because God alone is the "sole cause" over everything, such that all other so-called causes are merely "instruments of the divine working."[2]

Zwingli based much of this strong doctrine of sovereignty on philosophy; he began with a presupposed idea of God as necessarily the all-determining reality and drew from it the conclusion that everything must be a manifestation of the power of God or else God would not be God. Of course, Zwingli also appealed to Scripture, as have all defenders of the strong doctrine of God's sovereignty. It will be helpful to look at some allegedly supporting passages before plunging on to look at Calvin's doctrine and later Calvinists' interpretations of providence.

In chapter 3, we saw that Calvinists appeal to the stories of Joseph and Jesus' crucifixion to support a vision of God's providential sovereignty as detailed and meticulous, including evil. Of course, not all biblical scholars or interpreters deduce that doctrine from these stories and events. For example, isn't it possible that God "meant them for good" *in the sense that* he could have stopped the events but chose to allow them instead? Most Calvinists will claim there is little if any difference between that and their view, but I will argue the difference is great.

Calvinists appeal to statements in the Old Testament prophets, such as the already referred to Amos 3:6. But there are other passages, such as Proverbs 16:33; Isaiah 14:27; 43:13; 45:7; and Daniel 4:35. All of these indicate God's overseeing authority and rule down to the details. For example, Proverbs 16:33: "The lot is cast into the lap, but its every decision is from the LORD," while Isaiah 45:7: "I form the light and create darkness, I bring prosperity and create disaster; I, the LORD, do all these things." There is hardly any need to quote further; these passages alone seem to provide proof of the strong view of God's providence. Later in this chapter, of course, I will argue that there are alternative interpretations that better express God's sovereignty and that do not make God the author of evil.

Calvin picked up where Zwingli left off with his doctrine of God's sovereignty over history, God's meticulous providence, although he did not defend it from philosophy but primarily from Scripture (which is not to say he was not influenced by philosophy!). In a vivid illustration Calvin wrote:

> Let us imagine, for example, a merchant who, entering a wood with a company of faithful men, unwisely wanders away from his companions and in his wandering comes upon a robber's den, falls among thieves, and is slain. His death was not only foreseen by God's eye, but also determined by his decree. For it is not said that he foresaw how long the life of each man would extend, but that he determined and fixed the bounds which men cannot pass.... Yet, as far as the capacity of our mind is concerned, all things therein seem fortuitous [accidental]. What will a Christian think at this point? Just this: whatever happened in a death of this sort he will regard as fortuitous by nature, as it is; yet he will not doubt that God's providence exercised authority over fortune in directing its end.[3]

Calvin sums up his whole doctrine of God's providence thus: "No wind ever arises or increases except by God's express command."[4] In other places, he argues that God's providential governing of history cannot be expressed by means of permission; God does not merely permit anything but ordains it and brings it about most certainly. For Calvin, this is seen most clearly in the fall of Adam, which was foreordained by God. Just in case there would be any quibbling about how strong Calvin's doctrine of providence was, I will quote this passage from his *Institutes*:

> To sum up, since God's will is said to be the cause of all things, I have made his providence the determinative principle for all human plans and works, not only in order to display its force in the elect, who are ruled by the Holy Spirit, but also to compel the reprobate to obedience.[5]

How could Calvin put it any more bluntly and forcefully than that? God compels the reprobate, the wicked, to obey his will. In other words, even the evil done by wicked people is foreordained and rendered certain by God. Later Calvinists such as Sproul will claim that Calvinism *does not* say that God coerces the wicked to do evil acts. Calvin seemed to think it is so, even though he argues God remains unstained by the evil of their deeds because his motives are good while theirs are evil. (Of course, this just raises the question of the origin of evil motives!)

Jonathan Edwards

Later Calvinists' views of God's providence are largely consistent with Zwingli's and Calvin's. In other words, in general, high Calvinism from Zwingli to Calvin to Edwards to Boettner to Sproul to Piper amounts to *divine determinism* in spite of some Calvinists' strong objections to that terminology. We begin with Jonathan Edwards.

Edwards taught the strongest doctrine of God's rule possible. For him God is not only the all-determining reality; he creates the whole world ex nihilo (out of nothing) at every moment and does not work through secondary causes.[6] Everything without exception is directly and immediately caused by God, including evil. Edwards insisted that all things, including sin and evil, follow from "an infallible previous fixedness of the futurity of the event [meaning all events]," such that everything happens according to a "universal, determining providence" that imposes "some kind of necessity of all events."[7] Edwards nails it down:

> God does decisively, in his providence, order all the volitions of moral agents, either by positive influence or permission: and it being allowed on all hands, that what God does in the affair of man's virtuous volitions, whether it be more or less, is by some positive influence, and not by mere permission, as in the affair of a sinful volition.[8]

Readers should not be thrown off by Edwards' use of the language of permission because this must be understood in the context of his earlier quoted statements about "determining providence" and the "necessity of all events." Clearly, by "permission" Edwards only means that, in the case of evil, God does not force or coerce people to sin, but he does render it certain. One has to wonder why Edwards (and other Calvinists) fell back into using "permission" language when his (and their) overall explanation of God's providence requires something more direct and active?

Not only did Edwards affirm God's absolute, determining sovereignty over all events in the world; he also affirmed the necessity of God's own decisions. This nails down his belief in what I am calling divine determinism. For him, everything that happens, even in God's own mind and volition, is necessary. For those who doubt this, consider that Edwards affirmed "the necessity of the acts of God's will."[9] Of course, Edwards did not mean that some force outside of God or even within God coerces God to decide and act as he does. Rather, "the *necessary* determination of God's will in all things, [is] by what he sees to be *fittest* and *best*."[10] In other words, "God's will is determined by his own infinite, all-sufficient wisdom in everything."[11] The inexorable upshot of this must be that God's creation of the world is necessary and not contingent. That is to say, it is not free.

Some defenders of Edwards may object that the Puritan theologian claimed God's actions are free. Indeed he did. So how did he reconcile these things? Edwards argued that free will only means doing what is in accordance with one's strongest motive or disposition. For him, as for most Calvinists who wish to embrace some sense of free will in both God and creatures, free will is *not* being able to do otherwise than one does (power of contrary choice), which is the libertarian sense of free will, but only doing what one *wants to do even if he or she could not do otherwise.* According to Edwards, even one's wants are always determined by something. The heart, the seat of dispositions, determines the acts of the human will just as surely as God's wisdom determines his decisions and actions.

This has come to be called by philosophers "compatibilism"—belief that free will is compatible with determinism. It is probably not what most people think free will means. Most people probably mean by free will ability to do otherwise than one does. But according to compatibilism, the only time one is *not free* is when one is being forced to do something he or she does not want to do. In this sense, then, God's creation of the world is "free" because it is what God wanted to do. But that does not mean God could have done otherwise.

One has to question the orthodoxy of Edwards' view. The whole point of Christian orthodoxy traditionally affirming the freedom of creation is to assure that it is within the realm of grace and not necessity. Whatever is necessary cannot be gracious. Also, if God's creation of the world was necessary, then the world is *in some sense* part of God—an aspect of God's own existence. This is known as panentheism: the belief that God and the world are interdependent realities. Most orthodox Christians have always considered that heresy.[12]

I am not actually accusing Edwards of heresy; rather, I am accusing him of inconsistency because he clearly *did not* intend to make God in any way dependent on the world. The point is that his speculative musings about God's sovereignty led him to conclusions with which he probably was not comfortable and probably did not hold in the same way all the time. Nevertheless, in spite of Edwards' intentions, his strong doctrine of sovereignty—divine determinism—is a slippery slope that leads logically down into panentheism.

Another issue Edwards had to deal with was the problem of God's relationship to sin and evil. Doesn't his strong doctrine of providence lead inevitably to God being the author of sin and evil? Edwards was clearly uncomfortable with that, but at the same time he admitted it *in some sense*. First, his explanation of how God rendered the fall of Adam certain is that God withheld from Adam "those influences, without which nature will be corrupt," but this does not make God the author of sin.[13] To make the point clearer, Edwards stated that "the first arising or existing of that evil disposition in the heart of Adam, was by God's *permission*; who could have prevented it, if he had pleased, by giving such influences of his Spirit, as would have been absolutely effectual to hinder it; which, it is plain fact, he did withhold."[14] Even though God rendered certain the first evil disposition that gave rise to all others, Edwards argues, God is not guilty. Only Adam was guilty because his intentions were evil. God's intentions in rendering sin and evil certain were good. "In willing evil God does not do evil."[15]

Does this actually get God off the hook, so to speak, of being the author of sin and evil? Edwards finally concluded:

> If by "author of sin," is meant the permitter, or not hinderer of sin; and at the same time, a disposer of the state of events, in such a manner, for wise, holy and most excellent ends and purposes, that sin, if it be permitted or not hindered, will most certainly and infallibly follow: I say, if this be all that is meant, by being the author of sin, I don't deny that God is the author of sin.[16]

I suggest that most people would consider that being the author of sin. But many Calvinists, realizing that for most people "author of sin" means that God coerced Adam to sin against his will, reject that language while agreeing with Edwards. Neither Edwards nor any Calvinist believes that God forced Adam to sin against his will, but ordinary language dictates that one is the "author" of something simply by rendering it certain. Thus, I argue, Calvinism does make God the author of sin *in the sense that*, according to its account of God's sovereignty, God rendered Adam's sin certain.

My point here is simply this: When Calvinists deny that their doctrine makes God the "author of sin," what they usually mean is that God did not force Adam (or anyone) to sin against his will. However, they should admit, with Edwards, that their doctrine *does* make God the author of sin in the sense that God rendered it certain that Adam (and all his posterity) would sin.

R. C. Sproul

Similarly to Edwards, Sproul rejects the label "determinism" for this strong view of divine sovereignty *because* he understands "determinism" to mean "external coercion."[17] He admits, with Edwards and all other high Calvinists, that God determines all things, but he prefers to call this divine "determination," *not* "determinism."[18] One can only wonder what difference it really makes. I will continue to call this view divine determinism following the ordinary definition of "determinism" (as given in various dictionaries and encyclopedias), that "every event is necessitated by antecedent events and conditions."[19] Certainly that is the case with Edwards' and Sproul's and most other Calvinists' beliefs about God's sovereignty.

Let's turn now to Sproul's account of God's providential sovereignty. Sproul is well-known for making rather emphatic and extreme statements about Calvinist doctrine. For example, in *Chosen by God* he writes that anyone who does not agree with his belief (as expressed in the Westminster Confession of Faith) about predestination should be a "convinced atheist."[20] For Sproul (and many other Calvinists) predestination is more than a concept about God's sovereignty in deciding who will be saved and who will not be saved; it is also a concept about God's "total sovereignty" in all things. In chapter 3 I quoted Sproul's remark that there can be no single molecule in the universe not totally under the control of God. He is famous for asking audiences whether they believe in God's total sovereignty in the sense that I am here calling divine determinism.

Then he asks how many are atheists. Those who did not raise their hands in response to the first question, he says, should raise their hands to the second question. His reason, of course, is that "if God is not sovereign, then he is not God. It belongs to God as God to be sovereign."[21]

What's odd about this is that in *Chosen by God*, Sproul states that "good and learned men" can disagree about this doctrine, but then he says anyone who does not agree with him should be a convinced atheist. He shouldn't be surprised if some "good and learned men" take offense at that suggestion![22] Many Christians agree with him that God's sovereignty is an essential part of God's nature *without* agreeing with his *interpretation* of that sovereignty.

So what exactly is Sproul's doctrine of predestination/providence? We get a strong clue in his definition of predestination: "It includes whatever comes to pass in time and space."[23] In other words, predestination, in its broadest sense, is simply another word for God's determination of all events: meticulous providence. He affirms that everything that happens is God's will.[24] To nail it down he writes:

> The movement of every molecule, the actions of every plant, the falling of every star, the choices of every volitional creature [creatures who choose], all of these are subject to his sovereign will. No maverick molecules run loose in the universe, beyond the control of the Creator. If one such molecule existed, it could be the critical fly in the eternal ointment.[25]

In other words, "one maverick molecule could destroy every promise God has ever made about the outcome of history."[26]

Sproul goes on to make a distinction between two senses of God's will: God's *decretive will* and God's *permissive will*.[27] This might relieve some anxiety about God's role in evil, but then he takes back with one hand what he gave with the other: "What God permits, he *decrees* to permit."[28] In other words, God's permission is *willing and even determining permission*; it merely reflects and enacts God's eternal decrees. Thus, even sin lies *both* within God's decretive will *and* God's permissive will. The latter does not in any way determine the former or else God would not be sovereign. What God permits, he decreed to permit—including sin. The way Sproul explains the relationship between God's decretive will and God's permissive will tends to collapse them together. The specter of a God who wills sin and evil still hangs over it.

In order to obtain a more complete understanding of Sproul's doctrine of God's providential sovereignty, it is helpful to look at his view of free will. On the one hand, unlike some Calvinists, Sproul affirms that Adam and Eve fell by their own free will: "Calvinism sees Adam sinning by his own free will, not by divine coercion."[29] Furthermore, he says of the fall, "Adam jumped into the pit [of depravity and spiritual death]. In Adam we all jumped into the pit. God did not throw us into the pit."[30] Some of Sproul's readers take false comfort in this—as if it alleviates the problem of God's sovereign choice that Adam would sin. But that's not clear at all.

It's important to look more closely at what Sproul means by "free will." There he turns to Edwards' compatibilism, in which "free will" is simply doing what you want to do even if you couldn't do otherwise. Like Edwards (in many ways Sproul's mentor), Sproul argues that "we [always] choose according to our strongest inclination at the moment."[31] That would have been true for Adam, too, because both Edwards and Sproul are simply explaining what "free will" *always means*. Sproul explains further: "There is a reason for every choice we make. In a narrow sense every choice we make is *determined*."[32] Determined by what? By our inner motives and inclinations.

All one has to do to see that this really does not solve the problem of God and evil is think backward from Adam's first sin to the motive that controlled it and actually caused it. In other words, what Sproul is saying is that Adam's sin was predetermined by an inner disposition to sin. Adam could not have done otherwise than he did. Sproul says this is not determinism because he defines determinism as "coercion by external forces," which actually has nothing to do with it, as already noted. He seems to be inventing that definition arbitrarily simply to avoid calling his view of history, including the fall, determinism.

The question for Sproul and all Calvinists who take this approach is this: from where did Adam's evil inclination come? For them, it couldn't come from free will because free will is simply choosing to act on one's inclinations. I am going to explore this dilemma of Calvinism more fully later in this chapter. Here I simply raise it as a problem for Sproul's and other Calvinists' typical explanations of the fall of humanity into sin and evil and God's involvement in that. To hint at what is to come: it seems logically necessary by this account of free will and God's sovereignty to trace the first inclination to evil back to God as its source, which, of course, no Calvinist wants to do!

Loraine Boettner

I turn now from Sproul to Boettner. What did Boettner say about God's sovereign providence? I have already quoted his strong statements about God's sovereignty. Here I simply add to that earlier explanation. According to Boettner, the Reformed view of God's providence is that God "very obviously predetermined every event which would happen.... Even the sinful acts of men are included in this plan."[33] But, like Sproul, Boettner wants to say that God only *permits* the sinful acts of people; he does not cause them. Yet, also like Sproul, he takes back with one hand what he gives with the other by saying about this:

> Even the sinful actions of men [including Adam's first sin] can occur only by his [God's] permission. And since he permits not unwillingly but willingly, all that comes to pass—including the actions and ultimate destiny of men—must be, in some sense, in accordance with what he desired and purposed.[34]

In other words, even the first sinful act (and therefore the first inclination to sin) was willingly planned and purposed by God because he desired it. Boettner insists, however, that God never sins himself or even causes people to sin. Nevertheless, in order to bring about his purpose and plan he rendered even the first sin certain. How?

> All we need to know is that God does govern His creatures, that His control over them is such that no violence is done to their natures and that His control is consistent with His own purity and excellence. God so presents the outside inducements that man acts in accordance with his own nature, yet does just exactly what God plans for him to do.[35]

Later in this chapter I will explore this further and ask if it really gets God off the hook for being the author of sin and evil. Does it really differ from saying that God determines sin and evil and actively renders them certain? Is language of mere permission really appropriate for this account of God's role in sin and evil? If God presents people with "outside inducements" guaranteed to result in their sinning, doesn't that make God the author of their sin? If so, how are they responsible and God is not?

Paul Helm

I will now draw on Paul Helm, another Calvinist witness to the strong doctrine of providence that I believe gets Calvinism in hot water by inexorably leading to the "good and necessary consequence" that God *is* the author of sin, evil, and even all innocent suffering. Helm's *The Providence of God* is widely considered a contemporary classic of Calvinist thought. Here is how he expresses the sovereignty of God in providence: "Not only is every atom and molecule, every thought and desire, kept in being by God, but every twist and turn of each of these is under the direct control of God."[36] Then, "the providence of God is 'fine-grained'; it extends to the occurrence of individual actions and to each aspect of each action."[37] Of course, Helm recognizes that for many of his readers this strong view of God's sovereignty will raise to an intense pitch the problem of evil. Is God, then, the author of sin and evil? What of God's goodness?

This problem of evil and God's role in it becomes even more problematic when Helm turns to describing how God rules the evil in the world:

> For, according to the "no-risk" view [Helm's view of God's providence in which God takes no risks], God controls all events and yet issues moral commands which are disobeyed in some of the very events which he controls. For example, he commands men and women to love their neighbors while at the same time ordaining actions which are malicious or hateful.[38]

According to Helm, God has two wills: "what happens" (what he decrees and renders certain) and "what ought to happen" (what he commands that often goes against what he decrees). Some Calvinists refer to these as God's "decretive will" and God's "preceptive will." In other words, according to this view of God's providence, God commanded Adam and Eve not to eat of the tree of the knowledge of good and evil (preceptive will) while at the same time (or from all eternity) decreeing that they would eat of it. The crucial question this raises is how God is good and not in conflict with himself. God assures that his moral commands will be disobeyed. How can God do that without coercing people to sin? And how does he do it without being responsible for sin?

At this juncture Helm, like many Calvinists, turns to God's withholding of divine influence so that people naturally sin without God's causing them to sin: "What determines the action [e.g., the fall] in so far as it is an *evil* is divine *withholding*. God withholds his goodness or grace, and forthwith the agent forms a morally deficient motive or reason and acts accordingly."[39]

In other words, God renders evil certain without doing evil himself. The evil, after all, is in the motive with which the foreordained action is carried out by the creature. The sinner's motive is a bad one whereas God's motive in foreordaining and rendering it certain is good. The sinner is sinning because, from an evil motive (e.g., of selfishness) he or she disobeys God's preceptive will even though he or she could not do otherwise because God withholds the provision needed not to sin.

This raises many questions about God's goodness, human responsibility, and the source of the first evil motive. Helm affirms that, in spite of God's involvement in rendering evil certain, he is a perfectly good God such that "the goodness of God must bear some positive relation to the sorts of human actions we regard as good. Otherwise, why ascribe *goodness* to God?"[40] I will deal with the problems inherent in this account of God's providence later in this chapter. Suffice it to say here that it seems incoherent at best.

John Piper

What about the influential John Piper—probably *the* most important mentor of the new Calvinism among the young, restless, Reformed generation? What does he say about God's sovereignty and providence, including evil? He follows Edwards and parallels Helm closely. As explained earlier, Piper believes that everything without exception comes to pass according to God's foreordained plan and purpose and that God renders everything certain without participating in evil himself: "In some way (that we may not be able to fully comprehend) God is able without blameworthy 'tempting' to see to it that a person does what God ordains for him to do even if it involves evil."[41] With Helm Piper affirms two wills in God: "God decrees one state of affairs [including evil] while also willing and teaching that a different state of affairs should come to pass."[42] Piper denies, in his account of providence, that God is the author of sin or evil even though he does "see to it" that things that are contrary to God's commands come to pass.

Each of the authors quoted so far in this section somewhere says that whatever God foreordains and renders certain, including sin and evil, glorifies God. Boettner says it most succinctly: "God has a definite purpose in the permission [!] of every individual sin, having ordained it [!] 'for His own glory.'"[43] Even the works of Satan are foreordained and controlled by God for his glory![44]

Let us sum up the typical high Calvinist view of God's sovereignty. While there may be nuances of difference in each account, it's safe to say there are some overarching commonalities so that a general description can be offered. In high Calvinism, God's sovereignty in his providence means that everything down to the minutest details of history and individual lives, including persons' thoughts and actions, are foreordained and rendered certain by God. Even evil thoughts and actions are planned and brought about such that God "sees to it" that they happen to carry out his will. Nothing at all, whatever, falls outside God's predestining plan and activity.

Yet, God is not stained by the evil that creatures do even though he renders it certain because his motives are always good, even in bringing about the evil that he forbids. And God's ultimate plan is good such that evil serves its purpose. "God wills righteously those things which men do wickedly."[45] Yet creatures are solely responsible for the evil they commit.[46] God renders sin and evil certain not by coercing or forcing people to do them but by withdrawing or withholding that divine influence that they would need not to sin and do evil. Everything that happens, including sin, is ordained by God for his own glory.

THE PROBLEM OF GOD'S REPUTATION

Sproul states that "any distortion of the character of God poisons the rest of our theology."[47] Indeed, non-Calvinist Christians agree completely, but they regard the typical high Calvinist account of God's sovereignty as inexorably, logically leading to a distortion of God's character. Of course, no Calvinist admits this, but that's not the point. Calvinists frequently accuse Arminians and other non-Calvinists of stopping short of drawing out the "good and necessary consequences" of their admitted beliefs, so it is fair for Arminians to do the same with Calvinists. Generally speaking, with few exceptions, Calvinists affirm God's perfect goodness and love, but their belief in meticulous providence and absolute, all-determining sovereignty (determinism) undermines what they say. They seem to want to have their cake and eat it too.

Before plunging into my critique of Calvinism's account of God's sovereignty, I want to state clearly and unequivocally that all orthodox Christians, including non-Calvinists such as Arminians, also affirm God's sovereignty. Sometimes Calvinists smuggle their own definition of sovereignty into the meaning of the word itself so that anyone who does not agree with their divine determinism does not believe in divine sovereignty.[48] I have already demonstrated that Arminians believe in God's sovereignty, and once again, I point readers to *Arminian Theology: Myths and Realities*. Non-Calvinists take God's *permissive will* more seriously than Calvinists and explain biblical stories such as Joseph and his brothers (Gen. 50) and the crucifixion of Jesus in that way—God foresaw and permitted sinful people to do things because he saw the good that he would bring out of them.[49] But God by no means foreordained or rendered them certain.

Someone might ask how God could be sure they would happen. God knows the hearts of people and can foresee that, given certain foreseen circumstances, they will do sinful things. God does not have to manipulate them; he can simply predict them infallibly. Calvinists will scoff at this, but their own account of God's involvement raises greater problems that they may wrestle with but leave unsolved.

In short, the Calvinist account of God's sovereignty given earlier in this chapter inevitably makes God the author of sin, evil, and innocent suffering (such as the children of the Holocaust) and thereby impugns the integrity of God's character as good and loving. The God of *this* Calvinism (as opposed to, say, revisionist Reformed theology) is at best morally ambiguous and at worst a moral monster hardly distinguishable from the devil. Remember, according to this account of God's sovereignty and providence, *even the devil is only doing the works given him to do by God*. They, too, like everything else, have been foreordained, planned, willed by God, and rendered certain by God *for his glory*. I can only agree wholeheartedly with evangelical philosopher Jerry Walls who says, "The Calvinist must sacrifice a clear notion of God's goodness for the sake of maintaining his view of God's sovereign decrees."[50] About the Calvinist claim that even evil is willed and rendered certain by God Walls rightly says, "At this point the idea of goodness, as we know it, has simply lost its shape."[51]

Let me be perfectly clear that whatever objections Sproul and others may raise, the Calvinist account of God's sovereignty *is* divine determinism. No amount of caviling can get around it. To affirm that everything that happens, down to the minutest details including even God's own thoughts and actions, are determined *is by definition* to affirm determinism. Even if Sproul does not follow Edwards in arguing that God's own thoughts and actions are determined (which, given his agreement with

Edwards' compatibilist idea of free will, he would seem to have to), he *does* affirm that everything in the world is determined by God.

All of the Calvinists cited above *sometimes* fall back on permission language when talking about God's sovereignty over sin and evil, but a close examination of what they mean reveals that their idea of God's permission is different than ordinary permission. It is willing and even determining permission. Remember that God permits the fall of Adam but also renders it certain, because it is in his will and purpose, by withholding or withdrawing the moral power Adam would have needed not to sin.

This is an odd kind of permission indeed. Who would believe that a teacher who withholds the information students need to pass a course merely permitted them to fail? What if that teacher, when called on the carpet by parents and school officials, said, "I didn't cause them to fail. They did it on their own"? Would anyone accept that explanation or would they accuse the teacher of not merely permitting the students to fail but also of actually *causing* them to fail? And what if the teacher argued that he or she actually planned and rendered the students' failure certain for a good reason — to uphold academic standards and show what a great teacher he or she is by demonstrating how necessary his or her information is for students to pass? Would not these admissions only deepen everyone's conviction that the teacher is morally and professionally wrong?

Many, perhaps most, critics of Calvinism register extreme dismay at its divine determinism. There are many reasons, but the first and foremost one is that it renders God morally impure if not repugnant.

One day, at the end of a class session on Calvinism's doctrine of God's sovereignty, a student asked me a question I had put off considering. He asked: "*If* it was revealed to you in a way you couldn't question or deny that the true God *actually is* as Calvinism says and *rules* as Calvinism affirms, would you still worship him?" I knew the only possible answer without a moment's thought, even though I knew it would shock many people. I said no, that I would not because I could not. Such a God would be a moral monster. Of course, I realize Calvinists do not *think* their view of God's sovereignty makes him a moral monster, but I can only conclude they have not thought it through to its logical conclusion or even taken sufficiently seriously the things they say about God and evil and innocent suffering in the world.

Perhaps no one has taken a stronger stance against Calvinism's doctrine of God's providence than theologian David Bentley Hart, who examined the role of God in innocent suffering in *The Doors of the Sea: Where Was God in the Tsunami?*[52] There he calls the view espoused by high Calvinists "theological fatalism" and says that people who hold that view "defame the love and goodness of God out of a servile and unhealthy fascination with his 'dread sovereignty.'"[53] Then he says:

> If indeed there were a God whose true nature—whose justice or sovereignty—were revealed in the death of a child or the dereliction of a soul or a predestined hell, then it would be no great transgression to think of him as a kind of malevolent or contemptible demiurge, and to hate him, and to deny him worship, and to seek a better God than he.[54]

I find it helpful to quote Hart at some length as he expresses my own and most non-Calvinists feelings about Calvinism's divine determinism, including sin and evil and innocent suffering, so clearly and courageously:

> One should consider the price at which that comfort [viz., that of the Calvinist speaker who preached "God killed my son"] is purchased: it requires us to believe in and love a God whose good ends will be realized not only in spite of—but entirely by way of—every cruelty, every fortuitous misery, every catastrophe, every betrayal, every sin the world has ever known; it requires us to believe in the eternal spiritual necessity of a child dying an agonizing death from diphtheria, of a young mother ravaged by cancer, of tens of thousands of Asians swallowed in an instant by the sea, of millions murdered in death camps and gulags and forced famines (and so on). It is a strange thing indeed to seek peace in a universe rendered morally intelligible at the cost of a God rendered morally loathsome.[55]

With great reluctance, because I know it may deeply offend Calvinists, I can only say amen!

Without doubt some Calvinists will object and say God only *permits* sin and evil and innocent suffering; he does not actually *cause* them. And he permits them blamelessly without participating in the sin or evil themselves. The answer to this objection to Hart's devastating critique should be obvious from the Calvinist quotations provided above. Evangelical thinkers Jerry Walls and Joseph Dongell rightly point out in *Why I Am*

Not a Calvinist that the often-used language of *permission* "does not sit well with serious Calvinism,"[56] even though Calvinists such as Sproul and Helm fall back on it in order to avoid any implication that God is the cause of sin, evil, or innocent suffering.

Walls and Dongell rightly also point out that Calvin himself rejected this language of God's permission as inappropriate for God's sovereignty.[57] True, some Calvinists use it, but "if God only permits certain things without specifically causing them, it is hard to see how this would square with the Calvinist claim of all-embracing determinism."[58] (Philosopher Walls defines determinism as "the view that every event must happen exactly as it did because of prior conditions."[59])

According to Walls and Dongell and many other careful critics of Calvinism, a deep incoherence lies at the heart of Calvinists' assertion of exhaustive divine sovereignty, divine determinism, and mere permission of evil: "For a determinist—and this is the crucial point—no event can be seen in isolation from the events that cause it. When this is kept in mind, it's hard to see how Calvinists can speak of any events or choices as being *permitted*."[60] They take on Sproul's claim that evil springs from evil character made up of evil dispositions. This is Sproul's (and other Calvinists') attempt to avoid making God the author of evil because God is said to foreordain and render certain actions while the evil of them flows from the finite actors' sinful desires. God's motive in foreordaining and rendering certain the sin is morally pure, *and* he does not coerce anyone to sin. Thus, God is said merely to permit the sin or evil action while at the same time rendering it certain.

Walls and Dongell rightly question the coherence of this account of God's role in evil because the question inevitably arises: From where did the creature's evil disposition and evil desires come? Here's one of the Achilles' heels of Calvinism using Pharaoh as case study (because Sproul blames Pharaoh's evil actions on his evil character and not on God who foreordained them). Walls and Dongell point out that "Pharaoh did not become the person he was in a vacuum. Rather, his character was formed by a long series of events and choices, all of which were determined by God (according to Calvinism)."[61] In other words, to be consistent, Calvinism *must say* that even Pharaoh's evil character ultimately comes from God. (Imagine a universe in which only God and the very first creature exist. Where could the first evil impulse come from if not from the creature's free will, which Calvinism denies except in the compatibilist sense, or God?)

Walls and Dongell ask, then, "What sense, then, does it make to say that God permitted Pharaoh's actions, given this picture" of God's role in rendering everything certain without exception?[62] They point out that "the notion of permission loses all significant meaning in a Calvinist framework. Therefore, it is not surprising that Calvin himself was suspicious of the idea and warned against using it."[63] Finally, Walls and Dongell sum up the entire problem concisely and forcefully: "Calvinism is hard-pressed to account for sin and evil in a way that is morally plausible. For if God determines everything that happens, then it is hard to see why there is so much sin and evil in the world and why God is not responsible for it."[64]

Appeal, then, to God's permission of sin and evil does not square with high Calvinism's strong doctrine of divine sovereignty. Admittedly, many Calvinists *do* fall back on it, but that does not ameliorate what else they say about God's all-determining plan and action in rendering everything without exception certain.

Some Calvinists defend God's goodness based on what is called the "greater good" theodicy. (Theodicy is any philosophical or theological attempt to justify God's actions in the face of evil.) In fact, so far as I can tell, *all* Calvinists incorporate some version of the greater good defense of God's goodness in the face of sin and evil into their doctrines of providence. Walls and Dongell refer specifically to Paul Helm. The problem, they point out (and I would say another Achilles' heel of Calvinism), is belief in the divine decision to reprobate many people to hell by sovereignly "passing over them" when choosing some to save. In what sense can hell be said to serve a greater good? What good? I will say more on this issue in chapter 5, on unconditional election.

I would like to pause here and make something clear. *If* high Calvinism is saying anything distinctive in its doctrine of providence, it is that God purposefully plans and renders certain and controls everything without exception. Talk of God as merely permitting sin and evil and innocent suffering stands in stark contrast with this strong doctrine of providence. *If* it is logical for Calvinists to say God permits or allows evil, they can only mean that in a highly attenuated and unusual sense of "permits" and "allows"—one that falls outside the ordinary language of most people. Put bluntly but clearly, according to high Calvinism, God wants sin, evil, and innocent suffering to happen even if, as some Calvinists such as John Piper say, it hurts God. And he wants them to happen in a causal way; he renders them certain.

Let's examine a case study most Calvinists are reluctant to deal with. I find most of their case studies of God's sovereignty are about God's merciful allowing of suffering in Christians' lives to make them stronger. See, for example, Piper's *The Hidden Smile of God*,[65] in which he explains how intense affliction helped strengthen the spiritual lives of Christian heroes John Bunyan, William Cowper, and David Brainerd. But what happens if we turn from that kind of disciplinary affliction that Paul, in the New Testament, clearly says God *does* bring into Christians' lives for their own good and for his glory to two other kinds of affliction: the intense suffering of a child dying of cancer and the kidnap, rape, and murder of a child.

If high Calvinism is right, we have no choice but to attribute these horrible afflictions to God just as much as we must attribute Bunyan's, Cowper's, and Brainerd's afflictions to God. There is simply no way around it, given what Calvinists say about the "fine grained" sovereignty of God that controls every twist and turn of every atom and thought. The sufferings of children are not exempted by Calvinists even though they rarely bring them up.

So, return with me to the previously mentioned incident in the hospital where I visited my daughter's friend. Down the hall, not far away, I could hear a small child, perhaps two or three years old, screaming in agony between horrible, retching coughs. The poor child was being held by someone who talked soothingly to her as she coughed uncontrollably and then screamed some more. It was by no means a normal or usual childhood tantrum or cry of discomfort. I have never heard anything like it before or since or even on television. My constant thought was: "Why doesn't someone do something to alleviate that child's suffering?" I wanted to rush down the hall and see if I could help, but I could tell there were plenty of people around her in that room. What I heard haunts me to this day. It seemed that the child was possibly dying an agonizing death.

If Calvinism is true, God not only planned and ordained but also rendered certain that horrible suffering of that small child. He not only planned and ordained and rendered certain the child's illness but also the resulting agony. It won't do to reply that God suffers with her, as Piper says. In *The Pleasures of God* Piper offers his own case study of God's sovereignty in tragedy. He tells in some detail about his mother's death in a horrible car accident. (He makes a point of the fact that she suffered little, but what if she had suffered like that child I heard in the hospital?) Piper uses his mother's death to illustrate how whatever happens pleases God even if it also grieves him.[66] God, he avers, planned and saw to it that his mother's car accident and death would happen for his glory. But how does it render God any less monstrous to say that God plans, ordains, and renders certain the agony of a dying child but grieves over it? Piper says that everything in creation, including sin, evil, and suffering, is an expression of God's glory.[67] He says that God "loves a worldwide reputation"[68] and does everything to make his mighty power known.[69]

In *The Doors of the Sea* theologian Hart tells of a large Sri Lankan man of enormous physical strength whose five children were killed by the Asian tsunami of 2004. The man was featured in an article in the *New York Times*. He was unable to prevent his children from perishing and, as he recounted his futile attempts, he was "utterly overwhelmed by his own weeping."[70] Then Hart writes: "Only a moral cretin ... would have attempted to soothe his anguish by assuring him that his children had died as a result of God's eternal, inscrutable, and righteous counsels, and that in fact their deaths had mysteriously served God's purposes in history."[71] Of course, most Calvinists would advise their followers not to say such things in such moments to such people. However, Hart reflects that "if we would think it shamefully foolish and cruel to say such things in the moment when another's sorrow is most real and irresistibly painful, then we ought never to say them."[72]

Turn with me now to the second imaginary (but too often real) case study of innocent suffering. This one involves moral evil. Imagine a little girl being kidnapped by a vile sex maniac who places her in his car and drives from her neighborhood to an isolated forest alongside a river. In spite of her crying and protesting, he takes her down to the river bank where he rapes her, strangles her, and throws her body in the river. (This is not merely imaginary; it is based on a true story I saw on a television show called *Cold Case Files*.)

Calvin offers us the case of a merchant who foolishly wanders away from his companions and comes upon a thieves' den and is robbed and murdered. As earlier quoted, he says this event, like all events, was not only foreseen and allowed by God but actually caused and governed by God's secret plan. Nowhere does he suggest or allow that this is an exception to God's sovereignty; rather, he makes clear it is an illustration of how God works all things that are always being "directed by God's ever-present hand."[73]

We read about the foolish merchant or a similar event today and shake our heads and say, "Yup; I can see God foreordaining that. What a stupid man. And God could easily have a good reason for causing that to happen." But if Calvin is right (and if high Calvinists such as those we have quoted are right), it is not only the foolish merchant whose death is rendered certain by God; it is also the kidnap, rape, and murder of the little girl that was "directed by God's ever-present hand." Notice that this event was not a freak disaster of nature or the result of someone's stupidity. It was pure evil. But whether we take Calvin's illustration of the murdered merchant or the very real illustration of the little girl, according to Calvinism's view of God's sovereignty *both* are identical in that God planned, ordained, governed, and rendered them certain. Hart is right that this inexorably makes God "the secret architect of evil."[74]

But even worse, according to Piper, this makes God the "smiling face" hiding behind a "frowning providence." In *The Hidden Smile of God*, he quotes eighteenth-century Calvinist hymn writer William Cowper's song "God Moves in a Mysterious Way" approvingly: "Judge not the Lord by feeble sense, but trust him for his grace; behind a frowning providence he hides a smiling face."[75] That's all well and good when he is talking about the afflictions God brings into the lives of his heroes to make them stronger Christians. But what about when it applies equally, as it must if Piper is right about God's providence, to the scene of a sex maniac raping a little girl, then strangling her and throwing her into a river? It won't do to escape the difficulty by saying in such cases God merely allows the sin and evil and innocent suffering. If Calvinism is right, God also approves of it and renders it certain even if he also grieves over it. What kind of God is that?

Piper and other Calvinists talk much of God's great reputation and renown. What many of their listeners and followers fail to realize is their account of God's sovereignty makes God's reputation dubious at best—unless, of course, all one means by God's reputation is his power. But is that really what we mean by God's reputation? Isn't it more a matter of his character as good? As earlier noted, Helm says God's goodness cannot be so different from our highest and best ideas of goodness that it loses all meaning. But isn't that what has happened here—with Piper's and similar Calvinists' ideas of God's role in evil and innocent suffering? I think so.

I want to register the fact that some within the Reformed community agree with this assessment of high Calvinism's doctrine of God's sovereignty. James Daane, among others, blasts what he calls "decretal theology" (which is what I am calling divine determinism) for failing to take evil seriously. Drawing out the good and necessary consequences of this theology's explanation of God's role in sin and evil, Daane says, "With his eye of faith the decretal theologian can look out on a broken, bleeding humanity, on a world at war with itself, and see only a thing of beauty and peace."[76]

THE FREEDOM OF GOD AND HUMAN RESPONSIBILITY

At least two other problems arise directly out of high Calvinism's account of God's sovereignty. Not only is God's reputation as good impugned, but also God's freedom in relation to creation and human responsibility for evil are cast into doubt.

I have already touched on the problem of God's freedom. It will come up again throughout this book because it is an issue at the heart of the debate over Calvinism. Even some Reformed theologians believe classical, high Calvinism effectively, if inadvertently, undermines the freedom of God—which is highly ironic because *all* Calvinists claim that their view of God is designed to protect God's transcendence, including his freedom.

Many Calvinists argue that only Calvinism protects God from being made dependent on creatures. Boettner, for example, argues that Calvinism is all about God's absolute freedom from being conditioned by anyone or anything outside of himself. In fact, for Boettner, the whole scheme of Calvinism, although supported by Scripture, can be derived from the idea of God's infinity. Thus, when God created the world he did so with "perfect freedom."[77] Helm also leans on the idea of God's transcendence or wholly otherness to say that creatures cannot affect the divine will. God is wholly free from human or any other conditioning: "No human decision can change the divine will in any respect."[78] Sproul writes about God's self-sufficiency as absolutely crucial to God's deity and makes clear by that he means God is free from any dependence on anything outside himself for anything he is or does.[79]

These ideas of God are not unique to Calvinism; for the most part they are common stock in what is called "classical Christian theism"—a picture of God developed throughout the centuries but especially in the early church and medieval universities. In classical Christian theism God is said to be incapable of any kind of change or dependence on anything or anyone outside himself for anything. God is *actus purus*, to use the term of Thomas Aquinas, the great medieval scholastic philosopher and theologian. That means there is no potentiality in God, only actuality.

The question is, however, whether at least some versions of Calvinism inadvertently make God dependent on the world for something that he needs—his own self-glorification through the manifestation of all his attributes equally. This is a theme running throughout most high Calvinism—that everything God does in creation and redemption is for his glory. This idea of the purpose of God is traceable at least to Edwards, but Boettner expresses it best with his answer to why God has allowed sin into the world:

> Sin ... is permitted in order that the mercy of God may be shown in its forgiveness, and that His justice may be shown in its punishment. Its entrance is the result of a settled design which God formed in eternity, and through which He purposed to reveal Himself to His rational creatures as complete and full-orbed in all conceivable perfections.[80]

Piper, also like Edwards, claims that God's purpose in everything that happens is the display of his glory. Edwards clearly explained, as Piper agrees, that God's purpose in everything including evil is the full manifestation of all his attributes including justice and wrath.[81]

In an ironic twist, this explanation of God's purpose in creation and redemption, including sin and evil, comes back to haunt Edwards and most Calvinists after him. (Hints of it can also be found in Calvin.) Apparently, God *needs* the world to be as it is, including sin, evil, innocent suffering, redemption, and reprobation (hell), in order to manifest his attributes and thereby glorify himself. Could God have refrained from it? Not according to Edwards, who affirmed the "necessary determination of God's will in all things by what he sees to be *fittest* and *best*."[82]

Edwards' and other Calvinists' denials of libertarian freedom as incoherent and embrace of compatibilism even in God (i.e., God's free will is controlled by his strongest motives) lead straight into the idea that God's creation of the world as the "theater of his glory" (Calvin) was necessary and not truly free in the sense that it might have been otherwise. This logical conclusion from this strong view of sovereignty is contrary to the strong emphasis on God's transcendence and freedom from conditioning. It is also contrary to traditional Christian orthodoxy! And it undermines the whole idea of creation and redemption being *solely by grace* because what is necessary cannot be by grace.

Evangelical philosopher Bruce A. Little correctly criticizes Piper and others who think like him. According to Piper, he rightly notes, God ordains evil (as everything else) to glorify himself.[83] He notes that "Piper carefully uses his words to say that in all the evil on this earth, God has a purpose: to make the glory of Christ shine more brightly.... [A child's] torturous death is part of this will. This position not only makes evil necessary to the purpose of God, it makes God the one morally responsible for the evil."[84] Little and other critics come close to exposing the radical extent of this view of God's sovereignty including evil. It is that God *must create, allow sin and evil, redeem, and reject in order to fulfill the potential of his own self-glorification.*

Without the world, then, God would not be God in the same way; his glory would be less than it is with it. Evil, then, is necessary to God. God is dependent on the world, including evil. Evangelical philosopher Jeremy Evans rightly concludes: "If God needs creation to exemplify these properties [justice, wrath], then humans can rightly question whether God was free in His act of creation."[85]

Of course, few Calvinists will put it that way, but it is a "good and necessary consequence" of what some of them say about God's purpose in creation and the necessity of God's actions arising out of his character. The upshot is that God is not truly free in relation to creation in the sense of being able to do otherwise than create, permit (render certain) evil, redeem, and damn for his glory.

The second of the two problems following from Calvinism's doctrine of God's providence is the inevitable shift of responsibility for sin and evil from creatures to God. Again, all Calvinists say that God is not responsible for sin and evil even though he foreordains and renders them certain, and that creatures are responsible even though they could not do otherwise than they do.

In his *Institutes* Calvin claims that "God's providence does not exculpate our wickedness."[86] To those who claim that God's providence does make God and not the sinner responsible for evil he says: "Away ... with this doglike impudence, which can indeed bark at God's justice afar off but cannot touch it."[87] His explanation is that although people would not do evil things "unless he [God] willed it," they do them motivated by an "evil inclination." Therefore, even though they could not do otherwise than they do, and even though "their misdeeds are committed solely by God's dispensation,"[88] God is not guilty and they are.

Clearly, what Calvin means is that "evil" lies in the intentions of the heart and not in the actions themselves. Since God foreordains and renders certain the actions with a good motive (no doubt for his glory!), he cannot be held responsible for the evil of them. Rather, the person who does the evil thing he or she cannot avoid doing (because compelled by an evil motive and ultimately by God)[89] is the only guilty party.

What did Edwards say about this? We have already seen that Edwards believed and argued that God "renders sin certain infallibly" by "withholding his action and energy."[90] He wrote of sinners that "God leaves 'em [sic] *to themselves* [so that they] necessarily sin."[91] But, Edwards claimed, God does not do evil by willing evil.[92] This is because *guilt* lies entirely in the evil disposition of the heart that arose in Adam and in us by God's permission making it necessary. Here is Edwards' clearest statement on this matter: "For God ... to have the disposal [control] of this affair [the fall], as to withhold those influences, without which nature will be corrupt, is not to be the *author of sin*."[93]

Notice a couple of things here. First, Edwards believed and taught that human nature (and perhaps creaturely nature in general, including angels) would necessarily become corrupt and sin without supernatural divine influence. All Calvinists who follow Edwards' line here (and most do) must be making the same assumption. The necessary correlate of that is that human nature was not created good. This equates finitude with "not good." Of course, nobody has ever thought that finite nature is metaphysically perfect as God is perfect. It is capable of corruption. But to say it will necessarily become corrupt without God's supernatural influence is to call into question the goodness of God's creation.

Second, Edwards is saying that God withheld that necessary influence, and *he must mean withdrew it* because otherwise the fall would have happened immediately. Either way, God could have preserved Adam from sinning; he chose not to, knowing infallibly that Adam would fall if he withdrew his supernatural, preserving power.

Third, the fall of Adam and all its consequences (including the kidnapping, rape and murder of the little girl) were willed by God and rendered certain by God.

Fourth, Edwards nowhere explains the origin of Adam's evil disposition that made him and not God guilty. But his doctrine of divine providence, which is exhaustive sovereignty down to the minutest details, would seem to require that everything in creation, including all motives and dispositions, is under God's control and rendered certain by God. However, in this argument Edwards seems to be saying that Adam's evil disposition simply popped into existence out of nowhere. That is forbidden by Edwards' strong doctrine of God's sovereignty and by his denial of libertarian free will. Everything comes from somewhere! If the evil inclination that caused Adam to sin came from within himself autonomously, that would be a huge concession to Arminianism!

Edwards scholar John E. Smith, editor of *The Works of Jonathan Edwards*, comments that "it must be, then, that God in his wisdom counts a necessary evil nature subject to moral blame."[94] And, in light of Edwards' statement elsewhere that "nothing can come to pass but what is the will and pleasure of God should come to pass ... this extraordinarily strong language would seem to put Edwards in the position of making God the efficient cause of all evil and sin."[95] Smith criticizes Edwards for failing to account adequately for Adam's sin or God's blamelessness and says of Edwards' defense of God, "Edwards ended lamely."[96]

Let's move on to Boettner. What did he say about God's responsibility for sin and evil? True to his doctrine of meticulous providence, he did not hesitate to affirm "the absolute sway of God over the thoughts and intents of the heart [of man]."[97] However, he argued, people are enslaved to sin by their own fault. How did this enslavement to sin begin? Boettner repeats the arguments of Edwards. Even the fall of Adam and Eve was "ordained in the secret counsels of God,"[98] and God used his sway over their thoughts and intents to render the fall certain. "Yet," Boettner claimed, "God in no way compelled man to fall. He simply withheld that undeserved constraining grace with which Adam would infallibly not have fallen, which grace He was under no obligation to bestow."[99] According to Boettner, like Edwards before him, this is the reason God is not responsible for sin and evil and human beings are. All since Adam have inherited his corrupted nature and also act out of it sinfully because of it.

So, according to Boettner, the only way God could have been responsible for Adam's first sin is if he compelled him to sin. Simply rendering his sin certain by withholding the "constraining grace" in no way makes God responsible for it. Two questions automatically arise. First, who believes that a person who renders it certain that another person will commit a crime, such that the other person who actually commits the crime could not have done otherwise, is not complicit in it? Anyone who watches the television series *Law & Order* knows that a person or company that seduces a person to commit a crime even indirectly is just as guilty as the person who commits it. And the person who commits it is guilty only to the extent he or she was able to avoid doing it. I ask, if you were on a jury and you became convinced by the evidence that the defendant could not have done otherwise than commit the offense, would you vote guilty or for acquittal? I venture that common sense dictates that jurors vote for acquittal in such cases.

Second, Boettner believes that God in no way owed Adam that constraining grace needed not to sin. I regard that as debatable. But the issue is not whether God *owed* it to him but whether the God who is *love*, revealed most fully in Jesus Christ, would have removed it, thereby rendering it certain that Adam would fall with all the consequences of that. Boettner's argument that God in no way owed constraining grace to Adam certainly makes God seem callous, especially when God then blames Adam for sinning when God created him with a nature so weak that sinning was inevitable. It seems that, on this account, God set Adam up to fall. It reminds of the old limerick about the supralapsarian Dutch theologian Franciscus Gomarus, who harassed Arminius for not accepting this high account of God's sovereignty and all that comes with it:

> Franciscus Gomarus was a supralpsarius;
> He actually gave Adam an excuse.
> God had decreed,
> Foreordained Adam's deed.
> God pre-cooked Adam's goose.

What about other Calvinists? What do they have to say about God's responsibility and humanity's responsibility for the fall and all of its consequences? Helm repeats the arguments of Edwards and Boettner about God's ordaining evil and rendering it certain. God does not cause evil actions but "determines them" by "divine *withholding*."[100] He claims only the immediate cause of an evil act can be considered guilty of it.[101] I believe this is spurious because it flies in the face of common sense and natural law. Jeremy Evans is right: "Ultimate responsibility ... resides where the ultimate cause is."[102]

John Piper avoids the tortuous explanations of other Calvinists and simply says he does not know how it is that God foreordains and renders certain sin and evil and yet sinners are responsible and God is not. He says this is ultimately a mystery that cannot be relieved by human reasoning. The Bible simply says both: God foreordains evil and humans are responsible anyway.[103]

Many critics of high Calvinism, including this writer, believe a serious contradiction lies at the heart of this strong view of God's sovereignty that includes God's foreordination and rendering certain of evil—especially when it is explained by the mechanism of God's "withholding" or "withdrawing" of necessary grace such that Adam fell (and all his posterity with him) infallibly by God's design. I take seriously that Calvinists rarely attribute the guilt of sin to God; they almost always say that God is morally pure and stainless and that all guilt for sin lies with sinful creatures. But the problem is that this contradicts their strong view of God's sovereignty that includes God's determination to evil.

Who can blame those who fear that this inevitably leads to the good and necessary consequence that God is the author of sin and evil and thus bears primary responsibility for it? Other than a sheer act of will power to embrace what is unintelligible, what stops someone who believes this from continuing on to say that creatures are not guilty and God is? What one has to face is the question as to which side of this double-sided doctrine of God's absolute, determining sovereignty and humans' sole responsibility of evil to embrace. One cannot really embrace both without falling into contradiction. Appeal to mystery is not appropriate; contradiction is not mystery, as even Sproul emphatically argues in *Chosen by God*. I agree with him when he writes that "for a Christian to embrace both poles of a blatant contradiction is to commit intellectual suicide."[104] I will deal with this problem of unintelligibility more in the conclusion.

ALTERNATIVES TO DIVINE DETERMINISM

Does Scripture require acceptance of the high Calvinist doctrine of divine determinism? It does not. What about all those biblical passages that Calvinists use to argue their case for exhaustive foreordination and determination of all events, including sin and evil? Some of those have been mentioned earlier. Every single passage that supposedly teaches divine determination of evil, innocent suffering, and sin can be interpreted as referring to God's permission. Virtually all Christians agree that nothing whatever can happen without God's permission. The question is whether Calvinism is really permitted to fall back on permission language when it already says that God wills whatever happens, including sin and evil, and that God's permission is "willing permission" that actively renders them certain. The main alternative to this strong doctrine of God's sovereignty is *divine self-limitation.*

First, let it be clearly understood that those who appeal to divine self-limitation and passive permission as the explanation for sin and evil in the omnipotent, creator God's world *do not* say God *never* manipulates historical circumstances to bring about his will. What God *never does* is *cause evil.* God may and no doubt sometimes does bring about some event by placing people in circumstances where he knows what they will freely do because he needs them to do that for his plan to be fulfilled. Such seemed to be the case with Jesus' crucifixion. Even then, however, it was not that God tempted or manipulated individuals to sin. Rather, he knew what events, such as the triumphal entry, would result in the crucifixion.

But what we must not say is that the fall of Adam, which set off the whole history of sin and evil, was willed, planned, and rendered certain by God. God neither foreordained it nor rendered it certain, and it was not a part of his will except to reluctantly allow it. How do we know this? We know it because we know God's character through Jesus Christ. The doctrine of the incarnation proves that God's character is fully revealed in Jesus such that "no *interpretation* of any passage [in the Bible] that undercuts the revelations of the divine mind inculcated by Jesus can be accepted as valid. What he says and does is what God says and does. He had no hidden decrees to conceal, no dark side of his Father to protect from disclosure, no reason to be defensive about the [ways of] God."[105]

The high Calvinist doctrine of God's sovereignty including evil as part of God's plan, purpose, and determining power blatantly contradicts Scripture passages that reveal "God is love" (1 John 4:8), takes no pleasure in the death of the wicked (Ezek. 18:32), wants everyone to be saved (Ezek. 18:32; 1 Tim. 2:4; 2 Peter 3:9), and never tempts anyone (James 1:13). To be sure, Calvinists have clever but unconvincing explanations of these and numerous other passages of Scripture. For example, John Piper argues that God has "complex feelings and motives,"[106] such that he genuinely regrets that sin and evil have to be part of his world, genuinely wishes that all people could be saved, and is grieved when those he predestined to die and even suffer in hell for eternity for his glory experience that fate. But these are not convincing explanations of these important passages that reveal the heart of God. They make God double-minded.

So how might one deal with the reality of sin and evil in God's world without placing undue limits on God's power and sovereignty? The only way is to posit what Scripture everywhere assumes—a divine self-limitation in relation to the world of moral freedom, including especially libertarian freedom. That freedom is a wonderful and terrible gift of God to human persons created in his image and likeness. In other words, God allows his perfect will to be thwarted by his human creatures whom he loves and respects enough not to control them.

Thus, God does have two wills, but they are not ones posited by Calvinism. As a result of Adam's free choice to fall into sin (with free choice here meaning he could have done otherwise), God has *a perfect will*—also known as his *antecedent will.* ("Perfect" here means "what God truly wishes would happen.") God's perfect will is that none perish; this is God's antecedent will (antecedent to the fall and to its resulting corruption in the world). God also has a *consequent will*—consequent to creaturely rebellion. It is that he allows some freely to choose to perish. But his allowing is genuinely reluctant and not manipulative.

Evangelical theologian Stanley Grenz (1950–2005) offered a helpful distinction in God's providence that corresponds to the two wills—perfect/antecedent and consequent—mentioned above. It is the distinction between "sovereignty *de facto*" and "sovereignty *de jure*."[107] According to Grenz, with whom I agree, due to God's voluntary self-limitation he is now sovereign *de jure* (by right) but not yet sovereign *de facto* (in actuality). His sovereignty *de facto* is future. This reflects the biblical narrative in which Satan is the "god of this age" (2 Cor. 4:4) (where "world" clearly means "this present evil age"), and God will defeat him in the coming age to become "all in all" (1 Cor. 15:28). The entirety of 1 Corinthians 15 can be interpreted in no other way; it assumes the distinction between God's sovereign rule *de jure* now and *de facto* in the future. This is *not* to say, of course, that God is *not* actually sovereign now at all; it only says that God is *allowing* his sovereignty to be challenged and his will to be partially thwarted until then.

Doesn't this limit God's power and sovereignty? No, because God remains omnipotent; he *could* control everything and everyone if he chose to. For the sake of having real, personal creatures who can freely choose to love him or not, God limits his control. Still, God is sovereign in the sense that nothing at all can ever happen that God does not allow. Nothing falls totally outside of God's supervening oversight and governance.

But not everything that happens is what God wants to happen or determines to happen. There is no exhaustive divine determinism.

Of course, Jesus, being God, could have healed everyone in Nazareth when he visited there (Mark 6:5), but he "couldn't" do miracles there because of their lack of faith. As God, he had the sheer power to do miracles. But he had limited his power ordinarily to do miracles in the presence of faith. He did not want to go around unilaterally healing people without some measure of cooperating or receptive faith on their part. So it is with God's sovereignty. He could exercise deterministic control, but he has chosen not to do so. As theologian E. Frank Tupper says, God is not a "do anything, anytime, anywhere kind of God" because he has chosen not to be that kind of God.[108] He has chosen to make himself partially dependent on his human covenant partners while remaining the "superior covenant power of holy love."[109]

This is a book intended to point out the weaknesses and even fatal flaws of high Calvinism, that is, radical Reformed theology. It is not intended to be a defense of Arminianism or any alternative to Calvinism. That would make it a much longer book and therefore one many may decline to read. What is missing on bookstores' and libraries' shelves is not a book about Arminianism or even one about God's self-limiting sovereignty over against Calvinism. What is missing is a book demonstrating why high Calvinism is not biblically, theologically, or logically tenable. That's all this volume intends to be. Occasionally I will mention alternatives to high Calvinism, such as (about God's sovereignty) E. Frank Tupper, *A Scandalous Providence*; Gregory Boyd, *Is God to Blame?* Jack Cottrell, *What the Bible Says about God the Ruler*;[110] and especially David Bentley Hart, *The Doors of the Sea: Where Was God in the Tsunami?* Here I will offer a taste of that last little volume, which well expresses my and many other Christians' alternative (to Calvinism) vision of God's providence. Hart explains:

> How radically the gospel is pervaded by a sense that the brokenness of the fallen world is the work of rebellious rational free will, which God permits to reign, and pervaded also by a sense that Christ comes genuinely to *save* creation, to conquer, to rescue, to defeat the power of evil in all things. This great narrative of fall and redemption is not a charade, not simply a dramaturgical lesson regarding God's absolute prerogatives prepared for us from eternity, but a real consequence of the mystery of created freedom and the fullness of grace.[111]

FIVE

YES TO ELECTION; NO TO DOUBLE PREDESTINATION

I never discovered who did it, but I must say it was clever and intriguing if somewhat bizarre. My wife and I returned to my office to retrieve our coats after an evening Christmas program and banquet on campus. Pinned on my office door was a folded-over note. That's not unusual; I often get them from students, colleagues, or visitors. So I took the note down, opened my door, and turned on the light. Then I read the note: "Professor Olson, I talked to God; you're damned. Thought you'd like to know." It was unsigned. Of course, I took it as a joke; I had been involved in a light-hearted campus debate about "predestination versus free will," so I assumed the note was someone's attempt at humor. On the other hand, I have met Calvinists who think it is possible to know for sure who is predestined to heaven and who is predestined to hell.

That may not be as bizarre as some Calvinists think. They should study their own history. In the previous chapter I mentioned John Piper's book that includes a chapter on the Calvinist hymn writer William Cowper (pronounced "Cooper") (1731–1800), author of "There Is a Fountain Filled with Blood" and "God Moves in a Mysterious Way," as well as hundreds of other hymns. Cowper was a convinced Calvinist who strongly believed in "double predestination"—that God has from eternity chosen some people to save and others to damn. For much of his adult life he suffered bouts of extreme depression and even spent time in an asylum. During some of those times he was convinced that somehow he knew he was predestined to hell. Whether his conviction of damnation led to his depression or vice versa is, of course, unknown.

I spoke to an adult Sunday School class about Christian doctrine and spent one session on the doctrine of election, explaining how Calvinists view it as unconditional and Arminians (and others) view it as conditional (when referring to individuals and their eternal destiny). We talked about the strengths and weaknesses of this doctrine and especially the problem of God's goodness in light of his supposed decree to "pass over" or even positively select some to eternal perdition. The class debated among themselves whether this is consistent with the love of God shown in Jesus Christ. Afterward, a middle-aged gentleman with a PhD in psychology who was also the author of some well-known books on marriage came to me for a "one-on-one." He explained that he did not consider God's selection of some for damnation a problem because he had come to believe the reprobate are not really persons at all but automata (machines, robots). I had never heard such an explanation before and would have suspected it of being the imaginings of a somewhat unsophisticated mind, had this man not been who he was.

Without any doubt the doctrine of unconditional election, the "U" in TULIP, has been the subject of much debate and controversy among conservative and evangelical Christians. But it is crucial to all true Calvinists; it is the heart of their system of soteriology. To them, it is a sweet, comforting doctrine because it tells them their salvation is not dependent on anything they are or do but only on God's grace. To Calvinists it is inextricably linked to the foundational Reformation doctrine of justification by grace through faith alone. They believe that any view except theirs leads inexorably to a weakening of that Reformation doctrine. To others, however (such as Calvinists like Cowper), it is a doctrine of terror because of its unavoidable flip side—that God has chosen some, whom he could save, to suffer eternally in hell (even if only by passing over them when selecting others to salvation).

Whereas defenders of unconditional election see it as an expression of God's great goodness and mercy, opponents (such as John Wesley) see it as an expression of a dark and hidden God (Luther's term for the side of God that predestines some to hell) who cares more about his own glory than about the well-being of all people. Opponents say it cannot be reconciled with Scriptures such as "God is love" and "God [does not want] anyone to perish" (1 John 4:8, 16; 2 Peter 3:9). Most of all, it cannot be reconciled with the character of God revealed in Jesus Christ, who wept over Jerusalem when its inhabitants did not accept him as their Messiah (Luke 19:41–44).

Few people who know about the Calvinist doctrine of unconditional election (usually expressed by nontheologians as simply "predestination") are indifferent; most are either set against it (such as John Wesley) or adamantly for it (such as Jonathan Edwards). (I mention Wesley and Edwards here because they were born in the same year [1703], their lives significantly overlapped during the Great Awakening in Great Britain and North America, and they are usually considered the two great-grandfathers of the evangelical movement.) As I will explain more fully in this chapter, I am for unconditional election *as that applies to God's people but not specific individuals*, and I am for *conditional election of individuals*. But I am firmly and unalterably opposed to unconditional individual election's inevitable correlate—reprobation. I believe this so-called double predestination of individuals by God is inconsistent with his love, and the teaching makes it difficult to tell the difference between God and the devil.

UNCONDITIONAL ELECTION *IS* DOUBLE PREDESTINATION

Some Calvinists say that they believe in "single predestination." What they mean is that they do *not* believe God chooses to damn anyone; he only selects some of fallen humanity (St. Augustine's "mass of damnation") to save, and he leaves the rest to their deserved and freely chosen fate in hell. But does this make sense?

I begin as usual with Calvin, who wrote in the *Institutes* that "God is said to have ordained from eternity those whom he wills to embrace in love and those upon whom he wills to vent his wrath."[1] The surrounding context makes clear that he agrees with what is said. It would be difficult to argue that Calvin held anything other than double predestination. Passages from the *Institutes* quoted in chapter 3 make this clear; he talks about the reprobate being compelled to obedience by God. (Again, the context makes clear he does not mean compelled to obedience to God's *preceptive will*, that is, God's moral commands, but compelled to obedience to God's *decretive will*, that is, God's decrees of what shall be, including their sinfulness.) Calvin, I believe, would be shocked to hear of people calling themselves Calvinists but arguing that predestination is only single, that it applies only to election and not to reprobation—as if the two could be separated or as if God could be sovereign in that case.

Boettner also affirmed divine reprobation of some persons and even that God's will is the "decisive factor" in their damnation. First, he wrote of reprobation that "this, too," like election to salvation, "is of God."[2] Furthermore, "we believe that from all eternity God has intended to leave some of Adam's posterity in their sins and that the decisive factor in the life of each is to be found in God's will."[3] It is important to remember that for Boettner, as apparently for other Calvinist authors I have quoted, "the Scripture writers did not hesitate to affirm the absolute sway of God over the thoughts and intents of the heart."[4] Also, "God so governs the inward feelings, external environment, habits, desires, motives, etc., of men that they freely do what He purposes."[5] God, he confessed, "in a real sense" determines people's choices, and there is no such thing as "self-determination."[6] Thus, the reason is clear for Boettner's claim that reprobation is necessarily part of God's sovereign plan and purpose and is not ultimately conditioned by anything outside of God himself. God's will [obviously his "decretive will"] is the "decisive factor" in the life of the reprobate and their reprobation.

At the same time, however, like all Calvinists I am aware of, Boettner claims that the reprobate *deserve* their punishment (eternal suffering in hell) because they "voluntarily chose sin."[7] Ultimately, he leaves this apparent contradiction in the realm of mystery: "Predestination [including reprobation] and free agency are the twin pillars of a great temple, and they meet above the clouds where the human gaze cannot penetrate."[8] It seems to me, however, that this mystery is a blatant contradiction, something even Sproul rules out of bounds for Christian discourse. We must point out here the difference between mystery and contradiction; the former is something that cannot be fully explained to or comprehended by the human mind whereas the latter is sheer nonsense—two concepts that cancel each other out and together make an absurdity. Christian theology should never rest comfortably with the latter whereas the former is always going to be present in human talk of God.

Boettner has harsh words for those Calvinists who opt for single predestination: "'Mild Calvinism' [i.e., the attempt to believe in single predestination] is synonymous with sickly Calvinism, and sickness, if not cured, is the beginning of the end."[9] While admitting that reprobation is "admittedly an unpleasant doctrine,"[10] Boettner attempts to prove its necessity. For him, without it God's justice will not be fully displayed and thus God will not be fully glorified in the world and before angels.

Another witness that unconditional election necessarily includes reprobation as its "other side of the coin" is Calvinist pastor and theologian Edwin Palmer, author of *The Five Points of Calvinism*, in which he lays out and defends "Twelve Theses on Reprobation." First, he defines reprobation as "God's eternal, sovereign, unconditional, immutable, wise, holy, and mysterious decree whereby, in electing some to eternal life, He passes others by, and then justly condemns them for their own sin—all to His own glory."[11] Like Boettner and others, he admits this is a difficult doctrine but says that "our infinite God presents us with some astounding truths—truths that our sinful and finite minds rebel against."[12] He argues that sin comes about by the "efficacious permission of God"—something we have already noted in other Calvinist theologians who are reluctant to say sin is caused by God. It would seem that "efficacious permission" must mean, as God's permission of sin and evil means in Edwards, Boettner, and others, that God renders it certain without forcing people to sin. Palmer says: "All things, including sin, are brought to pass by God—without God violating His holiness."[13]

Palmer argues that the predestination of some necessarily implies reprobation of others: "If God chooses some, then He necessarily passes by others. Up implies down; back implies front; wet implies dry; later implies earlier; choosing implies leaving others unchosen."[14] (Notice that Palmer is using logic here and I agree with him!) He then goes on to argue that God does not "effectuate" sin and unbelief in the same way he effectuates faith.[15] "God wills sin and unbelief unwillingly; he takes no delight in them."[16] One can only wonder why this would be so *if* it is true that God does everything "for his glory." How can God not take delight in what glorifies him? Palmer forges on boldly and states that God's reprobation is both conditional and unconditional:

> Reprobation as condemnation is conditional in the sense that once someone is passed by, then he is condemned by God for his sins and unbelief. Although all things—unbelief and sin included—proceed from God's eternal decree, man is still to blame for his sins. He is guilty; it is his fault and not God's.[17]

This is enough to make anyone's head spin. And Palmer agrees and revels in it. "He [the Calvinist] realizes that what he advocates is ridiculous.... The Calvinist freely admits that his position is illogical, ridiculous, nonsensical, and foolish."[18] However, "this secret matter belongs to the Lord our God, and we should leave it there. We ought not to probe into that secret counsel of God."[19] Apparently Palmer agrees with Martin Luther who, when pushed to the wall by Erasmus in their debate about free will, urged his readers to "adore the mysteries" and not try to use logic. Palmer also echoes early church theologian Tertullian who said, "I believe it because it is absurd!" Perhaps many Calvinists will not agree with Palmer, but they should if they want to hold onto this teaching that God reprobates people unconditionally (because he himself foreordained sin and rendered it certain) *and yet* the reprobate are solely responsible and deserve their eternal punishment because their reprobation is "conditional."

What drives Palmer and other high Calvinists to such a sacrifice of the intellect? He makes no secret of it: Romans 9—the bedrock passage of Scripture for Calvinist belief in unconditional election and reprobation: "When God speaks—as he has clearly done in Romans 9—then we are simply to follow and believe, even if we cannot understand, and even if it seems contradictory to our puny minds."[20] Romans 9 says that God chose Jacob over Esau and loved Jacob and hated Esau before they were born or had done anything good or bad "in order that God's purpose in election might stand: not by works but by him who calls" (Rom. 9:11–12). Then Paul quotes Exodus where God said to Moses, "I will have mercy on whom I have mercy, and I will have compassion on whom I have compassion" (9:15). Then we read: "Therefore God has mercy on whom he wants to have mercy, and he hardens whom he wants to harden" (9:18).

Of course, Romans 9 says much more and I urge readers to read and study the entire book of Romans and interpret chapter 9 in the context of the whole book. Like all Calvinists, Palmer interprets these statements literally as applying to individual salvation and reprobation. As I will show later in this chapter, however, there are other valid interpretations that do not end up requiring the sacrifice of the intellect or regarding God as arbitrary or monstrous.

Sproul is another Calvinist who argues that there can be no unconditional election to salvation without reprobation so that "single predestination" is an impossible concept. He boldly promotes double predestination while registering some important caveats. "If there is such a thing as predestination at all, and if that predestination does not include all people, then we must not shrink from the necessary inference that there are two sides to predestination. It is not enough to talk about Jacob; we must also consider Esau."[21] In order to soften the blow (to God's goodness)

Sproul argues that these two decrees of God—to save some and damn others—must not be taken as "equally ultimate" or both positive. He criticizes what he calls hyper-Calvinism for making election and reprobation equally ultimate—placing them on the same plane in the plan of God and the outworking of that plan by God.[22] Against hyper-Calvinism Sproul expresses what he believes is the true Reformed doctrine:

> The Reformed view teaches that God positively or actively intervenes in the lives of the elect to insure their salvation. The rest of mankind God leaves to themselves. He does not create unbelief in their hearts. That unbelief is already there.... In the Calvinist view the decree of election is positive; the decree of reprobation is negative.[23]

One can only wonder how big a difference that is. Does saying that election and reprobation are not equally ultimate and that one is positive and the other negative really accomplish anything in terms of rescuing the integrity of God's character (which is clearly Sproul's concern)?

It is important for Sproul that double predestination be understood his way—as the unequal, ultimate *and* nonultimate decisions of God to save some fallen humans and let others suffer eternal punishment. First, he says, those whom God allows to suffer eternal punishment, those he passes over, deserve eternal punishment anyway. God is under no obligation to save them. His passing over them does not implicate him in their demise in any way that would imply moral imperfection in God.

A closer look at *how* Sproul says the reprobate are evil and deserving of eternal punishment reveals the flaw in his reasoning about the character of God in light of double predestination. He uses God's hardening of Pharaoh's heart to illustrate God's general way of rendering it certain that some portion of humanity, the nonelect or reprobate, deserve eternal punishment. "All that God has to do to harden people's hearts is to remove restraints. He gives them a longer leash.... In a sense he gives them enough rope to hang themselves."[24] He is affirming the normal Calvinist explanation that God renders the fall and all its consequent corruption, including sin and guilt, certain by withdrawing or withholding sufficient grace. God chooses certain people to harden their hearts so they won't repent and believe. Then he says:

> This is how we must understand double predestination. God gives mercy to the elect by working faith in their hearts. He gives justice

> to the reprobate by leaving them in their own sins. There is no symmetry here. One group receives mercy. The other group receives justice. No one is a victim of injustice. None can complain that there is unrighteousness in God.[25]

Does this make any sense? Not really. First, how is this not symmetry in light of the fact that sinners' sinfulness is foreordained and rendered certain by God such that they cannot do otherwise? How is God's decree of reprobation to pass over certain individuals merely negative and passive if God hardens their hearts? How does Sproul's account really differ from what he calls hyper-Calvinism?

Reformed theologian James Daane, an archenemy of double predestination, calls this kind of talk "verbalism"—"a theatrical game in which words really carry no ascertainable sense."[26] For Daane, as I will bring out later in this chapter, this applies to many words used by double predestinarians, whom he calls "decretal theologians." It seems to apply well to Sproul's talk of God's decrees not being equally ultimate because one is positive and the other negative and to his notions of justice and fairness.

All of the Calvinist theologians who argue *for* double predestination and *against* "single predestination" embrace and affirm the idea that God sovereignly predestines some of his own human creatures, created in his own image and likeness, to hell, and that this is consistent with God's goodness, justice, and love. I agree with them wholeheartedly that there can be no such thing as single predestination insofar as predestination is unconditional election of *some certain* people, a certain *number* out of all, to heaven. The automatic, unavoidable correlate to that is predestination to hell. It's double or nothing.

Where I disagree with them is that double predestination can be defended as good or that a God who does this can be considered good, loving, and just in any sense analogous to those virtues as they are revealed to us in Jesus Christ and in Scripture. If God does this the way they describe, then God's "goodness," God's "love," God's "justice" are mere words with no ascertainable meaning. Daane is right; it would be mere verbalism to continue to speak of God having those attributes as aspects of his eternal divine nature and character—something almost all Calvinists do.

Moreover, even if God merely passes over some whom he could save, why would he do that if he is good, loving, and just? What meaning could those attributes have, even when applied to God, if God does what Calvinists claim? In other words, it isn't just a matter of reprobation, although I do believe reprobation is necessarily implied in the Calvinist doctrine of election. Even if it were possible to hold on to the idea that God does not positively reprobate anyone but only mercifully chooses to save some and leave others to their "deserved damnation," what meanings would "goodness," "love," and "justice" have when attributed to a God who could save everyone because salvation is absolutely unconditional (i.e., not dependent on anything God sees in or about the persons being saved)?[27]

Here is another Achilles' heel of high Calvinism. In spite of their best efforts to avoid it, the "good and necessary consequence" of their soteriology—TULIP—is that God is morally ambiguous if not a moral monster. There is no human analogy for this "goodness." Any human being who had the ability to rescue a large number of people from a terrible calamity but rescues only some would never be considered good or loving or just. Some will say that these terms mean something different in God than in our world. Calvinist Paul Helm is right to reject that argument: "The goodness of God must bear some positive relation to the sorts of human actions we regard as good. Otherwise, why ascribe *goodness* to God?"[28]

A PROBLEM FOR GOD'S CHARACTER AND REPUTATION

Regardless of the above prima facie contradictions of double predestination, Calvinists do defend this theology in various ways. I think I have understood them correctly, but I still do not think these defenses hold up.

Some Calvinists simply turn aside objections to double predestination by saying: "It is not within the creature's jurisdiction to call [God] into question."[29] This is, of course, hardly a defense, but it is a response. Strangely, nearly all Calvinists do nevertheless attempt to defend God's goodness, so one wonders how seriously to take this response to criticism. Furthermore, it is not God whom critics of Calvinism are calling into question. It is Calvinists' *beliefs* about God that we are questioning! There is a difference. The frequency with which one encounters this rejection of criticism leads to the conclusion that at least some Calvinists have trouble distinguishing between their own *doctrine* of God and God himself. Like everyone else, Calvinists should be willing to at least consider the possibility that there are serious deficiencies and flaws in their doctrinal beliefs.

Many Calvinist theologians go beyond attempts to turn aside criticisms with statements about "not questioning God." Many do offer strategies for defending God's good character, God's reputation, in the face of critical questions from non-Calvinists. The main issue they address is simply this: How can God be said to *be good, loving, and just in the face of these doctrines of high Calvinism?* How is God good, loving, and just toward the reprobate? How is God not arbitrary in his choosing some to save unconditionally while leaving others to damnation? And a related critical question is: How can the gospel call be given out as a well-meant offer to all if some have already been chosen by God for damnation and thus have no chance at all, whatsoever, of being accepted by God? (This last question rises to an especially intense pitch in relation to the next point of TULIP—limited atonement.)

Another way of asking the same set of questions is to pose passages of Scripture to Calvinists and ask how they reconcile their belief in reprobation-predestination with them? For example, John 3:16: "For God so loved the world that he gave his one and only Son, that whoever believes in him shall not perish but have eternal life." Note also the verses quoted earlier: 1 Timothy 2:4; 2 Peter 3:9; and 1 John 4:8. How is God love if he foreordains many people to hell for eternity when he could save them because election to salvation is always completely unconditional and has nothing to do with character or choices? How is it that God wants all people to be saved if he determines some specific individuals to be damned? How is it that God has no pleasure in the death of the wicked (Ezek. 18:32) if he foreordains everything, including their reprobation and eternal punishment, for his good pleasure? How is God good if he purposefully withheld from Adam the grace he needed not to fall—knowing that Adam's fall would result in the horrors of sin and evil and innocent suffering of history?

First, some answers from John Calvin. Calvin had little interest in defending God's character; for him, whatever God does is right, and it is wrong to question God regardless of how unjust his actions seem to be. He frequently chided those who peer into God's mysteries too deeply (e.g., by seeking a cause or reason beyond simply *that* God willed something) or who accuse God of acting unjustly (by which he seems also to mean those who accuse his doctrine of God of ruining God's reputation).[30]

However, Calvin did attempt to explain some Scriptures that might seem to conflict with his arguments about God's double predestination. With regard to God's reprobation of some in light of the "all" passages of Scripture he wrote:

> God is said to have ordained from eternity those whom he wills to embrace in love, and those upon whom he wills to vent his wrath. Yet he announces salvation to all men indiscriminately. I maintain that these statements agree perfectly with each other. For by so promising he merely means that his mercy is extended to all, provided they seek after it and implore it. But only those whom he has illumined do this. And he illumines those whom he has predestined to salvation. These latter possess the sure and unbroken truth of the promises, so that one cannot speak of any disagreement between God's eternal election and the testimony of his grace that he offers to believers.[31]

This only seems to deepen the mystery. If this is intended to answer the question of how these statements agree perfectly with each other, I don't see how it accomplishes that. As great a thinker and communicator as Calvin was, I sometimes find his explanations obscure if not evasive.

Calvin says more about this problem. First, he argues that "none undeservedly perish."[32] That is why God is just in punishing the reprobate; they deserve it. Why do they deserve it? Because of their "malice and perverseness."[33] How does it come about that they continue in their malice and perverseness rather than repent and believe like the elect? "That they may come to their end, he [God] sometimes deprives them of the capacity to hear his word; at other times he, rather, blinds and stuns them by the preaching of it."[34] Why does God do this to the reprobate? "He who here seeks a deeper cause than God's secret and inscrutable plan will torment himself to no purpose."[35] Is Calvin getting anywhere toward resolving the problem? I don't see how that is the case; he seems merely to be deepening the dilemma of God's goodness.

How does Calvin interpret 1 Timothy 2:3–4, the clearest revelation that God desires the salvation of all men? "By this Paul surely means only that God has not closed the way unto salvation to any order of men; rather, he has so poured out his mercy that he would have none without it." In other words, all 1 Timothy 2:3–4 (and no doubt 2 Peter 3:9) means is that God wants some people of every tribe and nation to be saved but not every individual person. That hardly fits the language of 1 Timothy

2:4, however, which specifically says "all men," meaning "all people"—not all kinds of people.

So why does God reprobate some and not elect all to salvation? In some places Calvin leaves this in the realm of mystery, but in at least one instance he speculates: "The reprobate are raised up to the end [purpose] that through them God's glory may be revealed."[36] Those who accuse God of being unjust (or just accuse this doctrine of making God unjust!) are dismissed by Calvin as "foolish men [who] contend with God."[37] He impatiently declares that whatever God does is right and just simply because God does it, and there is no explanation for what God does other than "because he has willed it."[38] Nowhere does he even attempt to justify God or reconcile his doctrine with God's love. The only love of God he mentions is God's love for the elect.

Fortunately, many Calvinists have not been satisfied to leave the matter there. As one progresses forward toward the modern age and into the postmodern world of the early twenty-first century, one finds many Calvinists increasingly interested in justifying the ways of God.

Jonathan Edwards wrote an entire essay on "The Justice of God in the Damnation of Sinners." In it he stuck rather close to Calvin's approach, although somewhat more emphatically and defensively (perhaps because of the rising Enlightenment tendency to question God's justice). Again, as with Calvin, Edwards' emphasis falls on God's justice rather than his love, which he hardly mentions. Here is what Edwards says to those who question God's justice in damning for eternity to hell those he foreordained and even rendered certain to fall into sin and remain there:

> When men are fallen, and become sinful, God by his sovereignty has a right to determine about their redemption as he pleases. He has a right to determine whether he will redeem any or not. He might, if he had pleased, have left all to perish, or might have redeemed all. Or, he may redeem some, and leave others; and if he doth so, he may take whom he pleases, and leave whom he pleases.[39]

This hardly solves the problem of God's justice, however, as the "men" who are fallen, whom God has a right to dispose of as he wills, fell by God's foreordination and predestining power. Again, the question that naturally arises and that Edwards doesn't answer is this: What meaning do "goodness," "justice," and "love" have in such a context? Like Calvin, Edwards seems most interested in turning aside any and all questions about God's justice in reprobating and punishing people. The only answer he offers is that whatever God does is right and above fault. He simply assumes that his interpretation of what God does is the only reasonable one in light of Scriptures such as Romans 9.

What did Boettner say about God's goodness in light of his reprobation of people? He first makes clear beyond any doubt that God's sole purpose in reprobation is his glory; without it God's justice could not be sufficiently displayed—and that is one of the purposes of creation and redemption.[40] Of course, this raises the question of why it is just for God to punish the reprobate, and Boettner simply avers that they sinned "voluntarily."[41] In light of his explanations, cited and discussed in the previous chapter, it seems an odd use of "voluntarily" since God has determined it. For him, obviously, "voluntarily" does not mean they could do otherwise than they do. Is that a natural meaning of "voluntary," and does it answer or just raise more questions about God's justice? Boettner doesn't seem to recognize this problem, or he prefers to overlook it. And he doesn't really deal with the love of God *except to say* (oddly) that "God in his love saves as many of the guilty race of men as He can get the consent of His whole nature to save."[42] One can only respond with an astonished, "What?"

At least Boettner, in contrast to Calvin and Edwards and some other Calvinists, takes a shot at answering the question. But doesn't it raise more questions? Is God limited in some way? Why can't he get the consent of his "whole nature" to save everyone? The obvious implication, given everything else Boettner says, is that God *must* damn some in order to display his attribute of justice and thereby glorify himself. So God's need to glorify himself (and "need" is the right word, given Boettner's language of divine limitation in relation to the extent of salvation) overrides and controls his love.

This is exactly what non-Calvinists worry about with regard to Calvinism: that its deep, inner logic leads inexorably to exalting God's glory over and even against his love. Apparently, God can (or must) limit his love, but he can't limit his self-glorification. I would put it the other way around and say that in light of Christ's self-emptying (Phil. 2), God can limit his glory (power, majesty, sovereignty) but not his love (because God *is* love; see 1 John 4!).

Boettner argues that God is not arbitrary in his judgments, meaning that his choice of whom to save is not a matter of tossing the dice.[43] He says that God "has his reasons" even if we cannot even guess what they are.[44] Herein lies another problem. Like all Calvinists, Boettner states that God's choice of people to elect is absolutely unconditional; it has nothing to do with anything God sees in the ones he elects.[45] Just as reprobation is the necessary flip side of election, so choosing to pass over some in choosing to elect others must necessarily have nothing to do with anything especially bad God sees in them. All are equally worthy of eternal punishment. Once choosing on the basis of something particular about the ones chosen, either for election or reprobation, is ruled out, what is left? I argue all that is left, and this is a matter of sheer logic, is arbitrary choice—"eenie, meenie, miney, mo." There is no conceivable third alternative.

Imagine that you confront your child because you find his or her name written in crayon on the bedroom wall. He or she denies doing it. You ask, "Then who did it?" and the child says, "Someone else." Then you respond, "But wait, this is your room and your name is written on the wall and nobody but you has been here since I last saw the wall and then your name wasn't written on it." Your child says, "Okay, I didn't do it, but neither did someone else." What will your response be? Might you believe that explanation? Why not? Couldn't there be a third possibility? Unless you believe the house to be haunted or something, you probably won't seriously consider your child's explanation. The graffiti writer has to be either the child or someone else; there is no conceivable third possibility. So it is with Boettner's "explanation" (the same one used by most Calvinists) that God doesn't choose arbitrarily but also doesn't choose based on anything special about the persons he chooses. There is no third alternative. It has to be arbitrary if it is absolutely unconditional.

Unlike Boettner and other Calvinists, Edwards seems to have accepted, at least once, that God's choice between the elect and nonelect is arbitrary. This may come as a shock to many later Calvinists who object vehemently to this accusation about the Calvinist God. In his famous (or infamous) sermon "Sinners in the Hands of an Angry God," Edwards appealed to "God's arbitrary will" to explain God's treatment of the nonelect.[46] This is at least honest, bold, and consistent, but it raises serious issues for the character and ways of God.

How does Boettner deal with the "all" passages of Scripture? With regard to John 3:16 and similar verses, he says that "world" does not mean every individual person. It means all kinds of people.[47] Since so many Calvinists give this explanation, I'll save most of my critique of it for later in this chapter when I summarize problems with Calvinist explanations of God's reprobation. For now, suffice it to say this interpretation of "world" hardly works as it would require that numerous references to the whole world as fallen would mean only that people of all kinds are fallen.

For example, John 1:10 says that the "world" (same Greek word as John 3:16) did not recognize the Word when he came. If "world" in John 3:16 means "all kinds of people," then John 1:11 possibly means that only some persons—of all kinds of people but not everyone—did not recognize Jesus as the Son of God. No Calvinist interprets John 1:11 that way! Boettner's interpretation of John 3:16 seems forced. Although he does not come right out and say, "God hates the nonelect and that is why he reprobates them," he more than implies it. So, I judge it fair and safe to say that Boettner, like many Calvinists, does *not* think God *is* love as 1 John 4:8 says, *or* at least he falls into inconsistency in his handling of the matter. If God's very nature is love, then he loves everyone and not just some people "of every kind." (Of course, that assumes once again that "love" in God is analogous to and not totally different from the best of love as we know it. With Helm I assume that; otherwise the word means nothing.)

What about 1 Timothy 2:4 that says God wants "all people" to be saved? Boettner explains: "Verses such as 1 Timothy 2:4, it seems, are best understood not to refer to men individually but as teaching the general truth that God is benevolent and that He does not delight in the sufferings and death of His creatures."[48] One can only ask how that is a possible interpretation of that verse? Also, how can God not delight in what he has himself foreordained and rendered certain for his glory? Doesn't he delight in being glorified? This is a Calvinist conundrum, to be sure. But Boettner adds this: "It is true that some verses taken in themselves do seem to imply the Arminian position [i.e., that God really desires the salvation of everyone and makes it possible]. This, however, would reduce the Bible to a mass of contradictions."[49] One could just as easily turn that around and substitute "the Calvinist position" for "the Arminian position" and it would be truer.

Sproul wrestles admirably but ultimately unsuccessfully with the problem of God's goodness, love, and justice in the face of his reprobation of many human persons whom he could save. First, he admits that God foreordained sin, and I'm sure I have quoted him enough times to make clear that he also believes God rendered it certain.[50] Yet, he argues, God is not responsible for sin; we are.[51] God is just to condemn the reprobate because they hate him and are wicked: "Is there any reason that a righteous God ought to be loving toward a creature who hates him and rebels constantly against his divine authority and holiness?"[52] One can only respond ... yes. Because it is his *nature to love*! (1 John 4:8). Also, Romans 5:8–10 says that God loved sinners while they were still sinners and gave up Christ for them! Sproul verges on depicting God as not having a loving nature; he more than implies that God loves some and hates others when *all* have hated him and rebelled against his authority and holiness.[53] That brings us back to the issue of arbitrariness.

Sproul faces the issue of God's seeming arbitrariness and lack of fairness (and I would add apparent lovelessness) in double predestination: "The nasty problem for the Calvinist [is] ... if God can and does choose to insure the salvation of some, why then does he not insure the salvation of all?"[54] Indeed, why not? Here is Sproul's answer:

> The only answer I can give to this question is that I don't know. I have no idea why God saves some but not all. I don't doubt for a moment that God has the power to save all, but I know that he does not choose to save all. I don't know why.... One thing I do know. If it pleases God to save some and not all, there is nothing wrong with that. God is not under obligation to save anybody. If he chooses to save some, that in no way obligates him to save the rest.[55]

Sproul then objects to non-Calvinists raising this as an issue of fairness and says God does not have to answer to our standards of fairness.[56] Fair enough. But fairness isn't the main issue. The main issue, which Sproul skirts, is *love*. If God could save everybody because election to salvation is unconditional and if God is by nature love, why doesn't he? The only answers Sproul can offer are (1) he doesn't love everybody, and (2) God can do whatever he wants to do because he isn't obligated to do anything for anyone. These answers demean God and impugn his goodness and do damage to his reputation, which is based on his morally perfect character.

What does Sproul say about 1 Timothy 2:4? Nothing. I have not been able to find any explanation of that important passage in Sproul's writings, but he has written so much I may not have found it. However, in *Chosen by God* he does ask about 2 Peter 3:9, which says much the same but perhaps not as forcefully. Insofar as God does not want "anyone to perish, but everyone to come to repentance," Sproul says "anyone" means "the elect."[57] That doesn't work in light of 1 Timothy 2:4, however, which clearly refers to every person without exception. (Is that why Sproul passes over that passage without comment?)

Sproul takes another route as well. He suggests that the Bible speaks "more than one way" about God's will.[58] First, he says, there is God's "sovereign, efficacious will." This is what other Calvinists have called God's "decretive will." Then there is God's "preceptive will" (his commands). Finally, there is "God's disposition—what is pleasing to him."[59] So, according to this interpretation of 2 Peter 3:9 (and by extension 1 Tim. 2:4), it is saying that God *wishes* all could be saved even though he doesn't intend to save everyone.

Sproul says it makes God sad to punish the wicked.[60] He uses an analogy of a judge who must sentence his beloved son to prison. He has to do it, but it hurts him. The analogy, of course, breaks down entirely. The judge in the illustration did not foreordain and render certain his son's crime. If he had, he would be wrong to sentence him to prison! Also, the judge in the analogy *is* obligated to sentence his son to prison; according to Sproul, God is *not* obligated to save anyone and could save everyone. Finally, what if Sproul's judge sentenced his own son to prison but freed another young man who committed the same crime? Wouldn't everyone question the judge's love for his son?

Let's change the analogy a bit. Suppose a judge sat on his bench and wept as he sentenced his son to prison for armed robbery. Then it came to light that he used behavioral conditioning to make his son believe armed robbery is good and right *and* drove him to the bank to rob it. Then it also came to light that the judge granted clemency to another young man who also robbed a bank in exactly the same manner as his son. Who would think that judge was good? And yet that is a better analogy to Sproul's double predestination than his!

What about the problem of God's seeming arbitrariness in election and reprobation? Sproul says, "God doesn't do anything without a reason. He is not capricious or whimsical."[61] But *what* reason might he have for choosing John for salvation and Bob for damnation? He makes abundantly clear that election and reprobation are absolutely unconditional. So, his final word on the issue is that God chooses "according to the good will of his pleasure.... God predestines us according to what pleases him.... What pleases God is goodness.... Though the reason for choosing us does not lie in us but in the sovereign divine pleasure, we may rest assured that the sovereign divine pleasure is a good pleasure."[62] Once again, I can only respond with a stunned or bemused, "Huh?"

Back to the analogy I offered above in response to Boettner's claim that God's choice is not arbitrary but also not based on anything about the people he chooses. Sproul's appeal to God's "good pleasure" says nothing about *how* God chooses. After ruling out anything God sees in or about the people he chooses (e.g., a free response to the gospel enabled by his grace) and also ruling out arbitrary choice, what's left? Nothing conceivable. To say "God's good pleasure" *is*, then, to say (as Edwards did at least once) "arbitrary choice."

John Piper tackles the problem of God's love in relation to his choice of some to suffer in the flames of hell for eternity for his glory with great vigor and imagination. First, how does he deal with the "all" passages of the New Testament and Ezekiel 18:23—which he calls "the Arminian pillar texts?"[63] He appeals to two wills of God: "God decrees one state of affairs while also willing and teaching that a different state of affairs should come to pass."[64] In other words, God wills that some perish and at the same time wills that none perish. "As a hearty believer in unconditional, individual election I rejoice to affirm that God does not delight in the perishing of the impenitent, and that he has compassion on all people. My aim is to show that this is not double talk."[65]

So how does he show that it is not double talk? Piper writes about God's "complex feelings and motives."[66] On the one hand, God loves his glory above all else: "God elects, predestines, and secures for one great ultimate purpose—that the glory of his grace might be praised forever and with white-hot affection."[67] But in spite of the fact that God gets glory from election and reprobation (he agrees with those who argue they are inseparable as two sides of a coin), he also loves the nonelect and has genuine compassion on them. He claims that God has "universal love for all creatures" that is *not* the love he has for the elect. So this is his explanation of John 3:16 and 1 John 4:8. "There is a general love of God that he bestows on all his creatures."[68] But in spite of loving all people in some way, God only loves some people in the best way. His love for the nonelect appears in the temporal blessings he gives them. (I cannot resist saying again that Piper's view here amounts to saying that God provides the nonelect with a little bit of heaven to go to hell in!)

What about God's love and compassion for the nonelect? Piper avers that God has "a true compassion, which is yet restrained, in the case of the nonelect, by consistent and holy reasons, from taking the form of a volition to regenerate."[69] Moreover, "I affirm that God loves the world with a deep compassion that desires their salvation; yet I also affirm that he has chosen from before the foundation of the world whom he will save from sin. Election is the good news that salvation is not only a sincere offer made to all, but a sure effect in the life of the elect."[70]

To illustrate and defend his idea of these two wills in God Piper tells the story of George Washington and a certain Major Andre who had committed some treasonous acts during the Revolutionary War.[71] As the story goes, Washington sentenced Major Andre to death even though he had the power to pardon him. The future president and commander-in-chief of the Continental Army had great compassion on Major Andre as he signed his death warrant, which was judged necessary to uphold duty and policy. Piper compares this with God's complex feelings and emotions as he condemns the reprobate.

But does this analogy work any better than Sproul's analogy of the judge sentencing his son? The answer is no, it does not. First, if Piper is right, if Washington were truly comparable to God, he would have designed and governed Major Andre's crime and seen to it that he committed it. Who would consider Washington good for sentencing Major Andre to death if that were the case—no matter how "necessary" it was to uphold duty and policy?

Second, if Major Andre were truly comparable to the reprobate in Piper's theology, he would not have been able to do otherwise than commit his crime. Piper denies libertarian free will. Who would consider Major Andre deserving of death if he were controlled by someone else? (Remember that, even though Piper believes people always act according to their strongest motives—Edwards' view of "free will"—his God is also the all-determining reality and thus *must* be the ultimate cause of creatures' controlling motives.)

Third, the analogy implies a limitation of God—something surely Piper does not want to admit given his powerful elevation of God's supremacy in all things. Washington was obligated to sentence Major Andre to death; he felt duty bound to do it and he was accountable to others, such as the Continental Congress, his fellow officers and soldiers, and the citizens of the colonies. To whom is God accountable? If he feels such great compassion for the reprobate, why doesn't he just pardon them? He could, unless he is limited and controlled by something over which he has no power. After all, remember, in Calvinism God's election to salvation is absolutely unconditional. Back to the problem of Edwards' implicit dependency of God on the world!

Finally, the analogy breaks down because to be a valid analogy, Washington would have to have already pardoned at least one other person who committed exactly the same crime as Major Andre. After all, according to Piper, that's what God does—pardons (elects to salvation unconditionally) a lot of people who are no better than the ones he reprobates. Who would consider Washington "compassionate" in that case? Wouldn't he be considered arbitrary and capricious and suspected of just wanting to show his severity?[72]

What about the problem of the gospel call and invitation if God has already chosen some to be damned? Many of the Calvinist authors surveyed here do not directly address the problem: How can the gospel call be given out as a well-meant offer to all (which most Calvinists affirm) if some have already been chosen by God for damnation and have no chance at all of being accepted by God? Piper answers the question briefly in "Are There Two Wills in God?" He says, "Unconditional election [and by extension, of course, reprobation] ... does not nullify sincere offers of salvation to everyone who is lost among all the peoples of the world."[73] Of course, this is just an assertion; it falls short of an explanation.

This is a huge problem for anyone who believes it is appropriate for a preacher of the gospel to make an offer of salvation to everyone within his hearing. Yet, most evangelical Calvinists *do* believe that is legitimate *even though* the preacher knows there are probably many present who *cannot* respond and for whom the invitation is *impossible to accept* because God has closed the door on the possibility of their coming to faith and Christ did not die for them! (This is the subject of the next chapter.)

WITNESSES AGAINST DOUBLE PREDESTINATION

Although I have already made known my own qualms (to say the least!) about double predestination and especially the reprobation side of it, now I want to call on some other witnesses to give testimony to why it is unbiblical and unworthy of the character of God as revealed in Scripture and especially in Jesus Christ, and also why it is simply illogical in terms of its unwanted (by Calvinists themselves) "good and necessary consequences."

My first witness is theologian G. C. Berkouwer—that twentieth-century influential Reformed thinker. In his book *Divine Election*, Berkouwer expresses great discomfort with any form of divine determinism and especially any foreordination of individuals to eternal damnation. He argues that the Calvinist doctrine of predestination must be interpreted non-deterministically: "On the one hand, we want to maintain the freedom of God in election, and on the other hand, we want to avoid any conclusion which would make God the cause of sin and unbelief."[74] He expresses frustration with Calvin's approach, which says, on the one hand, that human beings are the sole cause of their rejection but also says, on the other hand, that God is the ultimate source of their "ruin and condemnation."[75]

Berkouwer rejects any divine causality of sin, evil, or reprobation and argues for a single predestination without calling it that. For him, reprobation is not a decree of God but "the shadow side" of "the light of election."[76] Of his own view, which he claims is consistent with the Reformed confessions, he says: "This doctrine opposes the so-called 'predestinationalists' who teach a double predestination in the sense that God from eternity has foreordained one group to salvation and another as decidedly to preterition [condemnation], and that Christ did not die for the reprobates."[77]

Most important for our purposes is that Berkouwer rejected the traditional Calvinist interpretation of Romans 9—the bedrock text of double predestination. Of Romans 9–11 he wrote: "It is being accepted more and more that this passage is not concerned primarily with establishing a *locus de praedestinatione* as an analysis of individual election or rejection, but rather with certain problems which arise in the history of salvation."[78] According to him, Paul's "vessels of wrath" are not individuals predestined to hell but Israel, which God temporarily abandoned in order to graft Gentiles into his people.[79]

Berkouwer is not as clear or forthcoming about his views on predestination as I would like. But one thing is clear, he rejects divine determinism especially with regard to evil and damnation. He opts for a dialectical or paradoxical approach that attempts to steer a course between the Scylla of indeterminism and the Charybdis of determinism. Both are rocks on which theology will crash if it is not careful. Ultimately, he claims about God's will and man's will that "every form of competition is made impossible. There are relations here which have no human analogies."[80] Sproul's trenchant critique of single predestination might apply to Berkouwer's explanation (if it can be called an explanation!), but the point here is simply that one of the twentieth century's most influential Reformed theologians argued vehemently against divine reprobation as inconceivable, given the character of God revealed in Jesus and throughout Scripture.

One of the main reasons Berkouwer rejects double predestination or any kind of divine determinism is that it undermines the preaching of the gospel. Here I will move on and come back to this important point in more detail when considering the objections of Berkouwer's main American disciple, James Daane, who wrote an entire book about the conflict between divine determinism and preaching the gospel.

Berkouwer takes the "all" passages of the Bible with ultimate seriousness and affirms God's love for the whole world without exception. He rejects the dualistic notion of two wills in God.[81] He says that the universalistic texts must be taken seriously without affirming "objective universalism"—the view that ultimately there are no damned. In the final analysis, Berkouwer's approach is only helpful in criticizing double predestination but not in offering a viable alternative because, although he says he takes the "all" texts seriously, he holds onto the idea of single predestination, which is finally untenable. I do not believe it is possible to take the "all" texts seriously while embracing any form of unconditional election—even Berkouwer's inconsistent single predestination view (unless one opts for universalism).

A Reformed theologian who moves further away from unconditional election than Berkouwer, but for the same reasons, is James Daane. In *The Freedom of God* he blasts the entire high Calvinist system of thinking of unconditional election in terms of God's choice of individuals and especially in terms of numbers. He calls high Calvinism "decretal theology" and "theology of the single decree" and "Reformed scholasticism"—all of which mean what I have called "divine determinism." This theology, he says, will not preach, and that is why there is so little preaching of election in Reformed churches. (He wrote this well before the renaissance of Calvinism in the new Calvinism of the young, restless, Reformed movement.) For him (as for me), unconditional election of individuals is not really good news because it necessarily implies reprobation of individuals: "Once one commits himself to the decree of decretal theology, it is theologically impossible for him to allow, justify, or explain preaching the gospel to all men."[82]

Daane argues that Calvin's followers increasingly defined election apart from grace by incorporating reprobation into their theologies. For him, "Scripture speaks of predestination to life but not to death"[83] And he recognizes that predestination to death is automatically the flip side of unconditional election of individuals to salvation. Daane rejects the whole approach of traditional Calvinism as it inevitably makes God the author of sin and damnation and has to appeal to two or three wills in God, including a secret will (to damn some in spite of revealing his will to save all).[84] It also contradicts itself by blaming humans for their depravity and condemnation when God decreed all of it from the beginning.[85]

Daane's analysis of high Calvinism penetrates right into its basic foundation: the doctrine of God. "The basic weakness of decretal theology appears to be precisely its understanding of God's relationship to the world."[86] This scholastic theology, he rightly argues, makes God and God's relationship to the world ahistorical, whereas the Bible portrays God as entering into history freely. "The possibility of taking history seriously, as real and not merely apparent, is foreclosed by the scholastic definition of the single decree."[87] For scholastic decretal theology, he says, nothing in the world can really affect God; everything including sin and evil and damnation are determined by God. The result, he says, is that "decretal theology is a profound rationalization of whatever is."[88] Also, in this theology, God's love is really his love for himself and Christ died for God rather than for the world.[89] Worst of all, according to Daane, this theology ends up depriving God of his freedom; whatever is, is what must be—even for God.

For Daane, Reformed theology needs to back up and take the biblical narrative more seriously than it has in its scholasticism. The God of the Bible *does* decree something; he decrees to "go historical by moving out of himself creatively toward and into both creation and redemption."[90] Daane says that "in creating the world, God conditioned himself, but with this condition—that he remains God."[91] This is God's freedom: to involve himself in the world, its time and history, its suffering and pain, in order to take it on himself and thus redeem it. Sin, then, is not foreordained by God as high Calvinism says. Daane rejects that notion: "Decretal theology is very vulnerable in its inability to maintain the gravity of sin."[92] He means that it makes sin, like everything else, a matter of course; it is decreed and foreordained by God necessarily and therefore is not really something opposed to God.

Daane seems to be moving toward a theology of God as taking risks, although he stops short of either Arminianism or open theism (the view that God does not foreknow the future absolutely). Why does he move in that direction? Because he takes history seriously—the biblical history of redemption that includes God in it as very involved rather than hovering over it as its author. Moreover, he takes the love of God in Jesus Christ very seriously; he takes God's freedom seriously as not his freedom *from* being affected by the world but as his freedom *to be* affected by the world.

What about election? If Daane is "Reformed," he *must* account for election. He does. And he calls it unconditional election. But it is God's unconditional election of Jesus Christ and his people, Israel and the church. It is not God's unconditional acceptance of some individual human persons to salvation and corresponding rejection of others to damnation. "The Bible knows nothing of an *isolated, individualistic* doctrine of election."[93] And it has nothing to do with historical determinism.

For Daane, election has nothing to do with numbers; to make it about numbers is inevitably to fall back into making reprobation a part of election, which makes election unpreachable. "Election in biblical thought is never a selection, a taking of this and a rejection of that out of multiple realities." Rather, "election is a call to service, a summons to be a co-laborer with God in the actualization of God's elective purpose and goal."[94] That elective purpose and goal revolves around Jesus Christ as God's mission in the world to save it.[95]

What about Romans 9–11 and Ephesians 1? These two New Testament passages are said to be the proofs of the high Calvinist doctrine of double predestination. Daane rightly says that "Romans 9–11 does not form a biblical commentary on the truth of individual election. Rather, it is a commentary on the fact of the inviolability of God's election of Israel as a nation."[96] Election to what? To service in blessing the nations with producing Jesus Christ—the real subject and object of God's electing grace. Ephesians 1, which speaks much about election, is not about individuals and their eternal destinies but about the people of God. The "you" repeated throughout the chapter as God's chosen is plural: God's new people, the church.[97]

Daane's revisionist Reformed approach is much preferable to high Calvinism's divine determinism and double predestination, including reprobation. And it goes considerably beyond Berkouwer in overturning Calvinist scholasticism. It is right to focus on the inability to preach that theology as good news because it inevitably includes sin, evil, innocent suffering, *and* hell as God's will—whatever its advocates may say. Furthermore, its "good and necessary consequence" is making God less than loving, less than free, and less than good. It also makes history unreal because nothing really happens; all is just the outworking of God's eternal, foreordained plan on a stage that is said to glorify the author and director of the play but, in fact, makes him monstrous.

Perhaps nobody in church history since the Reformation has attacked high Calvinism and especially double predestination as ferociously as John Wesley, author of two treatises on the subject: "Free Grace" and "Predestination Calmly Considered." I suggest that anyone who wants to read a relatively brief criticism of high Calvinism that simply blasts it out of the water look at one of these two writings. Unfortunately, at times Wesley's ferocity against this theology gets almost personal; his language against it contributed to the breakup of his friendship with revivalist George Whitefield (1714–1770), a five-point Calvinist.

Wesley rightly declares, with even Sproul and many Calvinists, that "single predestination" is impossible. His argument is worth quoting at length for those who still think it may be possible to believe in election without reprobation:

> You still believe that in consequence of an unchangeable, irresistible decree of God the greater part of mankind abide in death, without any possibility of redemption: inasmuch as none *can* save them but God; and he *will not* save them. You believe *he hath absolutely decreed not to save them*; and what is this but decreeing to damn them? It is, in effect, neither more nor less; it comes to the same thing. For if you are dead, and altogether unable to make yourself alive; then if God hath absolutely decreed your everlasting death—you are absolutely consigned to damnation. So then, though you use softer words than some [viz., single predestination], you mean the selfsame thing.[98]

Then he proceeds to destroy this doctrine: "You suppose him [God] to send them [the reprobate] into eternal fire, for not escaping from sin! That is, in plain terms, for not having that grace which God had decreed they should never have! O strange justice! What a picture do you draw of the Judge of all the earth!"[99]

In light of the "all" passages referred to several times in this chapter, Wesley says that unconditional election, which necessarily includes reprobation, calls God's sincerity into question. Referring to the universal call to repentance and salvation and God's expressed desire that all respond to it so as to be saved, Wesley poses an image to illustrate the problem: a jailor calling on prisoners to leave their cells without opening the doors.[100] "Alas! My brethren, what kind of sincerity is this, which you ascribe to God our Savior?"[101]

Then he takes on the issue of God's goodness and love clearly revealed in Jesus Christ and passages such as John 3:16 and 1 John 4:8. "How is God good or loving to a reprobate, or one that is not elected?"[102] To those who argue that God does love the reprobate in some way and is good to them, Wesley asks how God could be good to him in this world (i.e., in temporal gifts) "when it were better for him never to have been born?"[103] As for God's love for them: "Is not this such love as makes your blood run cold? . . . If, for the sake of election, you will swallow reprobation, well. But if you cannot digest this, you must necessarily give up unconditional election."[104]

Wesley goes on in his sermon "Predestination Calmly Considered" (which ought perhaps better be titled "Predestination *Not* So Calmly Considered"!) to argue that God is *not* exalted by unconditional election but rather "dishonored, and that in the highest degree, by supposing him to despise the work of his own hands."[105] But again, to those high Calvinists who say that God does love the nonelect and is good to them he scornfully asks:

> What would the universal voice of mankind pronounce of the man who should act thus? That being able to deliver millions of men from death with a single breath of his mouth, should refuse to save any more than one in a hundred, and say "I will not, because I will not!" How then do you exalt the mercy of God, when you ascribe such a proceeding to him? What a strange comment is this on his own word, that "his mercy is over all his works"![106]

At the conclusion of his tirade Wesley calls double predestination (which is necessarily the flip side of unconditional election) "an error so pernicious to the souls of men."[107]

What about Romans 9? How does Wesley deal with that all-important (to Calvinists) passage? He interprets it the way virtually all non-Calvinists have:

> It is undeniably plain, that both these scriptures [verses 12 and 13] relate, not to the persons of Jacob and Esau, but to their descendents; the Israelites sprung from Jacob, and the Edomites sprung from Esau. In this sense only did "the elder" (Esau) "serve the younger"; not in his person (for Esau never served Jacob) but in his posterity. This posterity of the elder brother served the posterity of the younger.[108]

In other words, "Jacob" and "Esau" are ciphers for Israel and Edom, and for Paul in Romans 9 they are referring to Israel and the Gentiles, which is the whole burden of Paul in this section of Romans! Wesley concludes: "So neither here is there any instance of any man being finally condemned by the mere sovereign will of God."[109]

To Wesley, the doctrine of double predestination is "a doctrine full of blasphemy,"[110] "such as [should] make the ears of a Christian tingle."[111] It destroys all of God's attributes (love, justice, compassion, etc.) and represents the most holy God as "worse than the devil, as both more false, more cruel and more unjust."[112] That is why Wesley finally concludes about Romans 9 and similar passages claimed by Calvinists as proof for their doctrine: "Whatever that Scripture proves, it can never prove this. Whatever its true meaning be, this cannot be its true meaning.... No Scripture can mean that God is not love, or that his mercy is not over all his works. That is, whatever it prove beside, no Scripture can prove predestination."[113]

ALTERNATIVES TO UNCONDITIONAL ELECTION/ REPROBATION

Fortunately, Wesley did not leave the matter there; he offered an alternative to the doctrine he called "blasphemy." His alternative is classical Arminianism, which is *not* what most Calvinists think. Too often the situation is represented as a definite either/or: *either* salvation by works righteousness *or* salvation by unconditional election. Like all true, classical Arminians Wesley affirmed as the beginning his first principle: "Whatsoever good is in man, or is done by man, God is the author and doer of it."[114] Contrary to what many think, Wesley, as a classical Arminian, affirmed that salvation is *all of grace and has nothing to do with man's merit*:

> [Salvation] is free in all to whom it is given. It does not depend on any power or merit in man; no, not in any degree, neither in whole, nor in

> part. It does not in any wise depend either on the good works or righteousness of the receiver; not on anything he has done, or anything he is. It does not depend on his endeavors. It does not depend on his good tempers, or good desires, or good purposes and intentions; for all these flow from the free grace of God.[115]

However, Wesley did not believe this "free grace" position on salvation required unconditional election. For him, salvation is given by God to the person who freely responds to the gospel with repentance and faith, which are not gifts of God *or* "good works" but human responses to God's gift of *prevenient grace.* He affirmed original sin, including total depravity in the sense of spiritual helplessness. But he also affirmed God's universal gift of prevenient or enabling grace that restores freedom of the will: "The very power to 'work together with Him' was from God."[116] This power to work together with God for salvation (which is all God's doing) is simply the calling, enlightening, enabling grace that God implants in a human heart because of his love and because of the work of Christ.[117] But this grace is resistible, not irresistible. It is given in some measure to everyone. Election is simply God's foreknowledge of who will freely receive this grace unto salvation (Rom. 8:29).[118] Reprobation is simply man's rejection of this grace and God's foreknowledge of that.

Wesley asks Calvinists and those tempted to join their ranks because they seem to make God most glorious: "How is it more for the glory of God to save man irresistibly, than to save him as a free agent, by such grace as he may either concur with or resist?"[119] For Wesley, the latter makes God more glorious because it does not require that God hate anyone or treat anyone unjustly. For Wesley, God's glory lies in his morally perfect character more than in his omnicausality—something he rejects as improper to God given the evil in the world.

Someone who has worked on the problem of Romans 9 and other passages about election without concluding they require belief in unconditional, individual predestination is Arminian biblical scholar William Klein, author of *The New Chosen People.* There he conducts a detailed study of the original languages of biblical passages that are claimed to support individual predestination to either heaven or hell and concludes that "the New Testament writers address salvific election in primarily, if not exclusively, corporate terms."[120] His systematic theological conclusion is that "God has chosen the church as a body rather than the specific individuals who populate that body."[121] Klein finds support for this view throughout Scripture but especially mentions 2 John 1 and 13.

Even more basic than corporate election, however, according to Klein, is God's election of Jesus Christ: "Christ is God's Chosen One, and the church is chosen in him."[122] The two are inextricably linked. He points to Romans 5, where Paul talks about "Adam" and "Christ" as representatives and, in a sense, corporate personalities.[123] Romans 9, then, presupposes this idea of corporate solidarity, which Klein says is everywhere presupposed in the biblical thought world.[124] Just as the "first Adam" represents fallen humanity in Romans 5 and there "Christ, the New Adam," represents the new humanity, so in Romans 9 "Jacob" represents God's people and "Esau" represents not God's people. According to Klein, then, how does one become one of God's elect persons? "As Israel became God's chosen people when God chose Abraham and Abraham responded with faith, so the church finds her election in solidarity with Christ and his election."[125] Through faith, a person enters into Christ, that is, into his church and thereby becomes "elect." "To exercise faith in Christ is to enter into his body and become one of the 'chosen ones.'"[126]

Here it will be helpful, almost necessary, to quote extensively from Klein because several paragraphs in his book nicely summarize *the main alternative* to high Calvinism's view of election and salvation. It is a brief statement of classical Arminian theology:

> When it comes to the provision of salvation and the determination of its benefits and blessings, the language of the New Testament writers is commanding. God decreed in his sovereign will to provide for salvation, and then he set Jesus on a course to secure it through his human life, death, and resurrection (Heb. 10:9–10). He purposed to extend mercy to his people and to harden and punish unbelievers. He predestined or predetermined what believers will enjoy by virtue of their position in Christ. We may trace salvation and all that it entails solely to the pleasurable will of God.
>
> *God's will does not determine the specific individuals who will receive that salvation.* The language of "willing" embraces all, not a select number. God's will is not restrictive; he wills all to be saved. Yet, people can procure salvation only on God's terms. Though Jesus desires to reveal God to all, only those who come to him in faith find God and the salvation he offers. That some fail to find sal-

> vation can be attributed only to their unwillingness to believe—to their preference for their own way rather than God's. If God desires salvation for all, he wills (in the stronger sense) to give life to those who believe. These are not incompatible. They place the initiative with God for providing salvation and the obligation with people to receive it on God's terms—faith in Christ. God has done more than merely provide salvation; he "draws" people (Jn 6:44) so they come to Christ. In fact, people come to Christ because God enables them (Jn 6:65). However, these actions of drawing and enablement are neither selective (only some are chosen for it), nor are they irresistible. Jesus' crucifixion was God's means of drawing all people to Christ (Jn 12:32). It was God's provision for their salvation. All may respond to God's overture, but they must do so by placing their trust in Christ. Since God draws all via the Cross, and he desires that all repent of their sins and find salvation, it is not God's will that determines precisely which individuals will find salvation. Though God surely has always known who they will be, and though he chose them as a body in Christ, individuals must repent and believe for God's will to be done.[127]

Someone might say "Well, that's all well and good *except*—it makes God less glorious!" The right response is "How so?" The critic might say: "It limits God." The response is: "Isn't God sovereign over his sovereignty? Can't God limit himself to give free will to human persons? If God's making salvation dependent on human persons' decisions is entirely based on God's own voluntary choice, how is that less glorious? Was the cross less glorious because it was not a display of power and might or majesty but suffering servanthood? Is it perhaps the case that the high Calvinist view of God's glory is based on a human notion of glory?"

A theologian who puts the idea of God's self-limitation to use to talk about God's greatness and goodness including *conditional* election of individuals is Jack Cottrell, author of many books of Arminian theology. Like other critics of high Calvinism, he argues that it inevitably leads to determinism and thus away from free will and a God of love and compassion. The God of Calvinism, he avers, is one whose sovereignty is marked by *omnicausality* and *unconditionality*.[128] In light of the sin and evil and innocent suffering of history and especially in light of the reality of hell, these are inconsistent with God's goodness. An omnicausally and unconditionally sovereign God would be the author of all that. The only way to avoid it, Cottrell rightly argues, is to believe in *divine self-limitation* and that of a kind beyond what Calvinists will normally allow. According to Cottrell,

> God limits himself not only by creating a world as such, but also and even further by the *kind* of world he chose to create. That is, he chose to make a world that is *relatively independent* of him.... This means that God has created human beings as persons with an innate power to initiate actions. That is, man is free to act without his acts having been predetermined by God and without the simultaneous and efficacious coactions of God. Ordinarily, man is allowed to exercise his power of free choice without interference, coercion or foreordination. By not intervening in their decisions *unless* his special purposes require it, God respects both the integrity of the freedom he gave to human beings and the integrity of his own sovereign choice to make free creatures in the first place.[129]

Of course, Cottrell is not the first theologian to think of this. One can find it, for example, in Swiss Reformed theologian Emil Brunner (and Cottrell quotes Brunner as a source). However, Cottrell explains the idea of divine self-limitation clearly and concisely and defends it well as necessary in order to understand how God is sovereign and yet not deterministically in control of everything, which would lead right into double predestination and thereby undermine, if not destroy, God's goodness.

By creating this particular world with its God-given human freedom to rebel and sin, God bound himself to react only in certain ways and not in other ways. This by no means detracts from his sovereignty because it is *an expression of his sovereignty*! According to Cottrell, and I agree with him, while this may not be explicitly taught in Scripture, it is everywhere assumed. For example, in the biblical narrative God grieves and relents and promises and reacts, and all those are expressions of conditionality, which implies voluntary limitation. God has obviously granted to human beings a degree of freedom even to hurt him and thwart his will (only up to a point, of course). God remains omnipotent and omniscient, and he is therefore omniresourceful and able to respond to whatever free people do in the wisest way to preserve his plan and bring about the ends he has decided upon.

One area where I disagree slightly with Cottrell is that he asserts that this self-limiting God retains "sovereign control." While rejecting determinism, he says that "God remains *completely in control of everything*" because "unless God is in *total* control, he is not sovereign."[130] That seems to me an a priori (entirely presupposed) statement and not really warranted by his own suggestion of divine self-limitation. A God who does not exercise deterministic power is not totally in control. I prefer to say God is "in charge, but not in control." It seems to me "completely in control of everything" implies something neither I nor Cottrell believe in—divine determinism.

After all, the context of Cottrell's statements about divine self-limitation is the doctrine of election (at least in the source I am citing here). If one says God is "completely in control of everything" and that includes who will be saved and who will not be saved, that teaching is not what Cottrell or any non-Calvinist believes. If we are going to exploit the idea of divine self-limitation to avoid double predestination, we might as well jettison the concept of total control, or else we are taking back with one hand what is given with the other.

At this point some Calvinist (or other) reader may be pulling his or her hair and yelling (figuratively speaking): "What about this free will business? What *is* free will? Hasn't Edwards proven that free will doesn't even exist except as doing what is in accord with one's strongest motive?" Cottrell and other critics of high Calvinism appeal to free will even to the point of saying it limits God (or, better stated, God allows it to limit his actions). For Edwards and most Calvinists, of course, it doesn't limit God because God controls even the free will decisions and actions of human beings.

But that leads right back into divine determinism—something many Calvinists deny but to no avail. After all, how can God control or even govern human decisions and actions unless he imparts motives? They are, after all, what controls decisions and actions. That makes God the source of sin and evil because those arise from and lie within motives (or what Edwards called dispositions).

I will take up the issue of free will in its Calvinist form (compatibilism) and its non-Calvinist form (non-compatibilism) in chapter 7 (on irresistible grace). Suffice it to say for now that I admit libertarian free will (the will not entirely governed by motives and able to act otherwise than it does) is somewhat mysterious, but I do not think it is impossible or illogical. Nor do many philosophers. And I do think, with Cottrell and

Wesley and other non-Calvinists quoted here, that without libertarian freedom, which presupposes divine self-limiting sovereignty, we are right back in divine determinism with all its deleterious good and necessary consequences.

So which mystery is better? With which one can a person live? The mystery of how God is good in spite of his foreordination and determination of sin, evil, and innocent suffering as well as the eternal suffering of the reprobate (who are reprobate by God's design and control), or the mystery of where libertarian free choices come from? I care more about preserving and defending the reputation of God as unconditionally good than solving the problem of free will.

I want to end this chapter about unconditional election (and its necessary correlate of reprobation) by appealing to certain specific texts of Scripture. Let's look again at John 3:16. Everybody knows it by heart. It says God loves the "world." Calvinists either do not believe that refers to everybody without exception, or they say (with John Piper) that God loves even the nonelect in some ways. Both explanations of John 3:16 fail to make sense. The best critical exegetes of John 3:16 affirm it does mean "the whole human race."[131] Even some Calvinists cannot agree with their fellow Calvinists that in that passage "world" refers only to the elect. They recognize all too well what the interpretation that limits "world" to only some people from every tribe and nation would do to other verses that mention "world" in John's gospel.

As for those Calvinists who think God loves "the whole world" but not in the same way, that is a strange kind of love and hardly fits the context of John 3:16: "For God did not send his Son into the world to condemn the world, but to save the world through him" (3:17). If "world" in verse 16 means all people, then verse 17 clearly says Jesus came to save everyone (or give everyone that possibility). That conflicts with Piper's and others' claim that God loves the nonelect (included in "world" in verse 16) because he surely wouldn't send Jesus into the world to save the nonelect! Both Calvinist interpretations of John 3:16 fall down as impossible. It stands as a monument against unconditional election with its necessary dark side of reprobation.

Finally, what about 1 Timothy 2:4, which says God wants "all people" to be saved and where the Greek cannot be interpreted any other way than every single person without exception? After all, the same Greek word for "all" is used in 2 Timothy 3:16 of inspired Scripture. If it doesn't mean literally "all" in 1 Timothy 2:4, then it doesn't mean "all" in 2 Timothy 3:16, but all Calvinists think it *does* mean literally "all" in 2 Timothy 3:16 ("all Scripture is God-breathed"). First Timothy 2:4 (which is not alone in universalizing God's will for salvation but is least open to any other interpretation) stands alongside John 3:16 as a proof text against unconditional election, which, except in the case of universalism, necessarily includes reprobation.

SIX

YES TO ATONEMENT; NO TO LIMITED ATONEMENT/ PARTICULAR REDEMPTION

During one of my class sessions with Calvinist speakers, a leader of the local Reformed University Fellowship (RUF) asked my students, "How many of you believe Christ died for everyone?" I knew he meant "for everyone in the same way—to suffer the punishment for their sins." Every student's hand shot up. "Then you have to believe everyone is saved; you have to be a universalist. How many of you are universalists?" All hands went down except one or two. "You see," the speaker said, "If Christ already suffered everyone's punishment for sins, including the sin of unbelief, then nobody can go to hell because it would be unjust for God to punish the same sin twice."

The speaker was bringing out one of high Calvinism's favorite "hooks" to get young people to consider including in their soteriology the "L" of TULIP—limited atonement. And if anyone does accept "L," Calvinists argue, they have to accept the rest of the system. After all, if all people are not going to be saved, then Christ died only for some—those he came to save. Who would they be? The unconditionally elected by God. Why would they be unconditionally elected by God? Because they are totally depraved and have no other hope than God's election of them and Christ's death for them. And how will God bring those for whom Christ died to benefit from his death on their behalf? By irresistibly drawing them to himself. How could anyone elected and drawn by God, whose sins are already paid for, ever be lost? It's impossible.

Clever. But does it work? Is limited atonement, which most Calvinists prefer to call "particular redemption," biblical? Is it consistent with the love of God shown in Jesus Christ and expressed in the New Testament many times in many ways (e.g., John 3:16)? Did Calvin believe in it? Did anyone in Christian history believe in it before Calvin's scholastic followers? Is it perhaps more a deduction from the T, the U, the I, and the P than a truth of revelation? Do high Calvinists actually embrace it because it is scriptural, or do they embrace it because logic requires it and they think Scripture allows it? Does rejection of limited atonement require universalism as a "good and necessary consequence," as the speaker claimed? These and other questions will be considered here in some detail.

My conclusion will be that limited atonement is another one of high Calvinism's Achilles' heels. It cannot be supported by Scripture or the Great Tradition of Christian belief (outside of scholastic Calvinism after Calvin). It contradicts the love of God, making God not only partial but hateful (toward the nonelect). Its rejection does not logically require universalism, and those who hold it do believe it because (they think) logic requires it and Scripture allows it, not because any clear portion of Scripture teaches it.

Another conclusion here will be that the T, U, I, and P of TULIP *do* require the L and that Calvinists who claim to be "four pointers" and reject the L are being inconsistent. Ironically, there I stand in agreement with all high Calvinists of the TULIP variety! I will also argue that belief in limited atonement, particular redemption, makes it impossible reasonably to make a well-meant offer of the gospel of salvation to everyone indiscriminately. Ironically, there too I stand in agreement with hyper-Calvinists!

Finally, the Calvinist speaker to my class aimed his last typical Calvinist argument at me and those students who agree that the atonement cannot be limited. "You may not know it, but you also limit the atonement. In fact, you limit it more than Calvinists do. It is actually you Arminians [and he meant to include all who say Christ died for everyone] who believe in limited atonement." That got the students' attention! I had heard it before and already knew where he was going with this. "You limit the atonement by robbing it of power to actually save anyone; for you, Christ's death on the cross only provided an opportunity for people to save themselves. We Calvinists believe the atonement actually secured salvation for the elect."

Here, as then, I will object to this attempt to turn the tables. I do not agree that non-Calvinists limit the atonement. This frequently heard complaint simply doesn't hold water because even Calvin did not believe the atonement saved anyone until certain conditions are met—namely, repentance and faith. Even if these are gifts of God to the elect, that means the atonement no more "saved" people than Arminians (and other non-Calvinists) believe.

CALVINISM'S DOCTRINE OF THE ATONEMENT

So far as I have been able to ascertain, all true Calvinists (as opposed to some revisionist Reformed theologians) embrace the so-called "penal substitution theory" of the atonement. Of course, they do not think it is "just a theory." With many non-Calvinists (such as Wesley) they regard it as the teaching of the Bible about Christ's saving death on the cross. According to this doctrine, Jesus' death was primarily a substitutionary sacrifice offered to God by Jesus (i.e., to the Father by the Son) as the "propitiation" for sins. "Propitiation" means appeasement. In this view, the cross event is seen as Christ's appeasement of God's wrath. He suffered the punishment for the sins of those whom God intended to save from their deserved condemnation to hell. Calvin puts it in a nutshell:

> This is our acquittal: the guilt that held us liable for punishment has been transferred to the head of the Son of God (Isaiah 53:12). We must, above all, remember this substitution, lest we tremble and remain anxious throughout life—as if God's righteous vengeance, which the Son of God has taken upon himself, still hung over us.[1]

Calvin, and most Calvinists, believed that Christ's death accomplished more (e.g., the "transmutation" or transformation of our sinful nature[2] and fulfillment of God's law in our place),[3] but the crucial achievement of Christ on the cross was the suffering of our punishment.

Other theories of the atonement have arisen in Christian history, and some of them find echoes in Calvin's theology. For example, the so-called "Christus Victor" view of Christ's saving death is popular especially since the publication of Swedish theologian Gustaf Aulén's classic book on the atonement, *Christus Victor*.[4] Calvin nods toward this image of the atoning death of Christ, that it conquered Satan and liberated sinners from bondage,[5] but his main focus is on Christ's satisfaction of God's justice by suffering the punishment deserved by sinners so that God can righteously forgive them. Contrary to many critics of this penal substitution theory, it does not rest on a view of God as bloodthirsty or as a child abuser! Calvin rightly underscores love as God's motive in sending his Son to die for sinners.[6]

Almost without exception high Calvinists since Calvin have held firmly to this view of the atonement and its achievement on behalf of God and sinners. They do not reject other dimensions of the atonement, but this one is central and crucial to the whole Calvinist soteriology. Many non-Calvinists agree. But the issue at stake here is whether Christ died in this way *for all people* or only for some—the elect. No Calvinist denies the *sufficiency* of Christ's death in terms of *value* to save the whole human race. What some have come to deny is that Christ actually suffered the deserved punishment for all people—something clearly taught by the Greek church fathers and most medieval theologians and even Luther. Classical, high Calvinism has come to believe and teach that God only *intended* the cross to be the propitiation for some people and not for others; Christ did not suffer for everyone (at least not in the same way, Piper would like to add) but only for those whom God has chosen to save.

This is the doctrine of "limited atonement," or what some Calvinists prefer to call "definite" or "particular" or "efficient" atonement. Boettner states the doctrine well: "While the value of the atonement was *sufficient* to save all mankind, it was *efficient* to save only the elect."[7] Lest anyone misunderstand and think this means God intended it for everyone, but it only effectuates the salvation of those who receive it with faith (the view of most non-Calvinist evangelicals), Boettner says the nonelect were excluded from its work by God: "It was not, then, a general and indiscriminate love of which all men are equally the objects [that sent Jesus to the cross], but a peculiar, mysterious, infinite love for the elect, which caused God to send His Son into the world to suffer and die," and he died only for them.[8] Like many Calvinists, Boettner claims that "certain benefits" of the cross extend to all people in general, but these are merely "temporal blessings" and not anything salvific.[9]

Non-Calvinists look at statements such as these and tremble. This would be, indeed, a "peculiar love" that excludes some of the very creatures God made in his own image and likeness from any hope of salvation. Moreover, these "temporal blessings," alleged to flow to the nonelect from the cross, are hardly worth mentioning. As I pointed out in the previous chapter, they amount to a little bit of heaven to go to hell in!

Steele and Thomas, authors of *The Five Points of Calvinism*, define and describe limited atonement, which they prefer to call particular redemption, this way:

> Historical or mainline Calvinism has consistently maintained that Christ's redeeming work was definite in *design* and *accomplishment*—that it was intended to render complete satisfaction for certain specified sinners and that it actually secured salvation for these individuals and for no one else. The salvation which Christ earned for His people includes everything involved in bringing them into a right relationship with God, including the gifts of faith and repentance.[10]

Like Boettner, these theologians aver that Christ's atonement was not limited in *value* but only in *design*. And they claim that Arminians (and other non-Calvinists) also limit the atonement in the manner mentioned above.[11]

Steele and Thomas claim support for limited atonement in biblical passages such as John 10:11, 14–18 and Romans 5:12, 17–19. However, even a cursory glance at these passages reveals they *do not* limit the atonement but only say it is for and applied to God's people. They do not deny that it is for others as well.

What about the "all" and "world" passages such as 1 John 2:2: "He is the atoning sacrifice for our sins, and not only for ours but also for the sins of the whole world"? Steele and Thomas explain these thus:

> One reason for the use of these expressions was to correct the false notion that salvation was for the Jews alone.... These expressions are intended to show that Christ died for all men without *distinction* (i.e., He died for Jews and Gentiles alike) but they are not intended to indicate that Christ died for all men without *exception* (i.e., He did not die for the purpose of saving each and every last sinner).[12]

One crucial question that arises in response to these claims is the distinction between the *value* of Christ's atoning death and its *design* and *purpose*. Apparently, Boettner and Steele and Thomas (and other Calvinists I will quote) believe that Christ's death on the cross was a *sufficient* sacrifice for the sins of the whole world. What, then, do they mean by saying that Christ did not die for all people? If it was a sufficient sacrifice for the sins of the whole world, including everyone, and had value enough for everyone, how is it *not* a contradiction to then say that Christ did not die for everyone?

Apparently, what at least *some* Calvinists mean is that Christ's death was great enough in scope and value for God to forgive everyone because of it, but God did not *intend* it for anyone but the elect. But why would God cause Jesus to suffer a punishment sufficient in scope for sins God intended not to forgive? And if his death was a sufficient punishment for all, then doesn't that imply he bore everyone's punishment? And if that's so, then even if God intended it only for the elect, the charge that universal atonement would require that everyone be saved (because sins cannot be punished twice) comes back to haunt Calvinists themselves. There is something terribly confused at the heart of the typical Calvinist claims about this doctrine.

This confusion becomes especially intense when Calvinist pastor-theologian Edwin Palmer ridicules the universal atonement view: "To them [he means specifically Arminians but this could apply to other non-Calvinists] the atonement is like a universal grab-bag: there is a package for everyone, but only some will grab a package.... Some of His [Christ's] blood was wasted: it was spilled."[13] But wouldn't this be true of *any* doctrine of the atonement that says it was a "sufficient sacrifice" for the whole world and that says its *value* is infinite? It would seem that advocates of limited atonement should say that Christ's death was *not sufficient* for the whole world and *did not* have infinite value *if* they are going to accuse believers in universal atonement of believing some of Christ's blood was wasted (because not everyone benefits from it). Doesn't their claim about its sufficiency and value amount to the same thing *even if* they go on to say God designed and intended it only for the elect? It seems so.

Palmer takes the same approach as Steele and Thomas with regard to the universal passages, including John 3:16–17: "For God so loved the world that he gave his one and only Son, that whoever believes in him shall not perish but have eternal life. For God did not send his Son into the world to condemn the world, but to save the world through him." According to Palmer, "In this passage 'world' does not mean every single person ... but ... people from every tribe and nation."[14] About the passages that say Christ died for "all" he says, "All is not all."[15]

Palmer calls the fact that Christ died only for the elect and yet God "freely and sincerely offers salvation to everyone" a "fundamental mystery."[16] As I will show, however, critics of the Calvinist view argue this is not a mystery but a contradiction—a distinction R. C. Sproul delineates (and he rejects contradictions in theology). How can a Calvinist preacher of the gospel, let alone God, say to any congregation or other assembly, "God loves you and Jesus died for you so that you may be saved if you repent and believe on the Lord Jesus Christ," without adding the caveat, "if you are one of God's elect"? He or she can't do it with a clear conscience.

Sproul, a Calvinist particularly strong on limited atonement, calls the doctrine "Christ's purposeful atonement."[17] This is, of course, a bit disingenuous insofar as it is intended to express what is distinct in the Calvinist view, because, of course, all Christians believe Christ's atonement was "purposeful." Right up front, at the beginning of his exposition of this doctrine, Sproul misrepresents and even caricatures non-Calvinist views. In order to support his belief in limited atonement, Sproul quotes Calvinist evangelical theologian J. I. Packer, who wrote: "The difference between them [Calvinist and Arminian views of the atonement] is not primarily one of emphasis, but of content. One proclaims a God who saves; the other speaks of a God who enables man to save himself."[18]

This is perhaps the most vicious calumny against non-Calvinists. No Arminian or other informed evangelical Christian believes in self-salvation. Sproul explains Packer's accusation by saying that for the Calvinist, Christ is a "real Savior," whereas for the Arminian, Christ is only a "potential Savior." I have demonstrated the falseness of this interpretation of Arminian theology in my *Arminian Theology*. I will explain below why it is wrong.

Sproul continues by throwing another tired accusation against Arminian theology *and any theology of universal atonement* (e.g., Lutheran). "If Christ really, objectively satisfied the demands of God's justice for everyone, then everyone will be saved."[19] Here Sproul is relying heavily on the theology of Puritan theologian John Owen (1616–1683), who was one of the early defenders of the theological novelty of limited atonement. According to Owen and Sproul, universal atonement, the belief that Christ bore the punishment for every person, necessarily leads to the universalism of salvation. After all, Owen argued, and Sproul echoes him, how can the same sin, including unbelief, be punished twice by a just God?

One has to wonder whether Sproul has never heard the obvious answer to this or if he is simply choosing to ignore it (see my answer later in this chapter). Suffice it for now to say simply that this argument is so easily turned aside that it makes one wonder why anyone takes it seriously. Then there is the problem I mentioned earlier: If Christ's death was a *sufficient satisfaction* for the whole world's sins, how is that different from Christ actually suffering the punishment for everyone? There really is no difference; the former *includes* the latter!

Sproul takes on the classical text of universal atonement (2 Peter 3:9) but ignores the equally important universal passages, 1 Timothy 2:5–6 and 1 John 2:2. According to him and many others who adhere to limited atonement, 2 Peter 3:9 should be interpreted as referring to "will of disposition," which is different from his "decretive will."[20] In other words, this verse does not express what God *decrees* to be the case but what God *wishes* could be the case. Whereas that might be a possible interpretation of 2 Peter 3:9 (though I doubt it), one cannot interpret 1 Timothy 2:5–6 in this manner, nor many other universal passages where Christ is said to give his life for "all" or "the world" or "everyone." Sproul also suggests that in 2 Peter 3:9, "any" refers to God's elect.[21] Again, as forced as this interpretation is, it might conceivably be possible. However, it is not possible as an interpretation for the other "all" texts, including 1 Timothy 2:5–6.

Evangelical statesman Vernon Grounds (1914–2010), longtime president of Denver Seminary and author of many books of theology, mentions the following universal passages about Christ's atonement: John 1:29; Roman 5:17–21; 11:32; 1 Timothy 2:6; Hebrews 2:9; and 1 John 2:2 (in addition, of course, to 2 Peter 3:9). Then he says of the view espoused by Sproul and other five-point Calvinists: "It takes an exegetical ingenuity which is something other than a learned virtuosity to evacuate these texts of their obvious meaning: it takes an exegetical ingenuity verging on sophistry to deny their explicit universality."[22] This observation is perhaps why Calvinists such as John Piper have so emphasized the idea that Christ died for all but not in the same way. I doubt that would satisfy Grounds or any other critic of limited atonement. It only raises more questions about God's love, sincerity, and goodness as well as about the value of "temporal blessings" provided by the atonement for the nonelect when they would be better off never born.

John Piper strongly defends limited atonement while at the same time arguing that there is a certain universality in it as well. This is his way, so it seems, of resolving the dilemma posed by the "all" passages in the face of belief in particular redemption and of solving the problem of how the believer in it can preach that Christ died for everyone in his or her audience. Piper's doctrine of the purpose of the atonement is interesting because it goes beyond the usual penal substitution theory into something like the governmental theory. The governmental theory is usually thought to be the typical Arminian doctrine of the atonement, although neither Arminius nor Wesley taught it.

According to the governmental view, Christ did not suffer the exact punishment deserved by every human being but an equivalent punishment to that. This was formulated by early Arminian thinker Hugo Grotius (1583–1645) to resolve the problem of how the atonement could be universal and yet not everyone be saved. (Like many Arminians, I think there's an easier answer to that problem than developing a new theory of how Christ's death satisfied the wrath of God.) According to Grotius and others who hold this view, the main purpose of the atonement was to uphold God's moral government of the universe in the face of two realities: (1) our sinfulness, and (2) God's forgiveness of our sinfulness. How can God be the righteous, moral governor of the universe and wink at sin by forgiving sinners? He can't be. So God resolves that inner dilemma by sending Christ to suffer a punishment exactly like the one sinners deserve—but not *their* punishment (which Grotius believed would be unjust and would result in all of them being saved). This upholds God's righteousness when he forgives sinners.

Piper does not reject the penal substitution view in favor of the moral government theory, but he does underscore the moral government motif. He asks: "Why did God bruise [i.e., kill] his Son and bring him to grief?" and then answers: "to save sinners, and at the same time to magnify the worth of his glory."[23] By laying "our sin on Jesus and abandoning him to the shame and slaughter of the cross," "God averted his own wrath."[24] Piper also makes clear that the cross is primarily a vindication of the righteousness of God for forgiving sinners. Many, if not most, Arminians and other non-Calvinist evangelical Christians can give a hearty amen to that. The only problems are (1) when Piper goes on to say, as he occasionally does in sermons, that Jesus died "for God," and (2) that the saving benefit of his death was intended only for the elect. Romans 5:8 clearly and unequivocally states Christ died "for sinners," and many verses already cited, including especially 1 John 2:2, say his death was an atoning sacrifice for the sins of the whole world.

Piper preaches that Christ died such a death only for some—the elect. For them and them only it actually secured justification by God. It did not just make it possible; it actually accomplished it. That is why, he argues, if Christ died for everyone, all would be justified and there could be no hell. So how does he explain verses such as 1 John 2:2? "The 'whole world' refers to the children of God scattered throughout the whole world."[25] But he also claims that "we do not deny that all men are the intended beneficiaries of the cross in some sense"[26] and that Christ died for every person but not in the same way. "There are many Scriptures which say that the death of Christ was designed for the salvation of God's people, not for every individual."[27] Then he cites John 10:15; 17:6, 9, 19; 11:51–52; and Revelation 5:9.

True, these verses mention Christ's death for "his sheep" and "for those whom the Father draws to the Son." Yet, not a single verse explicitly limits his death to these people. That Christ died for them [viz., Christians] by no means requires that he died *only* for them. Critic David Allen rightly points out that "the fact that many verses speak of Christ dying for His 'sheep,' His 'church' or 'His friends' does not prove that He did not die for others not subsumed in those categories."[28] To say he died for others in a different way, not suffering the punishment for them but only providing some vague temporal blessings, is hardly satisfying. What good would those be unless Christ also opened up the possibility of their salvation?

Overall, the high Calvinistic doctrine of limited atonement is confusing at best and blatantly self-contradictory and unscriptural at worst.

PROBLEMS WITH LIMITED ATONEMENT/ PARTICULAR REDEMPTION

Before delving into the numerous forceful objections to limited atonement, it is at least interesting to note that John Calvin himself did not believe in this doctrine. In 1979 researcher R. T. Kendall (b. 1935) published a powerful argument that Calvin did not believe in limited atonement: *Calvin and English Calvinism to 1649.*[29] Kevin Kennedy uses most of his arguments, along with others, in an article entitled "Was Calvin a 'Calvinist'? John Calvin on the Extent of the Atonement." Following Kendall, Kennedy admits that Calvin nowhere explicitly addresses the issue; he apparently did not even think of it as an issue or he would have boldly lined up on one side or the other (which Calvin was known to do!). But one cannot find in Calvin's writings a statement such as "Christ bore the punishment for every single person," a fact Calvinists who contend he believed in particular redemption use to their benefit.

However, as Kennedy keenly points out, Calvin *does* say things nobody *would say* who believed in limited atonement:

> For instance, if Calvin did profess limited atonement, one would not expect to find him intentionally universalizing scriptural passages that theologians from the later Reformed tradition claim are, from a simple reading of the text, clearly teaching that Christ died only for the elect. Furthermore, if Calvin truly believed that Christ died only for the elect, then one would not expect to find Calvin claiming that unbelievers who reject the gospel are rejecting an actual provision that Christ made for them on the cross. Nor would one expect Calvin, were he a proponent of limited atonement, to fail to refute bold claims that Christ died for all of humanity when he was engaged in polemical arguments with Roman Catholics and others. However, the truth is, Calvin does all this and more.[30]

But Kennedy does not have to infer Calvin's belief in universal atonement from what he does *not* say; he provides many quotes from Calvin, especially from his commentaries, that are unqualified universal statements regarding the atonement. Two must suffice here. In his commentary on Galatians Calvin wrote with regard to 1:14: "[Paul] says that this redemption was procured by *the blood of Christ*, for by the sacrifice of his death all the sins of the world have been expiated."[31] In his commentary on Isaiah Calvin wrote of Christ that "on him was laid the guilt of the whole world."[32] Again, Calvin wrote in a sermon on the deity of Christ:

> He [Christ] must be the redeemer of the world. *He must be condemned, indeed, not for having preached the Gospel, but for us he must be oppressed,* as it were, to the lowest depths and sustain our cause, since he was there, as it were, in the person of all cursed ones and of all transgressors, and of those who had deserved eternal death. Since, then, Jesus Christ has this office, and he bears the burdens of all those who had offended God mortally, that is why he keeps silent.[33]

After quoting numerous passages from Calvin's writings, Kennedy concludes: "These passages provide just a sampling of the many places where Calvin uses universal language to describe the atonement."[34]

Kennedy goes on to examine the one Calvin passage supporters of limited atonement tend to point to that seems to prove his belief in the doctrine: his remarks on the universalizing passage 1 John 2:2 in his commentary on this letter. Kennedy argues that there, Calvin was simply trying to avoid any interpretation of the verse as teaching universal salvation.[35] Besides, he rightly points out that one passage out of many that deal with the extent of the atonement should hardly be taken to contradict the rest.

Does it really matter whether Calvin believed in universal atonement or limited atonement? Not particularly. Nobody doubts that Calvin was solidly in favor of the other four points of TULIP. Had he lived longer, would he have found his way to "L?" Perhaps. Certainly some of his immediate successors did. However, the fact that Calvin apparently *didn't* see it explicitly taught in Scripture undermines the claims of those high Calvinists who say it is clearly taught there.

More important than whether Calvin believed in limited atonement is whether Paul did. Is there a verse in Paul's letters that clearly and unequivocally contradicts the doctrine of particular redemption? I believe there is. In all my reading of Calvinist and anti-Calvinist literature I have not run across any mention of 1 Corinthians 8:11, even though this single verse seems to contradict it. There Paul writes to the Christian who insists on flaunting his freedom to eat meat in a pagan temple, even in sight of Christians who have weaker consciences and might thereby "stumble": "So this weak brother or sister, for whom Christ died, is destroyed by your knowledge." Clearly, Paul is issuing a dire warning to those of "strong faith" to avoid offending the consciences of their weaker brothers and sisters. His warning is that by exercising Christian liberty from legalism too publicly, a "strong Christian" might actually cause a person loved by God, for whom Christ died, to be "destroyed."[36]

Now, if limited atonement is true, Paul's warning is an empty threat because it cannot happen. A person for whom Christ died cannot be destroyed. Christ died only for the elect, and the elect are drawn irresistibly to God (the subject of the next chapter) and will be kept by God (the "P" in TULIP) regardless of whatever happens.

Believers in limited atonement raise two objections. First, what does "destroyed" mean; might it only mean "damaged" or "hurt"? The Greek word translated "destroyed" is *apollytai*, which means to "destroy, perish, die." It is unlikely, if not impossible, that the word could mean anything else especially in this context. Second, I have heard some Calvinists insist it only means "harm" or "hurt." But why would Paul's warning be so dire in that case? "For whom Christ died"—it sounds as if Paul is saying this offense is serious business. The conjunction of "for whom Christ died" with "harm" just doesn't carry much weight.

The plain sense of the text is that Paul is warning Christians of stronger conscience to beware of causing the utter ruin and destruction, spiritually, of a weaker Christian or at least someone for whom Christ died. If that is so, and I am firmly convinced no other exegesis is reasonable, this one verse destroys the doctrine of limited atonement by demonstrating that Paul did not believe in it.

Before proceeding to other objections to limited atonement, I want to dispense with the argument that universal atonement necessarily implies universalism. It does not! First, even Calvin knew that there is a difference between Christ's atoning death on someone's behalf and the benefits of that atonement being applied to the person's life for forgiveness. Forgiveness is clearly conditional for Calvin; it requires faith and repentance.[37] That is, the elect person is *not* saved the moment Christ died for him or her; that personal salvation is a work of the Holy Spirit through the Word when God gives the gifts of faith and repentance for forgiveness. Even regeneration happens simultaneously with repentance and not, of course, when Christ died for the person.[38] Virtually every Calvinist I know believes that "salvation" is a person's experience only when the benefits of Christ's death are applied to his or her life; they are not saved already the moment Christ died for them.

Thus, the argument that universal atonement necessarily implies universal salvation fails to take into account the gap, as it were, between Christ's death for someone and the application of its benefit to the person's life. All for whom Christ died were not already saved when he died. Even in five-point Calvinism, Christ's death does not "accomplish" people's salvation but "secures" it, as Piper and others say. But even Piper and other proponents of limited atonement agree that the people for whom Christ died, in the sense of suffering their punishment, must have faith to be saved by Christ's death.

I believe, as do all Arminians and other non-Calvinist Protestants, that Christ died for every single human person in such a way as to secure their salvation without requiring it or making it certain. Subjective appropriation is a condition of said secured salvation being one's possession. Does that mean some of Christ's blood was wasted? Perhaps. And that is what makes spiritual death and hell so tragic—they are so absolutely unnecessary. But God, in his love, preferred to waste some of Christ's blood, as it were, rather than be selfish with it.

An analogy will illustrate my point here. Just one day after his inauguration, President Jimmy Carter followed through on his campaign promise and guaranteed a full pardon for all who resisted the draft during the Vietnam War by fleeing from the U.S. into Canada or other countries. The moment he signed that executive order, every single draft exile was free to come home with the legal guarantee that he would not be prosecuted. "All is forgiven; come home" was the message to every single one of them.

This cost President Carter dearly; some believe it was so controversial, especially among veterans, that it contributed to his loss to Ronald Reagan in the next election. Even though there was a blanket amnesty and pardon, however, many draft exiles chose to stay in Canada or other countries to which they fled. Some died without ever availing themselves of the opportunity to be home with family and friends again. The costly pardon did them no good because *it had to be subjectively appropriated in order to be objectively enjoyed.* Put another way, although the pardon was objectively theirs, in order to benefit from it they had to subjectively accept it. Many did not.

The claim that objective atonement necessarily includes or entails subjective, personal salvation is faulty. The argument, so frequently made at least since John Owen's *The Death of Death in the Death of Christ*,[39] that Christ either died for all and therefore all are saved, or he died for some and therefore some are saved, is logically absurd. It simply ignores the real possibility that Christ suffered the punishment for many people who never enjoy that liberation from punishment. Why would Christ suffer punishment for people who never enjoy its benefits? Because of God's love for all.

There is still the matter of Owen's (and most high Calvinists') argument that the same sin cannot be punished twice. Again, that's simply false. Imagine a person who is fined by a court $1,000 for a misdemeanor and someone else steps in and pays the fine. What if the fined person declines to accept that payment and insists on paying the fine himself or herself? Will the court automatically refund the first $1,000? Probably not. It's the risk the first person takes in paying his friend's fine. In such a case, the same punishment would be paid twice. It is not that God exacts the same punishment twice; it is that the sinner who refused the free offer of salvation by default subjects himself or herself to the punishment that has already been suffered for him or her. As noted above, that's what makes hell so terribly tragic.

So, there is a difference between the *provision* of forgiveness of sins and the *application* of forgiveness of sins. Calvin knew this. I suspect most Calvinists know it, but such knowledge takes a back seat to their desire to wield their argument that universal atonement would require universal salvation. Arminian theologian Robert Picirilli (b. 1932) is right when he says in relation to 1 Timothy 4:10: "That He [Jesus] is savior of all men speaks of provision; that He is savior especially of believers speaks of application."[40]

Many Calvinists have argued that belief in universal atonement leads to universalism. They point to certain Arminians of the eighteenth and nineteenth centuries who formed the basis of the Universalist movement (which later united with the Unitarian Church). However, it is my view that *Calvinism,* with its doctrine of *atonement as securing salvation* in a necessary way so that all for whom Christ died *must* be saved, leads to universalism. The reason is that for someone who takes utterly seriously the clear biblical testimony to the universal love of God for all people *and* believes atonement necessarily secures salvation, universalism is just a step away. The only way to hold back from it is by denying either the love of God in its fullest and truest sense *or* that atonement necessarily secures salvation for the person atoned for.

A case study in this trajectory from Calvinism to universalism is Karl Barth, who, I am convinced, did come to believe in the doctrine of *apokatastasis*—that everyone is or will be saved. He did that without sacrificing the T, the U, the I, and the P of TULIP. But he did retain the mistaken Calvinist notion that penal substitution necessarily secures personal, subjective salvation.[41] Once he came to believe that Christ died for everyone without exception, because God is "He who loves in freedom," universalism followed logically.

It seems to me, and to many other non-Calvinists, that any person who has a profound grasp of the biblical witness to God as revealed especially in Jesus Christ, but also in verses such as John 3:16 and 1 John 4:8, will have to give up particular redemption and, in order to avoid universalism, any necessary connection between redemption accomplished and applied. Four-point Calvinists, who try to deny "L" but hold onto the rest of TULIP, have to explain why Christ would suffer the punishment for the reprobate—sinners God intentionally rejects from possible salvation.

Most high Calvinists, including Boettner, Steele and Thomas, Sproul, and Piper, believe passionately in universal evangelism; they reject hyper-Calvinism that says a well-meant offer of salvation cannot be made to everyone either by God or by preachers. As already intimated, however, there is tension and even conflict between particular atonement and indiscriminate evangelism. Among other critics of limited atonement, Gary Schultz has argued convincingly that there is no sincerity in an indiscriminate preaching of the gospel and invitation to repent, believe, and be saved if limited atonement is true. "The crux of the issue," he rightly points out,

> is how the gospel can be genuinely offered to the non-elect if God made no payment for their sins.... If Christ did not pay for the sins of the non-elect, then it is impossible to genuinely offer salvation to the non-elect, since there is no salvation available to offer them. In a sense, when offered the gospel, the non-elect would be offered something that was never there for them to receive in the first place.[42]

Then Schultz also rightly drives the point home: "If the atonement was only for the elect, to preach this message to the non-elect would at best be giving them a false hope and at worst would be untrue."[43]

Some Calvinists may respond that a preacher never knows for sure who in his audience are the elect and who are not the elect, so he or she should offer salvation to everyone while thinking in his own mind that only the elect will respond. But two things block that objection. First, most, if not all, non-hyper-Calvinists believe that not only the preacher but also *God himself* offers salvation to all as a "well-meant offer" (as mentioned earlier as a declaration by the Christian Reformed Church against hyper-Calvinism). Surely *God* knows who the elect and nonelect are. Why would *God*, having that knowledge, offer salvation to those he intends to exclude and for whom Christ did not die? Second, if that is what the Calvinist preacher believes, why not offer the gospel of salvation to all indiscriminately, even if the preacher *does* know who is elect and who is not?

What's the practical application here? It is simply this: *if* you believe that there may be some in your audience who cannot be saved because Christ made no provision for their salvation, you *cannot in all honesty* preach that all may come to Christ through repentance and faith because Christ died for them. You have to tailor your offer and invitation to your theology and say something like this: "*If* you are one of God's elect and *if* Christ died for you, you can be saved by responding with repentance and faith." You cannot say to everyone, "Christ died for you so you can be saved; repent and believe so that God can forgive your sins and accept you as his child." But it *seems* non-hyper-Calvinism is saying *God* would give the second offer and invitation, so the preacher can also. But that would be insincere for God and the preacher. The point is, *insofar* as the preacher believes in limited atonement he or she should join the hyper-Calvinists and *not* offer the gospel of salvation to everyone indiscriminately. Also, the point is, how can belief in limited atonement *not* hinder evangelism?

THE ALTERNATIVE TO LIMITED ATONEMENT/ PARTICULAR REDEMPTION

Fortunately, limited/particular atonement is *not* the only option for Christians considering what Christ accomplished on the cross. A person can affirm penal substitution, including belief that Christ fulfilled the law for everyone and suffered everyone's punishment, and still believe that persons must subjectively appropriate those benefits by faith in order to be saved. This was, for example, Wesley's doctrine. It is also the doctrine of many Baptists and others who sometimes accept certain points of Calvinism but not limited atonement (however inconsistent that may be).

The vast majority of Christians down through the centuries, including *all the church fathers* of the first four centuries (i.e., before Augustine), believed in universal atonement. The great church father Athanasius, highly regarded by all Christians including Eastern Orthodox, Roman Catholic, and Protestant, adamantly insisted that by his death Christ brought salvation to everyone without exception:

> The Word perceived that corruption could not be got rid of otherwise than through death; yet He Himself, as the Word, being immortal and the Father's Son, was such as could not die. For this reason, therefore, He assumed a body capable of death, in order that it, through belonging to the Word Who is above all, *might become in dying a sufficient exchange for all*, and, itself remaining incorruptible through His indwelling, might thereafter put an end to corruption for all others as well, by the grace of the resurrection. It was by surrendering to death of the body which He had taken, as an offer-

> ing and sacrifice free from every stain, that He forthwith abolished death for His human brethren by the offering of the equivalent. For naturally, since the Word of God was above all, when *He offered His own temple and bodily instrument as a substitute for the life of all*, He fulfilled in death all that was required. Naturally also, through this union of the immortal Son of God with our human nature, all men were clothed with incorruption in the promise of the resurrection. For the solidarity of mankind is such that, by virtue of the Word's indwelling in a single human body, the corruption which goes with death has lost its power over all. You know how it is when some great king enters a large city and dwells in one of its houses; because of his dwelling in that single house, the whole city is honoured, and enemies and robbers cease to molest it. Even so is it with the King of all; He has come into our country and dwelt in one body amidst the many, and in consequence the designs of the enemy against mankind have been foiled, and the corruption of death, which formerly held them in its power, has simply ceased to be. For the human race would have perished utterly had not the Lord and Saviour of all, the Son of God, come among us to put an end to death.[44] (Italics added for emphasis.)

Clearly, Athanasius (together with all the Greek church fathers, Martin Luther, John Wesley, and numerous other great orthodox men and women in Christian history) believed that Christ died for all without exception, including suffering the penalty for everyone's sins. Clearly also, Athanasius *did not* believe (as a few Greek church fathers did) in universalism. He clearly stated, so that it cannot be misunderstood, that full salvation in the sense of eternal life comes finally only to those who repent and believe and that many souls will be lost forever because they reject Christ.

What the Greek fathers and nearly every Christian of renown believed about the scope and extent of the atonement (until Calvin's scholastic followers) was that Christ was the substitute for everyone without exception, such that every obstacle to God's forgiveness for every person was removed by his death. They also believed that the benefits of that sacrifice would only be applied to persons who believe—whether they are elect (Luther and Calvin) or freely choose to accept God's grace (Athanasius, Aquinas, the Anabaptists, Wesley).

This is orthodox church teaching; limited/particular atonement is aberrant church teaching. Just because it has been around among Calvinists for a long time (but only *after* Calvin!) does not make it any less aberrant. Even some of the Reformed divines gathered at the Synod of Dort rejected this point of TULIP, siding with the Remonstrants about this matter. Then, fifty years later, many Puritans at the Westminster Assembly that wrote the Westminster Confession of Faith opposed this doctrine.[45] What happened? Evidently, the louder and most insistent voices won the day in spite of not having truth on their side. To this day many Reformed people and many Calvinists cannot stomach this element of the TULIP system, extract it out, and reject it even if that brings them into conflict with the rest of what they believe and with their fellow Reformed and Calvinist believers.

SEVEN

YES TO GRACE; NO TO IRRESISTIBLE GRACE/ MONERGISM

Even though I had proven to him that my theology, classical Arminianism, does *not* say persons save themselves through their good works or contribute anything meritorious to their salvation, my Calvinist interlocutor wasn't convinced. "Your theology," he accused, "is still semi-Pelagian if not fully Pelagian."

Somewhat offended because I regard these as heresies, I asked him to explain more fully. I thought he had come to realize Arminians *do not* believe in works righteousness and *do* believe salvation is all of grace and has nothing to do with meritorious works. But he responded: "Because you make the decisive factor in salvation your own free will decision."

At that time, years ago, I had never heard that accusation, but I knew for sure that no Arminian says that. When pressed, my Calvinist friend said: "You see, if salvation isn't all God's work and has nothing whatever to do with anything we do, it isn't by grace and it isn't a gift. By making it dependent on the person's free acceptance of God's grace, you make salvation a good work and therefore not a gift; and that contradicts Ephesians 2:8–9." I've encountered this accusation against Arminianism (and all non-Calvinist theologies) many times since. Somehow this notion that non-Calvinists make their free will decision the "decisive factor in salvation" has become a mantra for many Calvinists.

While I do think this specific charge has a suitable answer (which I will explain below), the underlying issue in this conversation was really about grace as either resistible or irresistible. Close examination suggests this is exactly the issue underlying the charge that Arminianism amounts to "works-righteousness." How does the saving grace of God bring the benefit of Christ's atoning death, forgiveness, reconciliation with God, and justification into a person's life? Is it a gift imposed or a gift freely received?

The Calvinist view is called *monergism*—from two Greek words that mean "one" and "energy" or "action." Monergism is the belief that salvation is all God's doing from beginning to end without any cooperation from the person being saved other than what God instills in that person. The alternative is "synergism"—the belief that salvation is all of grace but requires free cooperation for it to be activated in a person's life.

THE CALVINIST DOCTRINE OF IRRESISTIBLE OR EFFECTUAL GRACE/MONERGISM

There's a reason why the "I" follows the T, the U, and the L in TULIP, and it's not just because that's how the flower is spelled. For Calvinists, irresistible grace, which many prefer to call "effectual grace," is both biblical and logically necessary because of total depravity, unconditional election, and limited atonement. For biblical support they usually point to John 6:44: "No one can come to me unless the Father who sent me draws them." They interpret "draws" as "compels" but without the connotation of external force against the person's will. In other words, God bends the elect person's will so that he or she *wants* to come to Jesus with repentance and faith.

As for logic, the argument is that because people are totally depraved and dead in trespasses and sins, unless God elects him or her, the person will never respond to the internal calling of the Holy Spirit. So, the Holy Spirit has to change the person inwardly in an effectual manner, which is regeneration. Then the born again person desires to come to Christ, in which case he or she is given repentance and faith (conversion) and justification (forgiveness and imputation of Christ's righteousness). This process is called "monergistic grace" or just "monergism."

Reformed theologian Henry Meeter, in *The Basic Ideas of Calvinism*, defines monergism this way:

> One might say, *God planned salvation, and he earned it in Christ.* Now the choice of acceptance or rejection is mine alone. In a sense it is so. But who causes a Christian to accept Christ? "For we are all gone astray. There is none that seeketh after God." So Christ sends the Holy Spirit into our stubborn hearts, regenerates us, and puts faith

> and love to God there, as well as new ambitions and desires. This he does with irresistible power—not, as the Arminians say, if we let him; we would never spontaneously let him. We only work out our own salvation because it is God that worketh in us.... Thus, the entire work of redemption in its essentials is the work of God. God the Father planned it. God the Son earned it. And God the Holy Spirit applies it, regenerating heart and life.[1]

Whether Meeter has Arminianism right is debatable, and I have challenged similar descriptions in my *Arminian Theology*. Nevertheless, his is a clear and concise expression of the monergism universally held and taught among Calvinists.

The point is that, for the Calvinist, any contribution that the human person makes to his or her salvation is really, however unnoticed, a work of God in him or her. Meeter partially quotes Philippians 2:12, which says: "Therefore, my dear friends, as you have always obeyed—not only in my presence, but now much more in my absence—continue to work out your salvation with fear and trembling." Verse 13, which Meeter omits (possibly by mistake), says, "for it is God who works in you to will and to act in order to fulfill his good purpose." For him and all Calvinists whom I have encountered, what Paul meant is this: "If you are working out your salvation with fear and trembling, remember it is God doing it all in and through you." Only in this way can all glory for salvation be given to God alone.

Did Calvin believe in monergistic grace? That he did is revealed in his *Institutes of the Christian Religion* where he referred to the "inner call." He declared: "The manner of the call itself clearly indicates that it depends on grace alone." He continues:

> Even the very nature and dispensation of the call clearly demonstrates [that] it consists not only in the preaching of the Word but also in the illumination of the Spirit.... When he first shines with the light of His word upon the undeserving, he thereby shows a sufficiently clear proof of his free goodness. Here, then, God's boundless goodness is already manifesting itself but not to the salvation of all; for a heavier judgment remains upon the wicked because they reject the testimony of God's love. [Of course, Calvin has previously made clear that this is because they were predestined to do so!] And God also, to show forth his glory, withdraws the effectual working of his Spirit from them.

> This inner call, then, is a pledge of salvation that cannot deceive us.... But lest the flesh boast that it did at least answer him when he called and freely offered himself, he declares that it has no ears to hear, no eyes to see, unless he makes them. Furthermore, he makes them not according to each person's gratefulness but according to his election.[2]

Here Calvin clearly expresses monergism or irresistible grace. God "makes" the elected sinner's ears to hear and eyes to see the gospel, and he "withdraws" that "effectual working" (irresistible grace) from the non-elect, the reprobate.

As I will explain later, most Calvinists claim that synergists want to be able to boast, even if just a little, that they contributed something to their salvation and/or are so in love with free will that they cannot bring themselves to accept that God does everything in salvation and they contribute nothing. That does not reflect the real statements made by synergists, however. The fact is, most synergists object to monergism because of the necessary implication stated plainly by Calvin that it requires God to withhold or withdraw monergistic grace from many of the very people he created in his own image and likeness to their eternal damnation and suffering "for his glory."

This Calvin states clearly about the reprobate: "They are raised up to the end that through them God's glory may be revealed."[3] Lest anyone misunderstand the source of their reprobation: "For when it says that God hardens or shows mercy to whom he wills, men are warned by this to seek no cause outside his will."[4] The *sole reason* non-Calvinist evangelical Christians object to monergism is because it makes God the ultimate, even if indirect, cause of the reprobates' unbelief and damnation. It does serious harm to God's reputation.

Lorraine Boettner follows Calvin closely by attributing everything in salvation to God to the exclusion of any free human cooperation with grace. He bases this on the doctrines of total depravity and unconditional election. "If man is dead in sin, then nothing short of ... supernatural life-giving power of the Holy Spirit will ever cause him to do that which is spiritually good."[5] So, regeneration must precede conversion: "Regeneration is a sovereign gift of God, graciously bestowed on those whom He has chosen."[6] It involves a fundamental change of character so that the person regenerated wants to repent and believe and serve God. Boettner avers that this doctrine of irresistible grace is *the only* evangelical theology because only it ascribes all the work of salvation to God, thus giving God alone the glory.[7] Arminianism is not evangelical, he claims, because it makes man and not God "ultimately the deciding factor" in salvation.[8] This is why he and other Calvinists attack Arminian theology as "man-centered" rather than "God-centered."

One has to wonder, however, who is the God at the center of this theology. Boettner admits that God could save everyone, because election to salvation is unconditional and regeneration and faith are solely gifts of God given only to the elect: "But for reasons which have been only partially revealed, He leaves many impenitent."[9] While non-Calvinists are willing to admit that high Calvinism is God-centered, they have good reason to wonder how exactly to distinguish between the God it centers itself on and Satan—except that Satan wants all people damned to hell and God wants only a certain number damned to hell. That may sound harsh, but it is the reason most Christians are not Calvinists. And it is no less harsh than Calvinists' frequent accusation that Arminians (and other non-Calvinists) place man, not God, at the center of their theology because they want to boast and rob God of his rightful glory.

Ironically and confusingly, Boettner goes on to claim that monergism involves no violation of the sinner's free agency. "This change [viz., regeneration] is not accomplished through any external compulsion but through a new principle of life which has been created within the soul and which seeks after the food which alone can satisfy it [viz., God's word]."[10] Then he compounds the confusion by saying that "the elect are so influenced by divine power that their coming is an act of voluntary choice."[11] One can only wonder what "voluntary choice" means in this context; I assume Boettner is referring to the compatibilist freedom of Edwards and other Calvinists—freedom compatible with determinism.

Steele and Thomas weigh in on this doctrine that they call "the efficacious call of the Spirit": "Simply stated, this doctrine asserts that the Holy Spirit never fails to bring to salvation those sinners whom He personally calls to Christ. He inevitably applies salvation to every sinner whom He intends to save, and it is His intention to save all the elect."[12] Like Calvin, Boettner, and most Calvinists, they distinguish between a "general, outer call" of the gospel, which is a universal invitation to all people to be saved, and a "special, inward call" that goes out only to the elect and effects their regeneration before they respond with repentance and faith. This special call is irresistible: "The grace which the Holy

Spirit extends to the elect cannot be thwarted or refused, it never fails to bring them to true faith in Christ."[13]

For biblical support Steele and Thomas turn to Romans 8:30: "And those he predestined, he also called; those he called, he also justified; those he justified, he also glorified." The omission of 8:29 appears convenient to their purpose of showing God utterly and solely responsible for regeneration. That verse says: "For those God foreknew he also predestined to be conformed to the image of his Son, that he might be the firstborn among many brothers and sisters." There election is based on God's foreknowledge—something Calvinists reject as an error. Also, verse 30 says nothing at all about grace being irresistible. Moreover, Paul skips over regeneration to justification. This verse, in its context and not treated eisegetically (reading meanings into a text that are not there), does not support irresistible grace.

Calvinist Palmer agrees entirely with Calvin, Boettner, and Steele and Thomas about irresistible grace, and for the same reasons; but he emphasizes more the active response to grace that is necessary on the elect person's part if he or she is to be saved. As we have already seen, like some Calvinists, Palmer revels in paradox. Here is another case:

> Although it is true that none would be saved were it not for the irresistible grace of God, no one may ever fall into the rationalistic trap of saying that he has nothing to do. He may not reason that since all depends on the Holy Spirit, he does not need to believe; or that he must simply wait for the Spirit to move him, and there is nothing that he can do to be saved.[14]

This warning sounds Calvinist and Arminian at the same time; Palmer apparently wants to have his cake and eat it too. Note especially the final words of his statement where he warns against believing there is nothing a person can do to be saved. Afterwards he writes: "If you do [believe], thank God for causing you to do so."[15] So, on the one hand, God "causes" the elect person to believe, and we are forbidden to suggest that is in any way an act of free will.[16] On the other hand, we are forbidden to suggest there is nothing a person can do to be saved. These ideas are difficult, if not impossible, to reconcile.

R. C. Sproul also champions irresistible grace: "God unilaterally and monergistically does for us what we cannot do for ourselves."[17] He prefers to call it "effectual grace" lest anyone misunderstand by thinking that in this belief God forces someone to be saved against his or her will. Rather, God graciously imparts the gift of faith so that the person wants to believe: "The faith by which we [the elect] are saved is a gift. When the apostle says [in Eph. 2:8–9] it is not of ourselves, he does not mean it is not our faith. Again, God does not do the believing for us. It is our own faith but it does not originate with us. It is given to us. The gift is not earned or deserved. It is a gift of sheer grace."[18] Also, "the whole point of irresistible grace is that rebirth quickens someone to spiritual life in such a way that Jesus is now seen in his irresistible sweetness."[19]

For Sproul, then, God "monergistically and unilaterally" saves the elect person by giving him or her the gift of faith, which then is the person's own faith *and* God regenerates the person so that they, for the first time, see Jesus "in his irresistible sweetness." All this without violating the person's will.

Like Boettner, Sproul regards irresistible grace or effectual calling as an even more basic and fundamental issue of Protestant (and therefore evangelical) theology than justification by faith alone. After all, he argues, if a person contributes anything to salvation, including a bare permission to allow God to work, then justification is not solely by grace alone. The issue of the graciousness of salvation is more important because it is more basic than the issue of salvation by faith alone. "Here we reach the ultimate point of separation between semi-Pelagianism and Augustinianism, between Arminianism and Calvinism, between Rome and the Reformation."[20]

Notice how Sproul is putting Arminianism, by which he means any Protestant view other than high Calvinism, on the side of "Rome"—meaning Roman Catholicism—over against the Reformation. What he is saying here is that Arminianism (i.e., any view other than his) is not really Protestant and therefore not really evangelical either. I live in Texas and around here we might say, "Them's fightin' words!" Seriously, one has to wonder why Sproul would be so blatantly offensive to fellow Protestant Christians, including everyone in the Wesleyan tradition, all Pentecostals, many if not most Baptists, and many other evangelical Christians who, for very good reasons, do not accept his point of view.

Sproul continues:

> In the Reformation view, the work of regeneration is performed by God and by him alone. The sinner is completely passive in receiving

> this action. Regeneration is an example of operative grace. Any cooperation we display toward God occurs only *after* the work of regeneration has been completed.[21]

The only support Sproul gives for his claim that this is "the Reformation view" is Luther's vicious response to Desiderius Erasmus (1466–1536) entitled *On the Bondage of the Will.* There, admittedly, Luther expressed this view. Does that make it "the Reformation view"? Hardly. Luther's right-hand man, Philip Melanchthon (1497–1560), was more of a synergist, agreeing with Erasmus that salvation involves some cooperation with God's grace by the human person even though he adamantly insisted there is no merit in this cooperation.[22] Reformation Anabaptists such as Balthasar Hubmaier (1480–1528) and Menno Simons (1496–1561) emphasized free will over against monergistic grace. For Sproul to pit his monergistic view of salvation as the only Protestant one over against all others as Roman Catholic is misleading at best and disingenuous at worst.

John Piper can be counted on to agree with Calvin, Boettner, Steele and Thomas, Palmer, and Sproul. Diving into paradox with them, he writes: "God will see to it that his elect hear the invitation and respond the way they should.... But he does not do this in a way that lessens our accountability to hear and believe."[23] He also argues that irresistible grace, together with unconditional election, forms the only reasonable motive for intercessory prayer and spiritual warfare. That is because, he argues, there is no point in praying for the salvation of the lost or the defeat of Satan, who he admits is "the god of this world," unless God intervenes powerfully to make these things happen. If people have free will, Piper argues, there is no point in praying for their salvation or that they not support Satan in his "devastation" of the world. "Either you give up praying for God to convert sinners or you give up ultimate human self-determination."[24]

Of course, anyone can see the profound irony in such claims. Elsewhere Piper has stated unequivocally that God ordains, governs, and even causes everything that happens.[25] Whatever is the case, God has foreordained it. If he responds to a prayer—for example, for the salvation of a lost loved one—it is because he has foreordained it. The prayer does not actually change anything; it is simply a foreordained means to a foreordained end. Piper is a divine determinist, whether he likes that label or not. So what role does prayer or spiritual warfare really play in his theology? Certainly not that they can actually bring it about that God acts in any other way than he already planned to act and necessarily will act.

MORE INJURY TO GOD'S REPUTATION

In the next section of this chapter, "Alternatives to Irresistible Grace/ Monergism," I will show that many of the accusations by Calvinists such as Sproul against non-Calvinist and especially Arminian views miss their targets entirely. In this section, I want once again to expose the fallacies of the Calvinist arguments for monergism and demonstrate that monergism actually injures God's reputation by necessarily undermining God's goodness and love.

I begin with refutations of typical Calvinist interpretations of Scriptures that supposedly require monergism. The most important such verses are John 6:44 and 65, where Jesus says that no one comes to him unless the Father "draws" him. Sproul and other Calvinists argue that the Greek verb here translated "draws" always and only means "compels."[26] In a brilliant but unpublished 2003 paper entitled "The 'Drawings' of God," pastor-theologian Steve Witzki conclusively proves that Sproul is wrong. He cites numerous Greek lexicons saying that the Greek word does not always mean "compels" but often means "draw, attract."[27]

Sproul cites a reference work many consider definitive in matters of interpreting the Greek New Testament—Kittel's *Theological Dictionary of the New Testament*—to support his definition of the term throughout the New Testament, including John 6:44 and cognate passages. However, Witzki quotes Kittel as allowing a broader range of possible meanings. With reference to John 6:44 and 12:32 the author of Kittel's article (Albrecht Oepke) writes:

> There is no thought here of force or magic. The term figuratively expresses the supernatural power of the love of God or Christ which goes out to all ... but without which no one can come.... The apparent contradiction shows that both the election and the universality of grace must be taken seriously; the compulsion is not automatic.[28]

The most devastating argument against Sproul's case that the term always means "compels" is John 12:32. There Jesus says that if he is lifted up from the earth, he will "draw all people" to himself. The Greek verb translated "draw" there is the same as in John 6:44 and 65. If Sproul is right and the verb must always mean "compel," then this verse teaches universalism. In fact, however, the word *can mean* simply draw or attract rather than compel or drag. The Arminian interpretation of these verses in John 6 and 12 is reasonable: that nobody can come to Jesus Christ unless he or she is drawn by God's prevenient grace that calls and enables but does not compel.

Are there Scriptures that contradict irresistible grace? Steve Lemke marshals many passages that disprove it. For example, Matthew 23 and Luke 13 describe Jesus' lament over Jerusalem:

> Jerusalem, Jerusalem, you who kill the prophets and stone those sent to you, how often I have longed to gather your children together, as a hen gathers her chicks under her wings, and you were not willing. Look, your house is left to you desolate. For I tell you, you will not see me again until you say, "Blessed is he who comes in the name of the Lord." (Matt. 23:37–39)

Lemke rightly notes that if Calvinism is correct, "Jesus' lament would have been over God's hardness of heart."[29] There are so many passages like this throughout the Bible, where God or Jesus or a prophet decries the people's hardness of heart sorrowfully as if it could be otherwise. If irresistible grace were true, of course, Jesus could have simply drawn the people of Jerusalem effectually to himself. Why didn't he if he was so sorrowful about their rejection? And why would he be sorrowful about their rejection if it, like everything else, was foreordained by God?

The usual Calvinist response to these passages is that God is sorrowful over people's hardness of heart and rejection of him. That he doesn't do anything about it can only be because he chooses not to, and that he chooses not to can only be because his strongest motive (Edwards' definition of free will) is not to. In brief, he doesn't want to but wishes he could. The only hint Calvinists give us as to why God doesn't do what he wishes is "for his glory." What kind of God is glorified by people rejecting him when he chooses not to overcome that rejection when he could?

Moreover, why would God be sad or sorrowful about what glorifies him? What possible analogy could there be to this in human experience? Suppose a father has a love potion that would cause all of his children to love him and never rebel against him. He gives it to some of his children but not others and then weeps because some of his children reject him and don't love him. Who would take him seriously? Or, if they took him seriously, who wouldn't think him insincere or a bit mad? Lemke concludes from the story of Jesus' lament over Jerusalem:

> If Jesus believed in irresistible grace, with both the outward and inward calls, His apparent lament over Jerusalem would have been just a disingenuous act, a cynical show because He knew that God had not and would not give these lost persons the necessary conditions for their salvation.[30]

Another interesting biblical passage mentioned by Lemke is Matthew 19:24, where Jesus says to his disciples: "Again I tell you, it is easier for a camel to go through the eye of a needle than for someone who is rich to enter the kingdom of God." What sense does this verse make in light of irresistible grace? Is Jesus saying it is harder *for God* to save a rich man than a poor one? How could that be? If everyone, without exception, only gets into the kingdom of God by God's work alone without any required cooperation on his or her part, then Jesus' saying makes no sense at all. Again, Lemke's comment is spot on:

> Of course, if Jesus were a Calvinist, He never would have suggested that it was harder for rich persons to be saved by God's irresistible grace than poor persons. Their wills would be changed immediately and invincibly upon hearing God's effectual call. It would be no harder for a rich person to be saved by God's monergistic and irresistible calling than it would be for any other sinner. But the real Jesus was suggesting that their salvation was tied in some measure to their response and commitment to His calling.[31]

Lemke also points to the numerous all-inclusive invitations for people to come to God and to Christ in Scripture, especially to the already discussed "all" passages that express God's desire for everyone to be saved and none to perish (Matt. 18:14; 1 Timothy 2:4; 2 Peter 3:9; 1 John 2:2). As I have already shown, these cannot be interpreted as referring only to some people.

Most devastatingly of all, Lemke rightly points out that "the Calvinists essentially blame God for those who do not come [to salvation]."[32] After all, while they would say that those who reject the gospel merely receive their just deserts when they are condemned, "there is really more to it than that. Calvinists say that God elected some to glory for His own reasons from before the world began, and He gave them irresistible grace through His Spirit so they inevitably would be saved."[33] This is the main point against this doctrine of Calvinism (as it is the main point against all of them!). It portrays God as a respecter of persons because he chooses some to save irresistibly and others not to receive that crucial gift, with the result that they are damned forever. That they deserve condemnation is not the issue. The issue is that *everyone* deserves it, but God is selective about saving some irresistibly and leaving others to die an eternal separation from him in hell. Calvinists offer no reason for this other than "God's good pleasure" and/or "God's glory."

Yet, all Calvinists claim that God is good and loving. What goodness and love is this? In fact, to put it bluntly, Calvinism necessarily implies, whether any Calvinist would say so or not, that God requires a better quality of love from us than he himself exercises! In Luke 6:35 and parallel passages Jesus commands us to love our enemies; there is no hint of any exception. But according to Calvinism, God doesn't do that. Of course, some Calvinists insist that God *does* love even his reprobate enemies. But there is no analogy to *that* kind of love in human experience. It would be a love in which a person could rescue some from terrible deaths but chooses not to in order to show how great he is. Is there any analogy to this "goodness" and "love" in human experience? If not, then I suggest, with Paul Helm, it is meaningless.

Walls and Dongell offer an analogy to test whether any human being would be considered loving or good if he or she acted as Calvinism says God acts in giving irresistible grace only to some of his fallen human creatures. (Remember, he created all in his own image and likeness.) In their illustration, a doctor discovers a cure for a deadly disease killing a group of camp children and gives it to the camp's director. The director administers it to some sick children so that they are cured and withholds it from others so that they die terribly. He has no shortage of the cure; nothing at all hinders him from curing all the children. Even though some of the children resisted the cure, the director had the ability to persuade all of them to take it; he only persuaded some. When the parents confront the director, he passionately contends that he loved all the children—even the ones who died. He cared for them while they were sick and made them as comfortable as possible.[34] Walls and Dongell rightly conclude:

> The director's claim to love all the children rings hollow at best, deceptive at worst. If love will not employ all available means to res-

> cue someone from ultimate loss, it is hard to hear it as love at all. In our judgment, it becomes meaningless to claim that God wishes to save all while also insisting that God refrains from making the salvation of all possible. What are we to make of a God whose walk does not match his talk?[35]

The plain fact of the matter is that the doctrine of irresistible grace, *without universal salvation which most Calvinists reject*, leads to the "good and necessary consequence" that God is not good and not loving. Now, of course, no Calvinist would admit that! But their teaching should lead a thinking person to that conclusion. And what they say is inconsistent and therefore highly problematic, if not downright incoherent. When I hear or read a high Calvinist saying that God loves everyone and is a good God, I really have no idea what that means.

Another problem with irresistible grace is that personal relationships require mutuality. Dutch philosopher-theologian Vincent Brümmer has demonstrated this conclusively in his *Speaking of a Personal God*, where he presents a step-by-step logical argument that mutuality, in the sense of free response that is resistible, is part of any personal relationship. Without freedom of will, which includes ability to resist, a person's acts are not really "acts" at all but "events."[36] By definition, realization of a personal relationship requires free acts of both parties toward the other:

> For the realization of a *personal relationship* the initiative of *both* partners in the relationship is necessary. Given that both partners in such a relationship are persons, both have by definition the freedom of will, by which it must be *factually possible* for both of them to say "no" to the other and so to prevent the relationship from coming into existence. It is only by means of the "yes" of one partner that the other receives the freedom of ability to realize the relationship. In this respect personal relationships are symmetrical and differ from purely causal relationships which are asymmetrical, because only one partner (the cause) can be the initiator. The other partner in a purely causal relationship is an object of causal manipulation and therefore lacks the freedom of will to be able to say "no" with respect to what happens to him or her.[37]

Brümmer argues further that in our relationship with God, God can be the initiator and must be because of our lack of "freedom of ability" due to our sinfulness. However, "a personal relationship with God assumes that the human partner also remains a person in the relationship and that his or her free choice is equally a necessary condition for the relationship to be brought about."[38] Finally, Brümmer negates the idea of irresistible grace by saying that even

> God cannot bring about our choice without it ceasing to be ours. By definition, a *personal* relationship with God cannot be factually unavoidable for the human partner. For this reason the doctrine of factual irresistibility excludes a personal relationship between God and human persons.[39]

It doesn't take a philosopher to establish these facts; they are common sense. But it helps for a philosopher to support them. And it won't do for Calvinists to complain about critics appealing to philosophy; they are good at using philosophy when it helps their arguments.[40] Common sense alone dictates that a truly personal relationship always involves free will; insofar as one party controls the other such that the other has no real choice whether to be in the relationship or not, it is not a real relationship. It makes no difference that both parties *want* to be in the relationship. Imagine a friendship where one person has manipulated the other one into being his friend. Perhaps he has plied him with money or even given him a drug that makes him friendly. Any objective observer of such a "friendship" would say it is really not a legitimate friendship—at least not a healthy one. Mutual, informed consent is a prerequisite to any good relationship.

But Brümmer doesn't leave the matter there. He aims his critique straight at high Calvinism's notion of salvation itself. Referring to high Calvinism with the metonymy of "Dordt" (referring to the 1618/1619 Synod of Dort) he says:

> It strikes me that the difficulties here have their source in the fact that the Dordt theologians did not view human salvation in terms of a personal *relationship* with God but in terms of a reborn *condition* in us. The only question then concerns the *cause* of this condition: is it God or us, grace or human will?[41]

But when salvation is regarded not as a mere causal condition but also, and even more, as a personal relationship, as most evangelicals do regard it, the idea that it can be founded on *both* grace *and* human will (with grace having priority) is compelling.

I will round out this description and critique of Calvinism's doctrine of irresistible grace, monergism, with an appropriate quote from Vernon Grounds, an evangelical theologian who agrees completely with Brümmer: "God deals personally with personal beings.... Grace that left no option whatever would not be grace, it would be something else. We should have to say, 'By force were ye saved, and not of yourselves.'"[42]

ALTERNATIVES TO IRRESISTIBLE GRACE/MONERGISM

Now I will tackle some of the objections to "evangelical synergism" raised by Calvinists. By "evangelical synergism" I mean roughly Arminian theology, although many who hold this view of salvation do *not* wish to be called Arminians. I respect that while also respectfully asking them to consider whether the label may be more appropriate than they think.

Over the centuries Calvinist theologians, by sheer repetition and misrepresentation, have brought about a situation where the term "Arminian" is widely thought of as designating a heresy. I have demonstrated conclusively in my *Arminian Theology: Myths and Realities* that it is *not* what they say. For example, contrary to Sproul and other misinformed or disingenuous Calvinist critics, it is not semi-Pelagian. Semi-Pelagianism is the heresy that says the initiative in salvation is ours, the human person's, and not God's.[43] Arminianism has always insisted that the initiative in salvation is God's; it is called "prevenient grace," and it is enabling but resistible. It would come as a shock to many Calvinists to know how much of salvation and the whole Christian life both Arminius and Wesley attributed to grace—*all of it.*

But Arminian theology assumes, because the Bible everywhere assumes, that God limits himself out of love so that his initiating, enabling grace is resistible. It is powerful and persuasive but not compelling in the determinative sense. It leaves the sinner a person, not an object. Baptist theologian Robert E. Picirilli says:

> What Arminius meant by "prevenient grace" was that grace that precedes actual regeneration and which, except when finally resisted, inevitably leads on to regeneration. He was quick to observe that this "assistance of the Holy Spirit" is of such sufficiency "as to keep at the greatest possible distance from Pelagianism."[44]

Another Baptist theologian, Stanley J. Grenz, was an Arminian without labeling himself such. In his systematic theology, *Theology for the*

Community of God, he describes prevenient grace in three ways: as illuminating, as convicting, and as calling and enabling.[45] He makes clear it is always resistible because it comes to persons and not machines through the hearing of God's Word. The point here is simply this: Arminian theology (and many non-Calvinist theologies that are not so labeled)[46] places the initiative in salvation and all the work of salvation squarely on the divine side of the equation. God's grace is the effectual cause of salvation, but the human person's faith as response to prevenient grace is the instrumental cause of salvation. What is that faith? Simply trusting God; it is not a "good work" or anything meritorious of which the saved sinner could boast.

But what about the Calvinist attacks on Arminian theology as a form of self-salvation and works righteousness akin to (they would say) Roman Catholic theology? Knowledgeable Calvinists do not say that Arminians believe they have to work for their salvation; they say that Arminians and other non-Calvinists make the human decision of faith the "decisive factor" in salvation and therefore bring it back, however unintentionally, to salvation by good works.

To Arminians, however, this accusation is ridiculous. Imagine a student who is starving and about to be evicted from his room due to lack of money. A kindly professor *gives* him a check for $1,000—enough to pay his rent and stock his kitchen with food. Imagine further that the rescued student takes the check to his bank, endorses it, and deposits it in his account (which brings his balance up to $1,000). Imagine also that the student then goes around campus boasting that he *earned* $1,000. What would everyone's response be who knew the truth of the situation? They would accuse the student of being an ungrateful wretch. But suppose the student said, "But my endorsing the check and depositing it was the decisive factor in my having the money, so I did a good work that earned at least part of the money, didn't I?" He would be ridiculed and possibly even ostracized for such nonsense.

In what situation in human experience is merely *accepting* a gift "the decisive factor" in having it? It is *a* factor, yes—but hardly the decisive one. Merely accepting a gift does not give one the right to boast. Oh, but the Calvinist will say, the student in the above illustration *could* boast *if* the professor offered a similar gift of money to *other* starving students and they rejected it. He could boast that in some way he is better than they are. I doubt it. He might try, but who would believe him? People would say to him: "Stop trying to take some credit for being rescued! That others didn't accept the money and were evicted and are begging for food on the street says nothing at all about you. Give all the credit where it belongs—to the kindly professor." Who can really argue with that?

Why do Arminians and other non-Calvinists reject irresistible grace? Because they love free will and don't want to give all the glory to God, as some Calvinists suggest? Not at all. That's a calumny unworthy of anyone who has bothered to study the matter. Every Arminian from Arminius to the present has always made clear the real motive behind rejecting the doctrine of irresistible grace: preserving the good and loving character of God. Of course, *if* a person could be a universalist, there would be no necessary obstacle to irresistible grace except possibly the one raised above about the nature of personal relationships. However, *if* the only possible way in which people could be saved was for God to overwhelm them and compel them to accept his mercy, I would have no fundamental objection to believing in it *so long as God did it for everyone.* Fortunately, there is another way: prevenient grace. And since I cannot believe in universal salvation, that is the only alternative to monergism that preserves God's character of perfect love, revealed in Jesus Christ.

Another common Calvinist objection to evangelical synergism/Arminianism is that it does not take human depravity seriously enough. After all, Calvinists aver, fallen human persons are literally dead in trespasses and sins. Their only hope is for God to resuscitate them. Indeed, but God's resuscitation does not include leaving them no option whether to accept him or not. Actually, Arminians and other synergists *do* believe that prevenient grace restores life to the person dead in trespasses and sins. However, it does not compel them to accept God's mercy unto salvation, which requires free repentance and faith (conversion).

So, in Arminian theology, a partial regeneration does precede conversion, but it is not a complete regeneration. It is an awakening and enabling, but not an irresistible force. This is how evangelical synergists interpret the "drawings" of John's gospel, including Jesus' words about drawing all people to himself if he be lifted up. In fact, *only* this interpretation of these drawings keeps them together meaning the same thing—God's powerful attracting and persuading power that actually imparts free will to be saved or not. Being saved is not a matter of doing a work; it is only a matter of *not resisting.* When a person decides to allow God's grace to save, he or she repents and trusts only and completely in Christ.

That is a passive act; it could be compared to a drowning person who decides to relax and let his rescuer save him from drowning.

This is how Arminians/evangelical synergists understand Philippians 2:12–13 quoted earlier. The apostle Paul, under the inspiration of the Holy Spirit, tells his Christian readers to remember to "work out" their salvation "with fear and trembling." Critics think Arminians and evangelical synergists generally stop there and ignore the next verse. But they don't. They realize and teach that *if* people are working out their salvation, from beginning to end, it is only because "God is at work" in them. That's prevenient, assisting grace: prevenient leading up to conversion and assisting throughout the entire Christian life. But it would be pointless for Paul to urge his readers to work out their salvation with fear and trembling if God were doing everything and they did not even have to cooperate by allowing God's grace to work in them.

I ask the reader's indulgence as I close this chapter by providing two rather homely illustrations of evangelical synergism that I believe do more justice to the biblical text and Christian experience *and the character of God* than Calvinist images and analogies. First, imagine a deep pit with steep, slippery sides. Several people are lying broken and wounded, utterly helpless, at the bottom of the pit.

- *Semi-Pelagianism* says that God comes along and throws a rope down to the bottom of the pit and waits for a person to start pulling on it. Once he does, God responds by yelling, "Grab it tight and wrap it around yourself. Together we'll get you out." The problem is, the person is too hurt to do that, the rope is too weak, and God is too good to wait for the person to initiate the process.
- *Monergism* says God comes along, throws a rope down into the pit, and climbs down it, wrapping it around *some* of the people and then goes back out of the pit and pulls them to safety without any cooperation. The problem is that the God of Jesus Christ is too good and loving to rescue only some of the helpless people.
- *Evangelical synergism* says that God comes along and throws a rope down and yells, "Grab onto it and pull and together we'll get you out!" Nobody moves. They are too wounded. In fact, for all practical purposes they are "dead" because they are utterly helpless. So God pours water into the pit and yells, "Relax and let the water lift you out!" In other words, "Float!" All a person in the pit has to do

> to be rescued is let the water lift him or her out of the pit. It takes a decision, but not an effort. The water, of course, is prevenient grace.[47]

Second, here is an illustration of grace and "working out your salvation" throughout the Christian life. During the hot summers I have to water my plants often. So I go to the outdoor faucet where the hose is attached, turn it on all the way, and then walk to the end of the hose and drag it around the side of the house to water a bush. Invariably when I get to the bush and press the handle of the attachment at the end of the hose, nothing comes out. I go back to the faucet and discover everything's fine there. The water pressure is strong; the water is flowing into the hose full force. Ah, I realize, there's a kink in the hose. So I go and find the kink that is keeping the water inside the hose from flowing and work it out.

In this illustration, the water represents God's assisting grace; it is always "full force" in a Christian's life. There are no "grace boosters." Grace is full and free from conversion and regeneration on into the life of sanctification. But if I am not experiencing the flow of God's grace in confidence and power for service, it isn't due to any lack of grace; it is due to kinks in the hose of my life. What are the kinks? Attitudes, besetting sins, lack of prayer. All I have to do is decide to remove those kinks and the grace that is already there is allowed to flow.

This is an imperfect illustration of Philippians 2:12–13 from an evangelical synergist perspective. The one alteration needed to make the illustration really "work" is that even my ability to remove those "kinks" is a gift of God. But I do have to do something—not a good, meritorious work of which I can boast but merely admitting my helplessness and utter dependence on God's grace and asking God to give me the ability and desire to remove the kinks.

The best exposition of this evangelical synergistic/Arminian soteriology in modern language is *The Transforming Power of Grace* by Thomas Oden. By all accounts an orthodox, biblically serious, and evangelical theologian, Oden winsomely and biblically articulates the theology briefly outlined above that I call evangelical synergism.[48] Of grace Oden says: "God prepares the will and co-works with the prepared will. Insofar as grace precedes and prepares free will it is called prevenient. Insofar as grace accompanies and enables human willing to work with divine willing, it is called cooperating grace."[49] "Only when sinners are assisted by prevenient grace can they begin to yield their hearts to cooperation with subsequent forms of grace." "The need for grace to prevene is great, for it was precisely when 'you were dead in your transgressions and sins' (Eph. 2:1) that 'by grace you have been saved' (Eph. 2:8)."[50]

EIGHT

CONCLUSION: CALVINISM'S CONUNDRUMS

Logic matters. Most Calvinists agree. Sproul, for example, insists that theology should contain no contradictions. Mysteries—yes; contradictions—no. Again, a mystery is something beyond our complete comprehension—like the Trinity. A contradiction is something impossible—a married bachelor, a round square, two plus three equals four. Few Calvinists want to embrace contradictions. Anyone who embraces or expresses a contradiction is dabbling in nonsense. What is a paradox? It's an apparent contradiction and therefore always a task for further thought.

But I would like to suggest there's a category between mystery and contradiction or between mystery and paradox—conundrum. A conundrum is a mental puzzle—something that jars the mind. It may be a contradiction, but it's hard to tell. It may be a sign of mystery, but it verges on nonsense. Everywhere and by everyone a conundrum is a signal of something wrong, something to be examined and thought about and hopefully solved.

An example from science is light. It manifests aspects of particles as well as waves. How it can be both even the best physicists aren't sure. It appears to be both, but there's no known way it could be both. So, science keeps working at the problem. Simply to sit back and say, "Well, isn't that wonderful; light is a mystery so let's just leave it at that and move on," wouldn't satisfy anyone with a reasoning mind. Inquiring minds want to know how a conundrum might be solved.

I believe Calvinism has too many and too profound conundrums that have no apparent solutions. They even appear at times like contradictions although they are not formal, logical contradictions. The most obvious and frequently mentioned one, even by Calvinists, is the combination of divine absolute sovereignty and human responsibility. As already seen, even John Piper, a scholar with a doctorate in New Testament studies from a major European university, admits he can't fathom it. He simply embraces it because he thinks Scripture requires it.

Most Calvinists admit it is a problem, a conundrum, how people can be foreordained and rendered certain by God to sin such that they could not do otherwise (e.g., Adam) and yet be responsible for it in the sense of guilt. Under no circumstances in human situations would a person be held accountable and punished for something he or she could not avoid doing. Yet that is what Calvinism says about God and sinners. This is, indeed, a conundrum. Some call it an "antinomy," which is simply another word for conundrum. There's nothing strictly illogical in the formal sense about the combination of determinism and responsibility, but it goes against the grain of all human thought and experience.

For many of us, this conundrum is too filled with tension to accept. It has to be resolved by being modified and, fortunately, Scripture allows it.[1] How? God's foreordination of people's sinful decisions and actions is nothing other than his decision to allow them. And he allows them by self-limitation, not "specific, willing permission" that renders them certain. Those who sin are responsible and accountable because they could have done otherwise with the free will God gave them.

Another tension-filled conundrum of Calvinism is this: if divine determinism is true, nothing is really evil. Think about it. If the good and all-powerful God has specifically willed and rendered certain every single event in history, how can anything really be evil? Must this not be the best of all possible worlds? Why would God foreordain and render certain anything but the best of all possible worlds? And how could anything in the best of all possible worlds really be ontologically (as opposed to merely in our perception) evil? If I were a Calvinist (in the strong, divine determinist sense) I would have a difficult time getting angry or worked up about anything because I would try to see everything as God's will—planned and purposed by God for a good reason, even if that good reason is simply "the greater glory of God." Even hell itself must be good because it manifests God's justice and thereby glorifies God. So why think hell is a bad place? Similarly child abuse, murder, rape, genocide—all willed and rendered certain by God. So why think they are evil?

Here is where Calvinists respond by appealing to two wills in God—decretive and preceptive. God decrees whatever comes to pass and therefore it is, in some sense, for the greater glory of God. But he also commands us not to do certain things and therefore doing them is evil. The result, of course, is that when a person murders another person, he is both doing evil and doing something good. Which is the higher reality? Well, obviously, God's good purpose is the wider lens through which the event should be seen. Therefore, it is not inherently evil, is it? Then some Calvinists will respond by saying that the evil in an act like murder lies in the murderer's disposition, intent, and motive, not in the act itself. God foreordains and renders certain the act (the murderer raising the knife and plunging it down into the victim's chest). But God's motive is good while the murderer's is evil. How does that help? After all, where did the murderer's evil motive and intention come from?

Simply to say "We don't know" is just to raise a bigger question: How can that be when the Calvinist has already said God foreordains and renders certain everything without exception, including creatures' thoughts and intentions? How can that not include the evil motive of the murderer's heart? Also, how could God render the murder certain without assuring that the murderer has an evil motive? Then most Calvinists will say that the evil motive or intention arose because God withdrew or withheld his inhibiting grace. How does that help? God is still the author of the evil motive by intentionally, purposefully, actively withdrawing or withholding that which he knew would have prevented it. And he supposedly authored it with a good motive for a good purpose—whatever exactly that is. That also implies a flaw in creation so that it was not inherently good. It seems the Calvinist explanation is going around in circles, never really managing to explain how anything is truly evil. I don't think most Calvinists have come to terms with this conundrum.

Another, closely related conundrum is that if Calvinism is true, nothing at all can possibly injure or lessen God's glory. A Calvinist friend wrote a book about an alleged heresy that supposedly lessens God's glory.[2] But how can that happen? It can't. Every heresy, like everything else, is foreordained by God for his glory. So, logically, it contributes to the greater glory of God. Even if it says that God is not glorious, that too glorifies God—like everything else. Logically, it seems a consistent Calvinist can never say that anything injures or lessens the glory of God. Everything without exception glorifies God and in the best possible way, or else God would not have foreordained it for his glory.

Right about now some readers might be saying: "Wait. I don't care about conundrums. So what? Isn't it spiritual to simply accept truths of God's Word even if they are confusing and even seemingly contradictory?"

First, nobody is saying not to accept truths of God's Word. The question is whether God's Word actually does require belief in conundrums or whether conundrums are always a sign of something wrong in our *interpretation* of God's Word. Presumably God is the author of logic and reason (at their best as functions of the image of God). All serious biblical interpretation seeks to iron out inconsistencies assuming that God is appealing to our minds as well as our hearts.

Second, even most Calvinist theologians want to avoid or resolve conundrums while occasionally and reluctantly admitting some seem unavoidable.

Third, even Calvinists attempt to undermine other theologies by pointing to their conundrums. It would certainly be a double standard to embrace conundrums comfortably and at the same time use them against Arminianism. For example, many Calvinists point to Arminians' belief that God knows the future exhaustively and infallibly as a conundrum when combined with belief that free will is the ability to do otherwise than one does. How could God know the future without foreordaining it? Insofar as Calvinists use such tactics when they critique other theologies, they are not permitted to embrace their own comfortably.

A conundrum I have already pointed out earlier is the Calvinist belief that God selects some people to save and others to "pass over," and that this selection has absolutely nothing to do with anything he sees in them or about them. Yet his selection is not arbitrary. I argued earlier that there is no middle ground between arbitrary and there being something about people that causes God to select them (such as a free response to God's invitation to be saved). An appeal to mystery is incorrect; this is not a mystery but a conundrum.

But the greatest conundrum of them all has to do with God's character. Nearly all Calvinists confess that God is the standard of moral goodness, the source of all values, the perfectly loving source of love. Then they also confess that God ordains, designs, controls, and renders certain the most egregious evil acts such as the kidnapping, rape, and murder of a small child and the genocidal slaughter of hundreds of thousands in Rwanda. They confess that God "sees to it" that humans sin, as with the fall of Adam and Eve. And they confess that all salvation is absolutely God's doing and not at all dependent on free will decisions of people (monergism), and that God only saves some when he could save all—assuring that some large portion of humanity will spend eternity in hell when he could save them from it.

Don't all theologies contain certain conundrums insofar as they attempt to be comprehensive and systematic? Probably so. One way to look at the choice between competing theologies (when Scripture is not absolutely clear)[3] is to decide on the basis of which conundrums one can live with. For me, and most non-Calvinists, nothing is more important to preserve, protect, and promote than the good name of God—God's reputation based on his good character. Insofar as Calvinism undermines that, I cannot live with its conundrums because they all ultimately injure God's reputation—making it difficult to tell the difference between God and the devil.

Some readers may question the sincerity of my pledge or the success of my effort to write about Calvinism with an irenic spirit. I ask, however, that you keep clearly in mind the difference between *persons* and *beliefs*. By no means do I wish to denigrate Calvinists; that I hold their belief system ultimately undermines the reputation of God is not any reflection on their integrity, sincerity, spirituality, or success as ministers and evangelists. I carry no hostility toward my Calvinist brothers and sisters on account of their mistaken beliefs. I struggle with some of their misrepresentations of my own theology, but I try not to have hard feelings toward them even for that.

Of course I would like to persuade fellow Christians to avoid Calvinism, not because I think it will kill their faith or spirituality but because I want people to think better about God than Calvinism allows. I believe God cares what we think about him and, because I love God, I want all people to think rightly about him.

As I have sought to make clear throughout this book, I believe high Calvinism inadvertently but inescapably impugns the good character of God. That I want to persuade people to avoid Calvinism does *not* mean I want them to avoid Calvinists. To be honest, I think evangelical Calvinists are some of the best Christians in the world. I just think they are terribly inconsistent and teach and believe doctrines contrary to Scripture, most of Christian tradition, and reason. And I think some of those doctrines dishonor God even though that is not Calvinists' intention. I also think some of those doctrines will lead at least some young Christians down theological and spiritual dead ends.

APPENDIX 1

CALVINIST ATTEMPTS TO RESCUE GOD'S REPUTATION

Throughout time, but especially in our time, certain Calvinists have recognized the problems their view of God's sovereignty poses for God's reputation and have offered solutions that allegedly relieve God of being the author of sin and evil. In other words, these are attempts to rescue God's goodness in light of God's absolute foreordination and rendering certain of all things down to the smallest details, but especially the evil decisions and actions of people. If God is absolutely sovereign over all, without self-limitation for the sake of creaturely free will (ability to do otherwise including the ability to thwart God's will), how is God *not* the author of sin and evil? And how are creatures rather than God responsible for evil?

Let's begin with a test case that will be used throughout to examine whether these strategies work to alleviate the problem: the fall of Adam in the garden of Eden. All Calvinists agree with Calvin himself that God foreordained and rendered certain the fall with all its consequences. We have already seen some of the ways in which Calvinists attempt to get God off the hook, so to speak, for being guilty of Adam's sin. How is it, then, that God is not guilty and Adam was?

The first strategy commonly used is to appeal to secondary causes. This is a philosophical concept derived from Aristotle's philosophy; medieval theologian Thomas Aquinas (1225–1274) drew on it to explain how God assures that everything happens but is not guilty of sin and evil. Calvin used this concept to put distance between God's sovereign power working out all things according to his purpose and the creature's evil decisions and actions. Contemporary Calvinist Paul Helm says:

> There is a long and honourable tradition according to which there are both *primary* and *secondary* causes. The primary cause (or causes) is

> the divine upholding; the secondary causes are the causal powers of created things; the power of the seed to germinate, of a person to be angry or to walk down the street, and so on.[1]

Few Christians (or theists in general) would disagree with this use of the concepts of primary and secondary causes. God is, of course, the creator and sustainer of everything outside himself and therefore has to uphold and even concur (even if only by bare permission) with whatever happens in the creaturely realm. Creatures have no absolute, autonomous power of their own over against God such that they can be and act totally apart from him.

However, problems arise when this distinction between primary and secondary causes is applied to divine providence to solve the problem of God's goodness and creatures' evil. For example, Calvinist Loraine Boettner argues that Satan was the "proximate cause" (the same as secondary cause) of the fall of Adam. This, he says, removes all blame from God even though God was the ultimate cause (same as primary cause).[2] Yet earlier, he admits that Satan was "God's instrument."[3] He also says God is never the "efficient cause" of sin.[4] This tangled web of causes creeps up frequently in Calvinists' attempts to shield God from being the author of sin, suggesting that the problems I have highlighted trouble Calvinists as well.

Theologian Henry Meeter tries to clear up the confusion:

> Consider the Calvinist's view regarding the universe of created things! Not only does he believe that it was created by God; but all that occurs in it, whether in nature or in human life, he holds to be but the unfolding of a divine plan of the ages. Even sin does not happen as an accident. God willingly permitted sin, lets it work according to its own inherent nature, and controls it for his glory. God works upon this creation in either of two ways. He works through the normal operations of the universe. Men, even sinful men, and nature act freely according to their own impulses or laws. They are, however, only the secondary causes; behind them lies God, as the First Cause of all things. He, without compelling any secondary causes to act contrary to their own nature and choice, brings to pass all that happens in the universe.... The Calvinist does not rest content ... until he has traced all events back to God and dedicated them to him.[5]

So, put in other words, God as the primary cause of everything that happens uses secondary causes to render certain what he wants to happen according to his foreordained plan. Even the fall of Adam is planned and rendered certain by God, but God is not responsible for the sin of Adam because secondary or proximate causes such as Satan and Adam's choice to sin actually bring it about. What is this but an appeal to *direct* and *indirect* causation? Ultimately, as Meeter admits, all events including the fall of Adam must be traced back to God, who renders them certain.

How does this appeal to secondary causes get God off the hook for evil or rescue his reputation? Helm recognizes the problem and pushes further by appealing to different *intentions* in such events as Adam's fall: "God ordains evil but does not intend evil as evil, as the human agent intends it. In God's case there is some other description of the morally evil action which he intends the evil action to fill. There are other ends or purposes which God has in view."[6]

So, God planned, foreordained, rendered certain, and controlled the fall, but God is not guilty and Adam is because of their different intentions as primary and secondary causes. But doesn't God ultimately serve as the instigator of the evil intention of Adam? Where else could it come from? If we trace everything back to God, as Meeter insists we must, isn't God still the initiator and instigator and ultimate cause of Adam's evil will? Does merely saying that God intended the fall for good release him from responsibility in such a case? I don't think so.

Is there any analogy to this Calvinist explanation of God's innocent role in sin and evil in human experience? I think not. Remember the analogy I offered earlier of the father who manipulated his son to rob money. I cannot think of a single example in human experience where one person who renders it certain that another person will do something evil is considered innocent—even if he meant it for good. In my analogy the manipulative father intended to use the money his son stole to help the poor, which would not lessen his legal liability for the robbery. As Evans (quoted earlier) wrote: "Ultimate responsibility ... resides where the ultimate cause is."[7]

It seems that the appeal to the distinction between primary and secondary causes fails to help the Calvinist solve the problem of God and evil. God is still the ultimate cause of evil and in more than the ordinary sense of being the creator and sustainer of the universe and the powerful one who must concur with the action of the doer of evil.

Another strategy employed by some Calvinists to rescue God's reputation in spite of divine determinism of sin and evil is appeal to what is known as "Molinism" or "middle knowledge." Calvinist theologian Bruce Ware uses this method to explain how God foreordains and renders certain even the evil actions of people such as Adam in his rebellion and yet is not the guilty party and bears none of the blame.[8] Molinism (named after sixteenth-century Jesuit theologian Luis de Molina [1535–1600]) is the belief that God possesses "middle knowledge"—knowledge of what any creature would do freely in any possible set of circumstances. The creature may possess libertarian freedom—freedom not compatible with determinism and able to do otherwise than it does—but God knows what he or she would do with that ability in any conceivable (i.e., logically possible) situation. A Calvinist Molinist such as Ware must alter the traditional Molinist idea of middle knowledge because he does not believe in libertarian freedom—the power of contrary choice. So Ware attempts to construct a version of Molinism that attaches not libertarian freedom but compatibilist freedom to middle knowledge.

Ware employs this idea of middle knowledge to explain God's blameless sovereignty over evil. According to Ware, God has the ability

> to envision, by middle knowledge, an array of situations in which his moral creatures (angelic and human) would choose and act as they would. More specifically, God [is] capable of knowing just what a moral agent would do in one situation, with its particular complex factors, as opposed to what that agent would do in a slightly different situation, with a slightly different complex of factors.[9]

In order to assure that the sin God wants to happen does happen without him being its direct cause or responsible for it (in a guilty sense), God simply places the creature (e.g., Adam) in a situation where he knows the creature will develop a controlling motive of his own accord and act sinfully out of it. Ware calls this an "indirect-passive divine agency," which controls human sinful choices without causing them. Ware explains further:

> When God envisions various sets of factors within which an agent will develop a strongest inclination to do one thing or another, the strongest inclination that emerges from those factors is not caused by the factors, nor is it caused by God. Rather, in light of the *nature of*

> *the person*, when certain factors are present, his nature will respond to those factors and seek to do what he, by nature, wants most to do. In short, the cause of the strongest inclination and the resultant choice is the nature of the person in response to factors presented to him.[10]

Ware thinks this gets God off the hook for evil while at the same time accounting for God's absolute sovereignty even over evil. He suggests that on this account, we should think of God "occasioning" a person's sinful decisions and actions while not "causing" them.

> Because God knows the nature of each person perfectly, he knows how those natures will respond to particular sets of factors presented to them. Thus, without causing a person to do evil, he nonetheless controls the evil they do. He controls whether evil is done, what evil is done, and in any and every case he could prevent the evil from being done. But in no case does he cause the evil to be done. In this way, God maintains meticulous control over evil while his moral creatures alone are the agents who do the evil, and they alone bear moral responsibility for the evil they freely do.[11]

Several questions arise from Ware's (and other Calvinists') account of God's involvement in sin and evil. First, given the strong view of God's sovereignty, how is it possible for a creature to have a nature that will then automatically develop an evil controlling inclination independent of God's ultimate causality? Where does such a nature come from? What is the source of the evil in it that causes it to develop a sinful strongest inclination or motive and then act upon it? Doesn't this account of human nature introduce an element of creaturely autonomy not allowed in traditional Calvinism?

To be specific, what flaw in Adam's nature made it inevitable that if he were placed in certain circumstances (namely, the garden of Eden with the serpent, etc.), he would sin? And where did that flaw come from if not from God? Ware's explanation seems to introduce into human existence a flawed nature given by God *or* a degree of autonomy from God not consistent with Ware's own high Calvinist view of sovereignty.

Second, and perhaps more obvious, how does this account of God's sovereignty over evil really get God off the hook, so to speak? After all, God is still the one manipulating the decisions and actions that occur. For example, according to Ware, God knew Adam so well that he knew he would develop an evil controlling motive and then sin if placed in the garden with the serpent and the tree. In what human experience would such a manipulative, controlling person not be at least equally guilty with the person who sinned (or committed a crime)? Ware offers a couple of illustrations of such experience, but they fail at crucial points. For example, he asks his readers to imagine a police sting operation in which the police know for sure that a certain criminal will break the law if drawn into a certain situation.

Such a scenario is not difficult to imagine; any viewer of the television show *Dateline* has seen it many times in the show's series *To Catch a Predator.* There vice officers (or persons being guided by them) use computer chat rooms to lure sexual predators to a house to have sex with a minor. When the predators show up, the police are there to greet and handcuff them. The police, of course, are innocent even though they have manipulated the predator into attempting to commit a crime. Ware offers such an example (without being that specific). But does it work? Is this really an analogy to God's use of middle knowledge to control evil in his view of God's sovereignty?

I submit it doesn't work. Here's why. First, the police who lure the predators had nothing to do with their becoming sexual perverts. They are not the persons' creators and they are not the sovereign rulers of the predators' universe. Here there is genuine autonomy; the predators are in no way dependent on the police for their existence or their natures. Ware seems to forget for the moment that, according to Calvinism, to which he fully subscribes, God is the creator of everything, including every nature. Calvinism radically rejects creaturely autonomy. He seems to think it compatible with Calvinism to say that a certain nature inclined toward evil can exist without God being its source. (Only libertarian free will can really explain how a good nature turns bad without God being responsible for that. But Ware's Calvinism rejects libertarian free will.)

Second, and closely related to the first objection, for the analogy to work, you would have to imagine the police not only luring an unknown person met online to a house. You would have to imagine the police also setting up the person to go online seeking a minor with whom to have sex. And you would have to keep going backward to keep the analogy between God and the police working. The police would have to somehow manipulate the potential predator to have abnormal thoughts, feelings, and desires. After all, Ware doesn't believe that God simply "finds" a person such as Adam and then uses his already independently existing twisted nature that will inevitably emerge as a rebellious inclination. God is Adam's Creator; everything about Adam is God's creation. To say otherwise is to introduce an element of creaturely autonomy ruled out by Calvinism's strong account of God's sovereignty.

Third, in a police sting such as *To Catch a Predator*, the police *never actually allow the predator to harm someone.* They only allow them to go so far in that direction. If the police, or the television show's agents under the watchful eye of the police, ever actually allowed the person to harm a minor, they would be liable for criminal charges themselves.

The main objection to Ware's use of middle knowledge as a tool to explain God's sovereignty over evil is that it makes God a master manipulator who renders sin and evil certain. In his view, Adam was placed in a precarious situation where God knew for sure he would fall. It doesn't matter whether he fell voluntarily or not; he would not have fallen had God not placed him in that specific situation *for the purpose of assuring that he sins.*

No matter how adamantly he avers otherwise, Ware still makes God the author of sin and evil. Even if he could somehow explain to our satisfaction how, in a purely legal sense, God was not responsible for the actual sin and Adam alone was (which I doubt is possible), there would still be the problem of God's intentionality in rendering the sin certain. Why would a good God, a God of perfect love, want to render sin certain even in such an indirect (but manipulative) manner? The explanation that God's intention is good in rendering evil certain simply doesn't convince for reasons already explained, especially when eternal suffering in hell awaits those God manipulated to sin.

In sum, then, many of the standard defenses of Calvinism, when probed deeply, reveal disturbing reliance on notions of God's sovereignty that make him the ultimate author of sin and evil. In spite of their intentions, they do not succeed in getting God off the hook, so to speak, for evil. That is, they do not rescue God's reputation from the corrosive effects of divine determinism.

APPENDIX 2

RESPONSES TO CALVINIST CLAIMS

1. Any other view of God's sovereignty than Calvinism diminishes the glory of God; only "the doctrines of grace" fully honor and uphold God's glory.

It all depends on what "God's glory" means. If it means power, then perhaps this is correct. But power isn't glorious except when guided by goodness and love. Hitler was powerful but obviously not glorious. Jesus Christ revealed God as "our Father" and therefore as good and loving. In fact, high Calvinism (TULIP), wrongly labeled "the doctrines of grace" by Calvinists, diminishes God's glory by depicting him as malicious and arbitrary. Furthermore, if Calvinism is correct, nothing can "diminish the glory of God" because God foreordained everything for his glory.

2. Non-Calvinist theologies of salvation, such as Arminianism, make salvation dependent on good works because the sinner's decision to accept Christ is made the decisive factor in his or her salvation.

It seems more the case that Calvinism makes salvation dependent on good works or something good about persons elected to salvation, or else how does God choose them out of the mass of people destined for hell? It's either something God sees in them, or else God's choice of them is arbitrary and capricious. Furthermore, Arminian theology does not make salvation dependent on good works; all the "work" of salvation is God's. The sinner is enabled to repent and believe by God's prevenient grace and the bare decision to accept God's salvation is not a good work; it is simply accepting the gift of grace. In no case is accepting a gift considered "the decisive factor" in its being possessed.

3. Only Calvinism can explain how God saw to it that Christ would die his atoning death on the cross. Unless God foreordained that certain sinful men would crucify him, God could not have assured it.

This is wholly unnecessary to suppose. Surely God in his wisdom and power can assure that a certain event happen without manipulating certain people to sin. Yes, God foreordained the cross of Christ, but he did not cause certain men (or "see to it" that they would) to sin. One alternative is that, at the right time, Jesus Christ rode into Jerusalem in the "triumphal entry," knowing it would provoke his crucifixion. There was no need to manipulate certain individuals to sin.

4. Unless Calvinism is true, we cannot trust the Bible to be without error. Only if God overrode the author's free will can the Bible be God's Word.

Neither Arminianism nor other non-Calvinist Christian theologies say that God never overrides a person's free will. What they say is that God never foreordains or renders certain sin or the choice to accept God grace. God puts pressure on people to do good, including to receive Christ, but never influences to evil or overrides free will in the matter of salvation.

5. Only Calvinism can account for God's sovereignty over nature and history; unless God foreordains and controls every event, down to the smallest puff of existence and down to every thought and intention of the mind and heart, God cannot be sovereign.

This is not what "sovereignty" means in any human context. A human sovereign is in charge but not in control of what goes on in his or her realm. God can steer the course of nature and history toward his intended goal and assure that they reach it without controlling everything. God is like the master chess player who knows how to respond to every move his opponent makes. There is no danger of God's ultimate will not being done. In fact, Calvinism cannot explain the Lord's Prayer that teaches us to pray, "Your will be done on earth as it is in heaven," which implies that God's will is not already being done on earth. According to Calvinism, it is!

6. Only Calvinism can explain passages such as Romans 9, which says that God shows mercy to whom he will show mercy.

Taken out of the context of the whole book of Romans, chapter 9 can seem to pose a problem for belief in free will. However, the Calvinist interpretation, that it teaches God's unconditional and even arbitrary choice of individuals to save and other individuals to damn was never heard of before St. Augustine in the fifth century. All the Greek church fathers interpreted it differently. A perfectly sound alternative interpretation says that Romans 9 is not referring to individuals or personal salvation but to groups and to service. God is sovereign in choosing Israel and then the Gentile church to play their respective roles in his plan of redemption.

7. Reformed theology, Calvinism, is the only solid foundation for conservative, biblical Christian theology. All other approaches, such as Arminianism, a man-centered theology, inevitably lead to liberal theology.

Arminianism is not a "man-centered theology" but a God-centered theology. It is driven entirely and exclusively by a vision of God's unconditional goodness and love. The one main reason Arminians and other non-Calvinists believe in free will is to preserve and protect God's goodness so as not to make him the author of sin and evil. Calvinism makes it difficult to recognize the difference between God and the devil except that the devil wants everyone to go to hell and God wants many to go to hell. Arminian theology does not lead into liberal theology. If anything, Calvinism does that. Friedrich Schleiermacher, the father of modern liberal theology, was a Calvinist! He never even considered Arminianism; he moved right from conservative, high Calvinism to universalism while holding onto God's meticulous providence even over evil. Most of the nineteenth-century liberal theologians were former Calvinists who came to abhor its vision of God and developed liberal theology without any help from classical Arminianism. Classical Arminianism has been preserved by many fundamentalists, holiness and Pentecostal Christians, and Free Will Baptists, none of whom can be considered liberal.

8. God has a right to do whatever he wants to with his creatures and especially with sinners who all deserve damnation. His goodness is shown in his merciful rescue of some sinners; he owes nothing to anyone. Those he passes over deserve hell.

While it may be true that everyone deserves hell, although even many Calvinists hesitate to say that about children, God is a God of love who genuinely desires all people to be saved, as the New Testament clearly testifies in 1 Timothy 2:4: "who wants all people to be saved and to come to a knowledge of the truth." There is no way to get around the fact that "all people" means every single person without exception. The issue is not fairness but love. A God who could save everyone because he always saves unconditionally but chooses only some would not be a good or loving God. He would certainly not be the God of 1 Timothy 2:4 and similar passages.

9. If God foreknows everything that will happen in the world he is going to create, including the fall and all its consequences, that is the same as foreordaining all of it, including sin and evil.

God foreknows because something is going to happen; he does not foreknow because he foreordains. In other words, according to Scripture, tradition, and reason, Adam's sin is what caused God to foreknow it. God did not envision Adam's sin and then decide to create the world in which Adam would sin. The difference lies in God's intentionality. The Calvinist must believe God intended Adam to sin and rendered it certain, making God the author of sin. Arminians and other non-Calvinists believe God never intended for Adam to sin even though he knew it would happen. It was not his will. Calvinism makes it God's will.

10. Non-Calvinist theologies undermine assurance and confidence of salvation because they make it dependent on human decisions. Only Calvinism provides comfort and assurance because it says everything is God's, including the gifts of repentance and faith.

Actually, Calvinism undermines comfort and assurance by making God arbitrary and morally ambiguous. A God who would predestine many people to hell when he could save them because his choice to save is always unconditional is untrustworthy. Also, how can people know for sure of their election? Many Calvinists have doubted their election. Calvinists talk about "signs of grace" that prove someone is elect, but what if a person is not sure he or she is displaying enough signs of grace? Calvinism no more provides comfort and assurance than Arminianism and other non-Calvinist theologies that assure people they are saved if they trust in Christ alone.

11. Non-Calvinist theologies such as Arminianism believe in something that is impossible: libertarian free will—belief that free decisions and actions simply come from nowhere. Calvinism and some other theologies, as well as many philosophers, know that "free will" simply means doing what you want to do and people are always controlled by their strongest motives, so being able to do otherwise—libertarian free will—is an illusion.

If "free will" only means doing what you want to do even though you couldn't do otherwise, how is anyone responsible for what they do? If a murderer, for example, could not have done otherwise than murder, then a judge or jury should find him not guilty—perhaps by reason of insanity. Moral responsibility, accountability, and guilt depend on ability to do otherwise—libertarian freedom. The Calvinist view of "free will" isn't really free will at all.

Moreover, if there is no such thing as libertarian free will, then God doesn't have it either, and that makes God's creation of the world necessary and not freely chosen, in which case it is not by grace but by necessity. The Calvinist view of "free will" robs both God and people of ability to do otherwise than they do and therefore renders their decisions and actions neither praiseworthy nor blameworthy. What is simply is, and what will be, will be. That goes contrary to all our instincts and intuitions about moral responsibility and God's transcendent freedom to create or not to create.

NOTES

Chapter One: Introduction: Why This Book Now?

1. Collin Hansen, *Young, Restless, Reformed: A Journalist's Journey with the New Calvinists* (Wheaton, IL: Crossway, 2008).

2. John Piper, *Desiring God: Confessions of a Christian Hedonist* (Portland, OR: Multnomah, 1986).

3. Hansen, *Young, Restless, Reformed*, 15.

4. Ibid., 21.

5. Ibid., 20–21. What exactly constitutes "feel good theology" is not always easy to tell, but many of the new Calvinists (and others, including this non-Calvinist author!) see it manifested in popular preaching and publishing that touts Christianity as the path to self-actualization and success if not material prosperity.

6. See Christian Smith and Melinda Lundquist Denton, "Summary Interpretation: Therapeutic Deism," in *Soul Searching: The Religious and Spiritual Lives of American Teenagers* (New York: Oxford Univ. Press, 2005), 102–71.

7. Loraine Boettner, *The Reformed Doctrine of Predestination* (Grand Rapids: Eerdmans, 1948).

8. Ibid., 7.

9. Ibid., 248.

10. R. C. Sproul, *What Is Reformed Theology?* (Grand Rapids: Baker, 1987); idem, *Chosen by God* (Wheaton, IL: Tyndale, 1988).

11. Michael Horton, *Christless Christianity: The Alternative Gospel of the American Church* (Grand Rapids: Baker, 2008).

12. Robert W. Jenson, *America's Theologian: A Recommendation of Jonathan Edwards* (New York and Oxford: Oxford Univ. Press, 1988).

13. My knowledge of this episode and development in Piper's career comes from a lengthy conversation with one of Piper's seminary professors, Lewis Smedes (1921–2002). Smedes was himself something of a Calvinist, but late in life he turned away from high Calvinism (the TULIP system) and confessed to me that he embraced open theism—the view that God limits himself so as not even to know the future exhaustively and infallibly. However, as one of Piper's mentors at Fuller Seminary years earlier, Smedes recalled recommending that Piper take on Edwards and immerse himself in his theology. His message to me was that, in his opinion, Piper took the assignment too seriously!

14. J. Todd Billings, "Calvin's Comeback? The Irresistible Reformer," *Christian Century* (December 1, 2009), 22–25.

15. John Piper, "Why I Do Not Say, 'God Did Not Cause the Calamity, but He Can Use It for Good.'" www.desiringgod.org/ResourceLibrary/TasteAndSee/ByDate/2001/1181_Why_I_Do_Not_Say_God_Did_Not_Cause_the_Calamity_but_He_Can_Use_It_for_Good/.

16. I have written an entire book about Arminian theology, a tradition often misrepresented by Calvinist critics as man-centered (among other things): *Arminian Theology: Myths and Realities* (Downers Grove, IL: InterVarsity Press, 2006). There I prove that

most of the criticisms of non-Calvinist evangelical theology by Calvinists (and perhaps some others) are false.

17. Hansen, *Young, Restless, Reformed*, 19.

18. Throughout this book I will use the phrase "rendered certain" to describe what high Calvinists believe about God's role in bringing about sin and evil. Few high Calvinists will say that God caused the Holocaust, but they will say God foreordained it and (to use John Piper's terminology) saw to it that it would happen. "Rendered certain" is a way of avoiding language of causation because Calvinists are uncomfortable with that, while at the same time expressing what must be believed within a high Calvinist view of providence.

Chapter Two: Whose Calvinism? Which Reformed Theology?

1. See, for example, Caspar Nervig, *Christian Truth and Religious Delusions* (Minneapolis, MN: Augsburg, 1941). Nervig's book was for years a widely used text by Lutherans on the pros and cons of denominations; it lists and describes under "The Reformed Churches" churches named Reformed, Presbyterian, Congregational, Protestant Episcopal (and its offshoots), Methodist, and Baptists. Many conservative Reformed and Calvinist people would be shocked to find Methodists and Baptists lumped into their category of Reformed. Methodists, for example, following John Wesley, reject the TULIP system.

2. www.warc.ch.

3. www.warc.ch/who/mc.html

4. Presumably this will continue to be the case with the WCRC although, at the time this is being written, its website does not offer such a list of criteria. The WCRC's website is www.wcrc.ch/.

5. Alan P. F. Sell, *The Great Debate: Calvinism, Arminianism, and Salvation* (Grand Rapids: Baker, 1982), 21.

6. Ibid., 23.

7. Ibid., 22.

8. Ibid., 23.

9. Alan P. F. Sell, *Doctrine and Devotion* (New York: Ragged Edge Press, 2000). The three volumes are *God our Father, Christ our Savior,* and *The Spirit Our Life.*

10. See my *Arminian Theology: Myths and Realities.* This is a theme that runs throughout the book. The issue is so-called Pelagianism, the theology condemned by both Catholics and Protestants that human persons initiate and contribute to their own salvation. I have demonstrated conclusively that classical Arminian theology has nothing in common with Pelagianism. As for Sell's affinities with Arminianism, consider this from *The Spirit Our Life*, 27: "It almost seems as if salvation is God's doing and ours: he regenerates, we have faith. Is salvation a co-operative effort in which God plays his part and we play ours? Yes—except that we can only play our part as God enables us."

11. See especially Berkhof's magisterial one-volume systematic theology *Christian Faith: An Introduction to the Study of the Faith* (Grand Rapids: Eerdmans, 1991), where he lays out a radically revised Reformed theology that virtually any Arminian could embrace.

12. James Daane, *The Freedom of God: A Study of Election and Pulpit* (Grand Rapids: Eerdmans, 1973).

13. Adrio König, *Here Am I! A Believer's Reflection on God* (Grand Rapids: Eerdmans, 1982).

14. Donald K. McKim, *The Encyclopedia of the Reformed Faith* (Louisville, KY: Westminster John Knox, 1992); idem, *The Westminster Handbook to Reformed Theology* (Louisville, KY: Westminster John Knox, 2001); idem, *Introducing the Reformed Faith* (Louisville, KY: Westminster John Knox, 2001).

15. McKim, *Introducing the Reformed Faith*, xiii.

16. Ibid., xv.
17. Ibid., 2.
18. Ibid.
19. Ibid., 7.
20. Ibid., 8.
21. Ibid., 7.
22. Ibid., 51–52.
23. Ibid., 52.
24. Ibid., 124.
25. Ibid., 183.
26. R. C. Sproul, *What Is Reformed Theology? Understanding the Basics* (Grand Rapids: Baker, 1997), 27.
27. Ibid., 141.
28. Richard J. Mouw, *Calvinism in the Las Vegas Airport* (Grand Rapids: Zondervan, 2004).
29. Ibid., 14.
30. Ibid., 15.
31. Ibid., 39–40.

Chapter Three: Mere Calvinism: The Tulip System

1. Boettner, *The Reformed Doctrine of Predestination*, 23.
2. Ibid., 24.
3. John Calvin, *Institutes of the Christian Religion*, Library of Christian Classics 20–21; ed. John T. McNiell; trans. Ford Lewis Battles (Philadelphia: Westminster, 1959), 1.16.9 (p. 210).
4. Boettner, *The Reformed Doctrine of Predestination*, 16.
5. Ibid., 14.
6. Calvin, *Institutes*, 1.18.1 (pp. 228–29).
7. Edwin H. Palmer, *The Five Points of Calvinism* (Grand Rapids: Baker, 1972).
8. David N. Steele and Curtis C. Thomas, *The Five Points of Calvinism: Defined, Defended and Documented* (Nutley, NJ: Presbyterian and Reformed, 1963).
9. H. Henry Meeter, *The Basic Ideas of Calvinism* (Grand Rapids: Baker, 1990).
10. Boettner, *The Reformed Doctrine of Predestination*, 59.
11. Ibid., 63.
12. Ibid., 62. This is a quote from the Westminster Confession of Faith.
13. Boettner, *The Reformed Doctrine of Predestination*, 72.
14. Ibid., 63.
15. Ibid., 72. I have contested this in *Arminian Theology: Myths and Realities*, 137–57.
16. Calvin, *Institutes*, 2.1.9 (p. 253).
17. Sproul, *What Is Reformed Theology?* 120.
18. Boettner, *The Reformed Doctrine of Predestination*, 77.
19. Sproul, *What Is Reformed Theology?* 123.
20. Calvin, *Institutes* 2.2.13–14 (pp. 271–74).
21. Sproul, *What Is Reformed Theology?* 120.
22. Ibid., 83.
23. Boettner, *The Reformed Doctrine of Predestination*, 102.
24. Ibid., 104.
25. Ibid., 105.
26. Calvin, *Institutes* 3.21.7 (p. 937).
27. Ibid., 3.27.1 (p. 947).
28. Ibid., 3.28.7 (p. 955). The actual phrase Calvin used in the original was "decretum horribile." It is translated by Battles as "the decree is dreadful indeed."
29. Sproul, *Chosen by God*, 137.

30. Ibid., 141.
31. Ibid., 142.
32. Ibid., 142–43.
33. Sproul, *Chosen by God*, 143.
34. John Piper, *The Pleasures of God* (Portland, OR: Multnomah, 1991), 132.
35. Ibid., 144.
36. Here I would like to note that some Lutherans believe in unconditional election but most do *not* believe in a decree of reprobation. This is what consistent Calvinists, anyway, find logically impossible. So, not only Calvinists believe in unconditional election, but apparently only Calvinists believe in a decree of reprobation.
37. Boettner, *The Reformed Doctrine of Predestination*, 98–101.
38. Ibid., 117.
39. Ibid., 152.
40. Some Calvinists are fond of saying that non-Calvinist views of the atonement such as universal atonement (that God intended the benefits of the cross for everyone) diminish the power and glory of the cross by making it only the creation of the *possibility* of salvation rather than the actual accomplishment of salvation. John Piper has said publicly that the cross actually accomplished the salvation of the elect. ("For Whom Did Christ Die? & What Did Christ Actually Achieve on the Cross for Those for Whom He Died?"): www.monergism.com/thethreshold/articles/piper/piper_atonement.html 2/26/2009.) The problem with this is fairly obvious and will be dealt with later. Just to hint at it: *If Christ's death actually accomplished salvation for someone, then that person would not have to repent and believe to be saved and even Calvinists believe actual salvation even of the elect "happens" not on the cross but when God imparts faith to that person.*
41. Boettner, *The Reformed Doctrine of Predestination*, 157.
42. Piper, "For Whom Did Christ Die?" Again, this raises some difficulties. Not all Calvinists will say that the cross actually saves anyone until God creates faith in the heart of the elect person and imputes to him or her the saving benefit of Christ's cross. Piper seems to be confused on this point. Or perhaps not. However, his words are confusing.
43. Sproul, *What Is Reformed Theology?* 177.
44. Boettner, *The Reformed Doctrine of Predestination*, 160.
45. Piper, "For Whom Did Christ Die?"
46. Piper, *The Pleasures of God*, 148.
47. Ibid., 144–46.
48. Boettner, *The Reformed Doctrine of Predestination*, 163.
49. Sproul, *Chosen by God*, 123.
50. Boettner, *The Reformed Doctrine of Predestination*, 177.
51. Ibid., 178.
52. Calvin, *Institutes* 3.22.7 (p. 941).
53. Sproul, *What Is Reformed Theology?*, 188.
54. Ibid., 191.
55. Ibid.
56. See "Declaration of the Sentiments of Arminius" in *The Works of James Arminius* (trans., James Nichols; Grand Rapids: Baker, 1996), 1:667.
57. Sproul, *Chosen by God*, 173.
58. Augustus Hopkins Strong, *Systematic Theology* (Valley Forge, PA: Judson, 1907), 772.
59. Millard Erickson, *Christian Theology* (Grand Rapids: Baker, 1984), 2:835.
60. Daane, *The Freedom of God*, 138.
61. Boettner, *The Reformed Doctrine of Predestination*, 129.
62. Sproul, *Chosen by God*, 142–43.
63. Ibid., 27.
64. Ibid., 31.
65. Ibid.

66. Paul Helm, *The Providence of God* (Downers Grove, IL: InterVarsity Press, 1994), 22.
67. Ibid., 172.
68. Vincent Cheung, "The Author of Sin." www.vincentcheung.com/2005/05/31/the-author-of-sin/.
69. Ibid.
70. "Interview with John Frame on the problem of evil." http://thegospelcoalition.org/blogs/justintaylor/2008/08/20/interview-with-john-frame-on-problem-of/.
71. This is in the earlier-mentioned sermon "Why I Do Not Say, 'God Did Not Cause the Calamity'...."
72. John Piper, "God's God-centeredness," sermon preached at Passion conference (Nashville, TN; Jan. 2–5, 2005).
73. Herman Hoeksema, *Reformed Dogmatics* (Jenison, MI: Reformed Free Publishing Association, repr. 1985).
74. Anthony Hoekema, *Saved by Grace* (Grand Rapids: Eerdmans, 1989), 72.
75. Ibid., 73.
76. Ibid.
77. Daane, *The Freedom of God*, 24.
78. Konig, *Here Am I!* 198–99.
79. I believe no statistical analysis is needed because the phenomenon is universally agreed on by those who teach biblical and theological studies in Christian colleges and universities. Few students know any hymns, and hymns were one way the Christian faith was passed on from generation to generation. Contemporary Christian music is notoriously shallow when it comes to doctrine and theology (with some exceptions, of course). I have encountered students raised in Christian homes and churches and even pastors' and missionaries' kids who claimed they never heard of the resurrection of the body as a Christian belief. Few can give even a cursory expression of the Trinity or deity and humanity of Jesus Christ beyond folk religious slogans such as Jesus was "God in human skin"—a popular expression of the ancient heresy of Apollinarianism.
80. The title of his book published in 2008 by Baker.
81. Piper, "For Whom Did Christ Die?"
82. When I contacted Piper about this quote, he pointed out that in the sermon he did not say Arminians *do* say this about the atonement and salvation but only that they *must* say this. I will leave it to readers to decide what most of his listeners and readers would think he meant. I know some who thought he meant this is actually Arminian theology. In my opinion Piper's statement here and many Calvinists' similar statements about Arminianism violate a basic rule of civil debate that should always guide not only Christians but all serious people: always describe your opponents' view as they describe it, and if you are going to accuse them of leading to a conclusion they do not actually embrace, say they do not actually embrace it. It seems to me that in this sermon Piper does what many Calvinists do with Arminianism—describe it most ungenerously by attributing to it conclusions considered logically necessary but not actually embraced by its adherents. I am not opposed to arguing against a theology because it necessarily leads somewhere considered bad. That is how I will attack Calvinism. But I am opposed to attributing to adherents of a theology certain beliefs they explicitly reject. That's unfair at best and dishonest at worst.
83. Two important expositions of Arminian theology that are also readable are Thomas Oden, *The Transforming Power of Grace* (Nashville, TN: Abingdon, 1993), and Robert E. Picirilli, *Grace, Faith, Free Will* (Nashville, TN: Randall, 2002).
84. This equation can be found on many pages of Sproul's published works, such as *What Is Reformed Theology?* 145, 149. Sproul does acknowledge Arminian belief in prevenient grace but then misrepresents the Arminian view when he asks of Arminians: "If the flesh can, by itself, incline itself to grace, where is the need of grace?" (188). No true Arminian says that the flesh (natural, fallen human being) can incline itself to grace;

such an inclination *always* comes from the Holy Spirit. The difference between this and Calvinism is that according to Arminianism, this work of the Holy Spirit called prevenient grace is resistible (because God chooses to allow it to be resisted!).

85. See Berkouwer's multivolume set with the overarching series title Studies in Dogmatics, published by Eerdmans.

Chapter Four: Yes to God's Sovereignty; No to Divine Determinism

1. Ulrich Zwingli, *On Providence and Other Essays*, eds. Samuel Jackson and William John Hinke (Durham, NC: Labyrinth, 1983), 137.

2. Ibid., 157.

3. Calvin, *Institutes* 1.16.9 (pp. 208–9).

4. Ibid., 1.16.7 (p. 206).

5. Ibid., 1.18.2 (p. 232).

6. Jonathan Edwards, *The Great Christian Doctrine of Original Sin*, ed. Clyde A. Holbrook (New Haven, CT: Yale Univ. Press, 1970), 402.

7. Jonathan Edwards, *Freedom of the Will*, in *The Works of Jonathan Edwards* (New Haven, CT: Yale Univ. Press, 1957), 1:431.

8. Ibid., 434.

9. Ibid., 395.

10. Ibid., 377.

11. Ibid., 380.

12. See John W. Cooper, *Panentheism: The Other God of the Philosophers* (Grand Rapids: Baker, 2006). Cooper explains well why panentheism is considered heretical by orthodox doctrinal standards and argues that Edwards' view of the God-world relation is panentheistic (77).

13. Edwards, *Original Sin*, 384.

14. Ibid., 393.

15. Edwards, *Freedom of the Will*, 411–12.

16. Ibid., 399.

17. Sproul, *Chosen by God*, 59.

18. Sproul, *What Is Reformed Theology?* 191.

19. See the *Stanford Encyclopedia of Philosophy* (http://plato.stanford.edu/).

20. Sproul, *Chosen by God*, 25. The passage of the Westminster Confession of Faith referred to by Sproul as requiring agreement in order not to be a "convinced atheist" is that "God from all eternity, did, by the most wise and holy counsel of His own will, freely, and unchangeably ordain whatsoever comes to pass."

21. Sproul, *What Is Reformed Theology?* 27.

22. Sproul, *Chosen by God*, 14–15.

23. Sproul, *What Is Reformed Theology?* 141.

24. Ibid., 172.

25. Ibid.

26. Ibid.

27. Ibid., 173.

28. Ibid.

29. Sproul, *Chosen by God*, 97.

30. Ibid., 98.

31. Sproul, *What Is Reformed Theology?* 133.

32. Ibid., 132.

33. Boettner, *The Reformed Doctrine of Predestination*, 24.

34. Ibid., 30.

35. Ibid., 38.

36. Helm, *The Providence of God*, 22.

37. Ibid., 104.

38. Ibid., 133.
39. Ibid., 171.
40. Ibid., 167.
41. John Piper, "Are There Two Wills in God," in *Still Sovereign: Contemporary Perspectives on Election, Foreknowledge, and Grace*, eds., Thomas R. Schreiner and Bruce Ware (Grand Rapids: Baker, 2000), 123.
42. Ibid., 109.
43. Boettner, *The Reformed Doctrine of Predestination*, 251.
44. Ibid., 243.
45. Ibid., 229.
46. Craig R. Brown, *The Five Dilemmas of Calvinism* (Orlando, FL: Ligonier, 2007), 45–58.
47. Sproul, *What Is Reformed Theology?* 40.
48. See, for example, Brown, *The Five Dilemmas of Calvinism*, 43–44.
49. This is not meant to be an exhaustive explanation of the existence of sin and evil in God's world; here I am only addressing the two biblical stories to which Calvinists so often point to prove their view of God's sovereignty even in the acts of sinful people. I affirm, with most non-Calvinists, that God also often simply allows sin in order to preserve the free will of people because God does not want to have robots but morally free agents who either choose freely to love and serve him or not.
50. Jerry Walls, "The Free Will Defense, Calvinism, Wesley, and the Goodness of God," *Christian Scholar's Review* 13/1 (1983): 29.
51. Ibid., 32.
52. David Bentley Hart, *The Doors of the Sea: Where Was God in the Tsunami?* (Grand Rapids: Eerdmans, 2005).
53. Ibid., 89.
54. Ibid., 91.
55. Ibid., 99.
56. Jerry Walls and Joseph Dongell, *Why I Am Not a Calvinist* (Downers Grove, IL: InterVarsity Press, 2004), 125.
57. Ibid., 126.
58. Ibid.
59. Ibid., 98–99.
60. Ibid., 129.
61. Ibid., 130.
62. Ibid., 131.
63. Ibid., 132.
64. Ibid., 133.
65. John Piper, *The Hidden Smile of God* (Wheaton, IL: Crossway, 2001).
66. Ibid., 67–69.
67. Ibid., 89.
68. Ibid., 102.
69. Ibid., 108.
70. Hart, *The Doors of the Sea*, 99.
71. Ibid., 100.
72. Ibid.
73. Calvin, *Institutes* 1.16.2 (pp. 198–99).
74. Hart, *The Doors of the Sea*, 101.
75. Piper, *The Hidden Smile of God*, 8.
76. Daane, *The Freedom of God*, 81. Of course, Calvinists often point to passages of Scripture that seem to portray God as monstrous. I cited some of these Old Testament passages near the beginning of this book. Daane, and most critics of Calvinism, believe the character of God is perfectly revealed in Jesus Christ and that we must interpret

other descriptions of God in that light. Jesus was genuinely grieved over sin and evil and clearly sought to alleviate suffering. Calvinists often accuse non-Calvinists of not taking Scripture seriously enough. What they mean is that they take Old Testament "texts of terror" more seriously than they take Jesus! At least that is how most non-Calvinists see it.

77. Boettner, *The Reformed Doctrine of Predestination*, 24.

78. Helm, *The Providence of God*, 138.

79. Sproul, *What Is Reformed Theology?* 37.

80. Boettner, *The Reformed Doctrine of Predestination*, 234.

81. John E. Smith, "God the Author of Sin," introduction to Edwards' *The Great Christian Doctrine of Original Sin*, 64.

82. Edwards, *Freedom of the Will*, 377.

83. Bruce A. Little, "Evil and God's Sovereignty," in *Whosoever Will: A Biblical-Theological Critique of Five-Point Calvinism*, eds. David L. Allen and Steve W. Lemke (Nashville, TN: Broadman & Holman, 2010), 283.

84. Little, "Evil and God's Sovereignty," 290.

85. Jeremy A. Evans, "Reflections on Determinism and Human Freedom," *Whosoever Will*, 266.

86. Calvin, *Institutes* 1.17.5 (p. 216).

87. Ibid., p. 217.

88. Ibid.

89. Remember the earlier quote from the *Institutes* that God "compels the wicked to obedience."

90. Edwards, *Freedom of the Will*, 404.

91. Ibid.

92. Ibid., 411–12.

93. Edwards, *Original Sin*, 384.

94. Smith, "God the Author of Sin," 46.

95. Ibid., 62

96. Ibid., 52.

97. Boettner, *The Reformed Doctrine of Predestination*, 209.

98. Ibid., 234.

99. Ibid., 235.

100. Helm, *The Providence of God*, 170–71.

101. Ibid., 171.

102. Evans, "Reflections on Determinism and Human Freedom," 263.

103. One of the clearest and least complicated expressions of this view is Piper's talk "The Sovereignty of God and Human Responsibility," at www.youtube.com: "Commending Christ Q & A Desiring God 2009 Conference for Pastors February 4, 2009."

104. Sproul, *Chosen by God*, 41.

105. William G. MacDonald, "The Biblical Doctrine of Election," in *The Grace of God, the Will of Man: A Case for Arminianism*, ed., Clark H. Pinnock (Grand Rapids: Zondervan, 1989), 213.

106. Piper, *The Pleasures of God*, 146.

107. Stanley J. Grenz, *Theology for the Community of God* (Nashville, TN: Broadman & Holman, 1994), 140.

108. E. Frank Tupper, *A Scandalous Providence: The Jesus Story of the Compassion of God* (Macon, GA: Mercer Univ. Press, 1995), 334–35.

109. Hendrikus Berkhof, *The Christian Faith: An Introduction to the Study of the Faith* (Grand Rapids: Eerdmans, 1991), 146.

110. Frank E. Tupper, *A Scandalous Providence*; Gregory A. Boyd, *Is God to Blame?* (Downers Grove, IL: InterVarsity Press, 2003); Jack Cottrell, *What the Bible Says about God the Ruler* (Eugene, OR: Wipf & Stock, 2001).

111. Hart, *The Doors of the Sea*, 97.

Chapter Five: Yes to Election; No to Double Predestination

1. Calvin, *Institutes* 3.24.17 (p. 985).
2. Boettner, *The Reformed Doctrine of Predestination*, 104.
3. Ibid.
4. Ibid., 209.
5. Ibid., 214.
6. Ibid., 215, 217.
7. Ibid., 125.
8. Ibid., 222.
9. Ibid., 105.
10. Ibid., 108.
11. Palmer, *The Five Points of Calvinism*, 95.
12. Ibid., 97.
13. Ibid., 101.
14. Ibid., 106.
15. Ibid.
16. Ibid., 107.
17. Ibid., 105–6.
18. Ibid., 85.
19. Ibid., 87.
20. Ibid., 109.
21. Sproul, *Chosen by God*, 141.
22. Ibid., 142.
23. Ibid.
24. Ibid., 145.
25. Ibid., 147–48.
26. Daane, *The Freedom of God*, 71.
27. Some Calvinists may object to my wording here and say that while "election" is unconditional, "salvation" is not. In other words, according to their theology, God chooses people to save without regard to anything about them, but he saves them only on the condition of their repentance and faith (conversion). However, it seems right and fair to say that salvation itself is also unconditional because God provides even repentance and faith to the elect before and apart from any decisions or actions they make. In my opinion, the distinction between election *to* salvation as unconditional and salvation *itself* as conditional is a distinction without a difference.
28. Helm, *The Providence of God*, 167. Here it would be possible and right to get into the whole "nominalism" versus "realism" debate about universals such as "goodness" and about whether God has an eternal nature that determines his character or simply chooses to do things, making them automatically good because God chooses them. The vast majority of orthodox Christians down through the centuries have rejected nominalism for good reasons. Luther was an exception, perhaps Zwingli also. However, most Calvinists clearly do not want to be nominalists; they believe God has an eternal, immutable nature and character and acts in accordance with it. So to say that "whatever God does is automatically good, loving, and just simply because God does it" is to fall back into nominalism and its attendant "hidden God" idea, which makes God unknowable and untrustworthy and makes talk of God's moral attributes meaningless.
29. Steele and Thomas, *The Five Points of Calvinism*, 31.
30. Sometimes Calvin *sounds* like a nominalist—someone who denies that God has a nature that guides or controls what he does. This comes across whenever he says that God can do whatever he wants, such that his actions do not need to be consistent with virtues such as goodness, love, or justice. At other times, however, Calvin *sounds* like a realist—someone who believes God has a nature—in which case his objections that God

cannot be accused of being unjust (or unloving) because whatever he does is automatically just (or loving) ring hollow.

31. Calvin, *Institutes* 3.24.17 (p. 985).

32. Ibid., 3.24.12 (p. 979).

33. Ibid.

34. Ibid., 3.24.12 (p. 978).

35. Ibid.

36. Ibid., 3.22.11 (p. 947).

37. Ibid., 3.23.2 (p. 949).

38. Ibid.

39. Jonathan Edwards, "The Justice of God in the Damnation of Sinners," 2.3, in *Jonathan Edwards: Representative Selections, with Introduction, Bibliography, and Notes*, rev. ed., Clarence H. Faust and Thomas H. Johnson, eds. (New York: Hill and Wang, 1962), 119.

40. Boettner, *The Reformed Doctrine of Predestination*, 79, 117.

41. Ibid., 125.

42. Ibid., 306.

43. Ibid., 97.

44. Ibid.

45. Ibid., 83.

46. Jonathan Edwards, "Sinners in the Hands of an Angry God," in *Jonathan Edwards: Representative Selections*, 156.

47. Boettner, *The Reformed Doctrine of Predestination*, 293.

48. Ibid., 295.

49. Ibid.

50. Sproul, *Chosen by God*, 31.

51. Ibid.

52. Ibid., 33.

53. In fact, in *What Is Reformed Theology?* 161, Sproul as much as says that God hates the reprobate.

54. Sproul, *Chosen by God*, 35.

55. Ibid., 37.

56. Ibid.

57. Ibid., 197.

58. Ibid., 195.

59. Ibid., 195–96.

60. Ibid., 196.

61. Sproul, *What Is Reformed Theology?* 156.

62. Ibid., 158.

63. John Piper, "Are There Two Wills in God?" 108.

64. Ibid., 109.

65. Ibid., 108.

66. Piper, *The Pleasures of God*, 146.

67. Ibid., 137.

68. Ibid., 148.

69. Ibid., 145.

70. Ibid., 146.

71. Piper, "Are There Two Wills in God?" 128.

72. Some Calvinists, and I suspect Piper is one of them, would no doubt respond to my claims that their doctrine of election makes God arbitrary by saying that God has "consistent and holy reasons" for his decisions, reasons we cannot understand. However, this is just a phrase; it doesn't inform us of anything. Once Piper and other Calvinists rule out anything God sees in or about the elect that causes him to choose them, the only alternative left is arbitrary choice. I challenge Calvinists to say what God's "consistent

and holy reasons" for choosing one person over another might be once everything about the chosen person is ruled out as a cause of God's choice.

73. John Piper, "Are There Two Wills in God?" 107.

74. G. C. Berkouwer, *Studies in Dogmatics: Divine Election* (Grand Rapids: Eerdmans, 1960), 181.

75. Ibid., 187.

76. Ibid., 195.

77. Ibid., 198.

78. Ibid., 212.

79. Ibid., 215.

80. Ibid., 216.

81. Ibid., 238–39.

82. Daane, *The Freedom of God*, 33.

83. Ibid., 37.

84. Ibid., 39.

85. Ibid.

86. Ibid., 63.

87. Ibid., 86.

88. Ibid., 81.

89. Ibid., 67, 92.

90. Ibid., 149.

91. Ibid., 63–64.

92. Ibid., 80.

93. Ibid., 114.

94. Ibid., 150.

95. Ibid., 109.

96. Ibid., 114.

97. Ibid., 139–40.

98. John Wesley, "Free Grace," in *The Works of John Wesley*, Vol. 3, *Sermons 71–114* (Grand Rapids: Zondervan, n.d.), 547.

99. John Wesley, "Predestination Calmly Considered," in *The Works of John Wesley*, Vol. 10, *Letters, Essays, Dialogs and Addresses* (Grand Rapids: Zondervan, n.d.), 221.

100. Ibid., 227.

101. Ibid.

102. Ibid.

103. Ibid., 227–28.

104. Ibid., 229.

105. Ibid., 255.

106. Ibid., 235.

107. Ibid., 256.

108. Ibid., 237.

109. Ibid.

110. Wesley, "Free Grace," 554.

111. Ibid., 555.

112. Ibid.

113. Ibid., 556.

114. Ibid., 545.

115. Ibid.

116. Wesley, "Predestination Calmly Considered," 230.

117. Ibid., 232–33.

118. Ibid., 210.

119. Ibid., 231.

120. William Klein, *The New Chosen People* (Eugene, OR: Wipf & Stock, 2001), 257.

121. Ibid., 259.

122. Ibid., 260.
123. Ibid., 262.
124. Ibid., 260–61.
125. Ibid., 264.
126. Ibid., 265.
127. Ibid., 281–82.
128. Jack Cottrell, "The Nature of Divine Sovereignty" in *The Grace of God, The Will of Man*, ed. Clark H. Pinnock (Grand Rapids: Zondervan, 1989), 106–7.
129. Ibid., 108.
130. Ibid., 111.
131. For example, A. T. Robertson as quoted by Jerry Vines, "Sermon on John 3:16," in *Whosoever Will: A Biblical-Theological Critique of Five-Point Calvinism*, ed. David L. Allen and Steve W. Lemke (Nashville, TN: Broadman & Holman, 2010), 17.

Chapter Six: Yes to Atonement; No to Limited Atonement/Particular Redemption

1. Calvin, *Institutes* 2.16.5 (pp. 509–10).
2. Ibid., 2.16.6 (p. 511).
3. Ibid., 2.16.5 (p. 507).
4. Gustaf Aulén, *Christus Victor: An Historical Study of the Three Main Types of the Idea of the Atonement* (New York: Macmillan, 1969).
5. Calvin, *Institutes* 2.16.7 (p. 512).
6. Ibid., 2.16.4 (p. 506).
7. Boettner, *The Reformed Doctrine of Predestination*, 152.
8. Ibid., 157.
9. Ibid., 160.
10. Steele and Thomas, *The Five Points of Calvinism*, 39.
11. Ibid.
12. Ibid., 46.
13. Palmer, *The Five Points of Calvinism*, 41.
14. Ibid., 45.
15. Ibid., 53.
16. Ibid., 51.
17. Sproul, *What Is Reformed Theology?* 163.
18. Ibid., 163.
19. Ibid., 166.
20. Ibid., 169.
21. Ibid., 171.
22. Vernon C. Grounds, "God's Universal Salvific Grace," in *Grace Unlimited*, ed. Clark H. Pinnock (Minneapolis: Bethany, 1975), 27.
23. Piper, *The Pleasures of God*, 165.
24. Ibid., 165, 167.
25. Piper, "For Whom Did Christ Die?"
26. Ibid.
27. Ibid.
28. David L. Allen, "The Atonement: Limited or Universal?" in *Whosever Will*, 93.
29. R. T. Kendall, *Calvin and English Calvinism to 1649* (Oxford: Oxford Univ. Press, 1979).
30. Kevin Kennedy, "Was Calvin a 'Calvinist'? John Calvin on the extent of the atonement," in *Whosoever Will: A Biblical-Theological Critique of Five-Point Calvinism*, ed. David L. Allen and Steven W. Lemke (Nashville, TN: Broadman & Holman, 2010), 195.
31. Ibid., 198.
32. Ibid.

33. Ibid., 199–200.
34. Ibid., 200.
35. Ibid., 211.
36. Some readers may wonder about the relevance of this passage to what is sometimes called "eternal security"—the unconditional perseverance of the saints. It seems to me possible to interpret it either way—as referring to someone who is already a believer and might lose his or her salvation because of the offense of the stronger brother, *or* as referring to a person not yet a Christian (but for whom Christ died) who might be driven away by the offense.
37. Calvin, *Institutes* 3.3.19 (p. 613).
38. Ibid., 3.3.9 (p. 600).
39. Many editions of this book by John Owen (1616–1683) are available, such as: *The Death of Death in the Death of Christ*, ed. J. I. Packer (London: Banner of Truth Trust, 1963).
40. Picirilli, *Grace, Faith, Free Will*, 136.
41. For a detailed, thorough analysis of Barth's move from five-point Calvinism to universalism, see G. C. Berkouwer, *The Triumph of Grace in the Theology of Karl Barth* (Grand Rapids: Eerdmans, 1956). While Berkouwer does not accuse Barth of blatant universalism, he does indicate that universal salvation is implicit in Barth's doctrine of election. I agree with that assessment.
42. Gary L. Schultz, Jr., "Why a Genuine Universal Gospel Call Requires an Atonement That Paid for the Sins of All People," *Evangelical Quarterly* 82:2 (2010): 122.
43. Ibid., 115.
44. Athanasius, *On the Incarnation of the Word* 2.9, in *Select Writings and Letters of Athanasius, Bishop of Alexandria*, trans. Archibald Robertson, *Nicene and Post-Nicene Fathers*, second series, vol. 4 (Grand Rapids: Eerdmans, 1980), 40–41.
45. For these historical facts see Allen, "The Atonement: Limited or Universal?" 67–77.

Chapter Seven: Yes to Grace; No to Irresistible Grace/Monergism

1. Meeter, *The Basic Ideas of Calvinism*, 45.
2. Calvin, *Institutes* 3.24.2 (p. 967).
3. Ibid., 3.22.11 (p. 947).
4. Ibid.
5. Boettner, *The Reformed Doctrine of Predestination*, 163.
6. Ibid., 164.
7. Ibid., 173–74.
8. Ibid., 175.
9. Ibid., 169.
10. Ibid., 177.
11. Ibid., 178.
12. Steele and Thomas, *The Five Points of Calvinism*, 48.
13. Ibid., 49.
14. Palmer, *The Five Points of Calvinism*, 66.
15. Ibid.
16. Ibid., 60.
17. Sproul, *What Is Reformed Theology?*, 188.
18. Ibid., 119.
19. Ibid., 123.
20. Ibid., 186.
21. Ibid.
22. See Melanchthon's *Commentarius De Anima* (1540) (Whitefish, MT: Kessinger Publishing, 2009) in which he identifies three "concurrent causes" of justification: word, Spirit, and free will. Although some strict monergists wish to "rescue" Melanchthon's

reputation from the claim that he adopted a synergistic view of salvation, most Melanchthon scholars recognize his fundamental agreement with Erasmus on this question even though he always rejected any notion that the free human acceptance of grace amounts to an act of merit.

23. Piper, *The Pleasures of God*, 202.

24. Ibid., 226.

25. See his sermon (or blog posting) dated September 17, 2001, just after the terrorist attacks on New York and Washington, D.C., the title of which is, "Why I do not say, 'God did not cause the calamity, but he can use it for good.'" (www.desiringgod.org/ResourceLibrary/TasteAndSee/ByDate/2001/1181_Why_I_Do_Not_Say_God_Did_Not_Cause_the_Calamity_but_He_Can_Use_It_for_Good/). Clearly, then, he *does say* that God causes sin and evil!

26. Sproul, *Chosen by God*, 69.

27. Steve Witzki, "The 'Drawings' of God" (unpub. paper, 2003), 2–3.

28. See *Theological Dictionary of the New Testament (Abridged Edition)*, ed. Gerhard Kittel and Gerhard Friedrich; trans., Geoffrey W. Bromiley (Grand Rapids: Eerdmans, 1985), 227.

29. Lemke, "A Biblical and Theological Critique of Irresistible Grace," in *Whosoever Will: A Biblical-Theological Critique of Five-Point Calvinism*, ed. David L. Allen and Steve W. Lemke (Nashville, TN: Broadman & Holman, 2010), 120.

30. Ibid.

31. Ibid., 121.

32. Ibid., 122.

33. Ibid., 122–23.

34. Walls and Dongell, *Why I Am Not a Calvinist*, 54–55.

35. Ibid., 55.

36. Vincent Brümmer, *Speaking of a Personal God* (Cambridge, UK: Cambridge University Press, 1992), 75.

37. Ibid.

38. Ibid.

39. Ibid., 75–76.

40. Anyone who doubts this has never studied the theology of Jonathan Edwards, who saw in Locke's empiricism an ally in establishing God's sovereignty and the lack of libertarian free will. One of Edwards' most noted interpreters says: "Locke's treatment of the human faculties and his theory of the 'simple idea' became useful for Edwards in a description of the internal dynamics of the act of faith." See Conrad Cherry, *The Theology of Jonathan Edwards: A Reappraisal* (Bloomington, IN: Indiana Univ. Press, 1966), 15.

41. Brümmer, *Speaking of a Personal God*, 75, 76–77.

42. Grounds, "God's Universal Salvific Grace," 28.

43. See Rebecca Harden Weaver, *Divine Grace and Human Agency: A Study of the Semi-Pelagian Controversy* (Macon, GA: Mercer Univ. Press, 1996), 110–11.

44. Picirilli, *Grace, Faith, Free Will*, 153.

45. Stanley J. Grenz, *Theology for the Community of God* (Grand Rapids: Eerdmans, 2000).

46. For example, Anabaptists such as Mennonites do not call themselves Arminian, but their soteriology is also synergistic. When I use the terms "Arminian" and "evangelical synergism" I intend to include them.

47. Another aspect of this illustration I find helpful is that the water meant to save the helpless people in the pit becomes their destruction by drowning if they resist it—an image of God's wrath?

48. I want to make clear that my homely illustrations are not from Oden and I don't know what he would think about them. He is not to blame for their imperfections.

49. Oden, *The Transforming Power of Grace*, 47.

50. Ibid.

Chapter Eight: Conclusion: Calvinism's Conundrums

1. In *The Pleasures of God* John Piper criticizes theologian Clark Pinnock for embracing open theism because "logic required it and Scripture allowed it." But I think that is an invalid criticism. Every Christian believes some things because reason requires them and Scripture allows them—even John Piper. Perhaps he is not aware of it, but it seems clear to me that he believes in limited atonement in that same way that Pinnock believes in open theism. After all, no place in Scripture explicitly says or requires belief that Christ died only for the elect; it is an inference from some passages in John. Why do people like Piper believe it? I think it is because the logic of TULIP requires it.

2. Bruce Ware, *God's Lesser Glory: The Diminished God of Open Theism* (Wheaton, IL: Crossway, 2000).

3. Of course, some people on both sides of the monergism/synergism divide will argue that Scripture *is* absolutely clear about these disputed matters. But how can it be, if equally sincere, God-fearing, Jesus-loving, Bible-believing Christians have disagreed for hundreds of years and continue to disagree in spite of equally penetrating analyses of the biblical texts? One Calvinist speaker declared publicly that non-Calvinists do not "honor" Scripture. Similar statements can be heard from non-Calvinists about Calvinists. I do not think Calvinists, even high Calvinists of the "five point" variety, dishonor Scripture. What I do think is that they are blind to the "good and necessary consequences" of their theological system.

Appendix 1: Calvinist Attempts to Rescue God's Reputation

1. Helm, *The Providence of God*, 87.
2. Boettner, *The Reformed Doctrine of Predestination*, 251.
3. Ibid., 241.
4. Ibid.
5. Meeter, *The Basic Ideas of Calvinism*, 44.
6. Helm, *The Providence of God*, 190.
7. Evans, "Reflections on Determinism and Freedom," 263.
8. The view discussed here is also the one suggested by evangelical theologian Millard Erickson in *Christian Theology* (Grand Rapids, Mich.: Baker, 1983), 1:356–62. Erickson calls it "a moderately Calvinistic model." It's difficult to see what's "moderate" about it as Erickson ends up where all Calvinists do—with divine determinism. But, like Ware later, Erickson uses middle knowledge to attempt to reconcile divine determinism with human (compatibilist) freedom and rescue God's reputation by relieving God of causing sin and evil.
9. Bruce Ware, *God's Greater Glory: The Exalted God of Scripture and the Christian Faith* (Wheaton, IL.: Crossway, 2004), 120.
10. Ibid., 122.
11. Ibid., 124.